FULFILLING
GOD'S
END-TME
MISSION

A Comprehensive Evangelism Training Manual

MARK AND ERNESTINE FINLEY

 Pacific Press®
Publishing Association

Nampa, Idaho | Oshawa, Ontario, Canada
www.pacificpress.com

Cover design by Gerald Lee Monks
Cover resources from iStockphoto.com
Inside design by Kristin Hansen-Mellish
Inside images on pages 5, 9, 17 (bottom), 21, 25, 40, 45 (bottom), 75, 76, 78, 79, 83, 102, 182 (bottom) from Pacific Press® Publishing Association. All other inside images are provided by the authors, who assume full responsibility.

The authors assume full responsibility for the accuracy of all facts and quotations as cited in this book.

Unless otherwise attributed, all Bible references are taken from the NKJV, The New King James Version, copyright © 1979, 1980, 1982, Thomas Nelson, Inc., Publishers.

You can obtain additional copies of this book by calling toll-free 1-800-765-6955
or by visiting http://www.adventistbookcenter.com.

Library of Congress Cataloging-in-Publication Data

Finley, Mark, 1945-
 Fulfilling God's end-time mission : a comprehensive evangelism training manual / Mark and Ernestine Finley.
    pages cm
 ISBN 13: 978-0-8163-4675-2 (pbk.)
 ISBN 10: 0-8163-4675-5 (pbk.)
 1. Evangelistic work—Seventh-day Adventists—Study and teaching. I. Title.
 BV3796.F55 2013
 269'.2—dc23
                           2013023136

13 14 15 16 17 • 5 4 3 2 1

Contents

Appendix

INTRODUCTION

Evangelism is heaven's top priority. There is **nothing more important** to God than **saving lost mankind.** For He "**desires all men to be saved** and to come to the knowledge of the truth" and He is not willing that any should perish" **(1 TIMOTHY 2:4; 2 PETER 3:9).** God had only one Son and He sent Him as an evangelist. The **focus of Jesus' life was saving lost people.** It is written of Jesus,

"for the **Son** of Man **has come** to **seek** and to **save** that which was lost" **(LUKE 19:10).**

Jesus gave the totality of His life in winning lost men and women. Certainly, we can do no less. To **follow Jesus means** to follow Him in the path of soul winning. God has **raised up His church** to participate with Him in reaching out to win the lost. **We are ambassadors for Christ,** priests of God, lights in a dark world to share His grace and truth with those around us. **There is no higher calling and no greater privilege.**

The **urgency of our times** demands that we do something great for God. What a time to be alive! **What a time to be a full-time Adventist preacher or a part-time lay preacher.** This is our time now! In a world seeking for answers, **God has called us to give His final appeal to a dying world.** The **greatest joy** in life is to participate with Christ in the closing work. The **greatest satisfaction** in life is to see men and women, boys and girls saved for eternity. One of our delights in heaven will be to meet people who have come to our evangelistic meetings, people who have heard our preaching and we have

visited with in their homes and they have made eternal decisions for Christ and His kingdom. In a special sense, **Seventh-day Adventist Christians** have been **commissioned** by God **to take** *the three angels' messages* **to the world.** This message of **"present truth"** is to be **proclaimed to the ends of the earth** to prepare people for the second coming of Christ. It is just as **important** in our day as Noah's message was in his day and John the Baptist's message was in the first century. Once again, God has sent a **special message** at a **special time,** to prepare a **special people** for a **special event**—the second coming of Christ. **REVELATION 14:6–12** presents an **urgent, last-day message** for all humanity. Listen to its dynamic pathos once again:

"Then I saw another **angel** flying in the midst of heaven, having the **everlasting gospel** to **preach** to those who dwell on the earth—**to every nation, tribe, tongue, and people**—saying with a loud voice, '**Fear God** and **give glory** to Him, for the **hour of His judgment has come;** and **worship Him** who made heaven and earth, the sea and springs of water.'

"And another **angel** followed, saying, '**Babylon is fallen,** is fallen, that great city, because she has made all nations drink of the wine of the wrath of her fornication.'

"Then a **third angel** followed them, saying with a loud voice, 'If anyone **worships the beast** and his image, and receives his mark on his forehead or on his hand, he himself shall also drink of the wine of the wrath of God, which is poured out full strength into the cup of His indignation. He shall be tormented with fire and brimstone in the presence of the holy angels and in the presence of the Lamb. And the smoke of their torment ascends forever and ever; and they have no rest day or night, **who worship** the **beast** and **his image**, and whoever receives the mark of his name.'

"Here is **the patience of the saints**; here are those who **keep the commandments of God and the faith of Jesus.**"

The **proclamation of the three angels' messages** is our **unique task** and our primary reason for existence as an end-time movement. Now is the time **for Adventist Christians to proclaim the three angels' messages to the world.** Now is the **time to proclaim God's eternal message of truth to cities, villages, and every nation, kindred, language, and people group in the world.** Ellen White states in the book *Evangelism:*

"To **all people** and nations and kindreds and tongues **the truth is to be proclaimed.** The time has come for much **aggressive work** to be done in the **cities**, and in all neglected, **unworked fields**" (P. 59).

The **greatest joy** in life is to **participate with Christ** in His mission of bringing the gospel to the world in these **closing days of earth's history.** The greatest satisfaction in life is to see men and women, boys and girls saved for eternity. There is no greater joy on this side of heaven than in winning souls to Christ.

We **are not alone in our evangelistic ministry.** The Father and the Son cooperate with us in reaching out to others. **All heaven is interested in winning souls.** The Holy Spirit touches hearts, drawing the unsaved to the Father's heart. The holy righteous angels engage in spiritual warfare with the forces of hell for the souls of men and women. Christ's final words to His disciples echo down the corridors of time, **"Lo, I am with you always, even to the end of the age"** (MATTHEW 28:20).

These words are still true. **The One who has called us to the task has empowered us to do it.** The One who has commissioned us stands by our side. He guarantees success. He promises to make our words effective in the hearts of people. The power that brought the worlds into existence is ours! Only eternity will reveal what the Lord has done through our evangelistic efforts.

Welcome to the most exciting work in the entire universe—winning lost men and women to Christ. There is nothing more fulfilling. God is going to work powerfully through many humble pastors and lay members.

"As the **time comes** for it [the **message of the third angel**] to be given with greatest power, the **Lord** will **work** through **humble instruments,** leading the minds of those who consecrate themselves to His service. The **laborers** will be **qualified** rather **by the unction of His Spirit than by the training of literary institutions.** Men of faith and prayer will be constrained to go forth with holy zeal, declaring the words which God gives them" **(THE GREAT CONTROVERSY, P. 606).**

Heaven's mandate is clear. The Great Commission of MATTHEW 28:19, 20 rings in our ears. The three angels' messages of REVELATION 14:6-12 moves our hearts. The promise of the Holy Spirit's power compels us to share Jesus' love and truth now. We hear the call of God:

" 'Advance, **enter new territory;** lift the standard in every land. "Arise, shine; for thy light is come, and the glory of the Lord is risen upon thee." [ISA. 60:1.]' "

"The time has come when **through God's messengers** the **scroll** is being **unrolled** to the world. The **truth contained** in the **first, second,** and **third angels' messages must go to every nation, kindred, tongue, and people;** it must lighten the darkness of **every continent,** and extend to the islands of the sea. There **must be no delay** in this work.

"Our **watchword** is to be, **Onward,** ever **onward!** Angels of heaven will go before us to prepare the way. Our burden for the regions beyond can never be laid down till the **whole earth** is **lightened** with the **glory of the Lord**" **(GOSPEL WORKERS, P. 470).**

As you carefully study the pages of this manual, **Fulfilling God's End-Time Mission,** you will discover basic Bible principles that guarantee success in evangelistic outreach. **In this manual, you will learn how to:**

- **Develop** an ongoing, comprehensive evangelistic outreach out of your church.
- **Motivate** your members to be actively involved in service.
- **Organize** the essential committees for a successful series.
- **Advertise** effectively to draw a crowd.
- **Plan** a logical order of topics anchored in the three angels' messages.
- **Visit** with a purpose.
- **Make** effective appeals.
- **Answer** objections.
- **Nurture** new converts and much, much more.

As you put these principles into practice, you will experience new success in your evangelistic meetings. **You will be amazed at what God does through you,** for when we do God's work, God's way, **He guarantees the results,** so read on and let God use you in ways you never imagined.

CHAPTER 1

WHY EVANGELISM?

Introduction

The pastor sat quietly in his study hoping to spend an hour or two preparing for his sermon. His reflections were interrupted by a knock on his study door. He was surprised to meet a group of his church's elders. "Pastor, we need to talk. This is a large institutional church and we are a little nervous with all of your preaching on the priority of evangelism.

"You have been **emphasizing evangelism—evangelism—evangelism.** We have a question.

- "Why all this emphasis on **soul winning**?
- "Why focus on witnessing?
- **"Why place priority on evangelism?"**
  - Have you ever asked these same questions? Have you ever wondered if **evangelism** really **makes** a **difference**?
  - Isn't **God doing everything** He can to win people without our help?
  - What is the **purpose** of **sharing our faith** if God is already working to win the person we are witnessing to?

The New Testament presents **eight powerful reasons** for **evangelistic outreach** and **witnessing.** As you understand these basic scriptural principles, it will make a dramatic difference in your ministry.

Eight Reasons for Biblical Evangelism

01 | Evangelism is God's means of saving lost people.

The New Testament is clear. **God had only one Son** and **He became an evangelist. Jesus** left the glories of heaven, the worship of the angels, and the fellowship of the Father to save lost mankind.

His **purpose** in coming to earth was to reveal the Father's love to a planet in rebellion, model heaven's principles in a sinful world, and **redeem** lost humanity. Luke states it succinctly:

"For the Son of Man has come to seek and to save that which was lost" (LUKE 19:10).

Jesus did not come to simply inspire us. **He came to save us.**

This is the purpose of all authentic evangelism. Evangelism is the **proclamation** of the **gospel** in every way possible so that every person possible may have every **opportunity possible to believe** and **be saved.**

This concept of the lostness of humanity is clearly seen in the book of Romans:

- In ROMANS 1-3, the apostle sets forth the eternal truth that without Jesus **all humanity is lost.**
- In ROMANS 3-6, he reveals that **justification** is by faith in Christ. In justification, Christ imputes to us His own righteousness.
- In CHAPTERS 6-9, he reveals that **sanctification** is by faith in Christ. In sanctification, Christ imparts to us His own righteousness.
- In ROMANS CHAPTER 10 VERSES 13 AND 14, Paul **summarizes** the essence of his arguments and practically applies the natural outworking of salvation through Christ.
- In ROMANS 10:13-17, the apostle Paul urgently appeals to the church at Rome and to all Christians that salvation comes in response to an act of faith in Christ resulting from the proclamation of His Word. He declares, "For '**whoever calls** on the name of the **LORD shall be saved**' " (ROMANS 10:13).

Then the apostle asks these thought-provoking questions:

"How then shall they **call** on Him in whom they have not believed? And how shall they **believe** in Him of whom they have not heard? And how shall they **hear** without a preacher? And how shall they **preach** unless they are sent?" (VERSE 14).

ROMANS 10:14
- To be saved, you must **call.**
- To call, you must **believe.**
- To believe, you must **hear.**
- To hear, you must have a **preacher.**

You and I are sent by God to share the eternal message of God's truth about His saving grace so that people can hear and respond.

Listen to the clarity of the apostle's words, "So then **faith** comes by **hearing**, and hearing by the **word of God**" (ROMANS 10:17).

God has ordained preaching or faith sharing as His means of saving lost humanity.

"For since, in the wisdom of God, the world through wisdom did not know God, it pleased God through the foolishness of the message **preached to save** those who believe" (1 CORINTHIANS 1:21).

The sharing of the gospel does not give people their only chance to be saved, but it does give them their best chance. **God reveals Himself** through **nature**, His **providence**, and the **impressions** of His Spirit, but each of these is liable for misinterpretation.

- **Nature** reveals good and evil (earthquakes, tornados, floods, etc.).
- **Providences** are sometimes difficult to understand.
- **Impressions** are always funneled through fallen human nature.

The clearest **revelation** of **God's truth** and **character** is **God's Word.**
The **preaching** of the gospel **provides** the **greatest opportunity** to:

- **Understand God's character**
- **Know His love and**
- **Respond to His grace.**

The New Testament reveals this eternal truth. **People** are **saved** as they respond to the gospel. There will be people saved because of your **witness.**

- God will use the **Bible studies you give**
- the **literature** you distribute
- **the small groups** you conduct
- **the CDs and DVDs** you loan and
- **the evangelistic meetings** you conduct.

Our responsibility is to *give* **them an** *opportunity*. **It's God's responsibility to** *impress* **their hearts.**

People are not:
- Misguided
- Misdirected
- Misinformed
- Mis-anything else
- They are **lost without Christ**

LUKE 15 reveals this clearly:
- The **sheep** is lost.
- The **coin** is lost.
- The **prodigal son** is lost.

The **sheep is lost**, knows it's lost, but can't find its way home.
The **coin is lost** in the house and has no idea it is lost. Coins can't think.
The **boy is lost** and comes home to the loving arms of his father.
In each instance, the **lost are found.** God's grace is great enough to save lost people.
We witness so lost people will respond to God's grace and be saved.
What about those who have **never heard** the name of **Jesus**?

- Every coin has **two sides.**
- **Will** God save some people that do not know the story of salvation?
- **Will** there be some people saved based on God's wisdom?
- **God is both sovereign and all wise.** If in His infinite wisdom He chooses to save

someone who has never heard the name of Christ but **He knows that if they had heard they would accept,** that is totally up to God.

PSALM 87:5, 6 says: "And of Zion it will be said, '**This one** and **that one were born in her;** and the Most High Himself shall establish her.' "

The Lord will record, when He registers the peoples: "**This one was born there.**"

JUDE 20-22 says: "But you, beloved, building yourselves up on your most holy faith, praying in the Holy Spirit, keep yourselves in the love of God, **looking for the mercy of our Lord Jesus Christ unto eternal life.** And on **some** have **compassion,** making a **distinction.**"

In His infinite wisdom and abounding grace, God will save some who never have had a chance to know Him, but that decision is totally up to God. As far as we are concerned, **there is no salvation outside of a saving knowledge of Jesus,** and the message of His love and grace must be shared with all humanity.

02 | Evangelism is God's way to a vibrant spiritual life.

Without outreach, spiritual rigor mortis sets in.

- There is an **arthritis** of the **soul.**
- There are the **clogged arteries** of the **heart.**
- There is a **malignancy** (cancer) of the **spirit.**
- There is a **retardation** of real, genuine **spiritual growth.**

Throughout Scripture, giving away your faith is indissolubly linked to a **growing faith.** The simple fact is this:

You cannot **receive continual spiritual nourishment** unless you are **sharing** what God has already given you.

ACTS 20:35: "I have shown you in every way, by laboring like this, that you must support the weak. And remember the words of the Lord Jesus, that He said, '**It is more blessed to give than to receive.**' "

Who is **more blessed,** the one who gives the Bible study or the one who receives it?
Who is **more blessed,** the one who distributes literature or the one who receives it?
In God's plan, **the one who witnesses receives a greater blessing** than the one witnessed to. Ellen White refers to a time when the early Christian church grew and became spiritually weak. Notice this insightful comment about the church when it became popular.

"Forgetting that **strength to resist evil** is best gained through **aggressive service.**" (THE ACTS OF THE APOSTLES, P. 105).

God could have reached His object in **saving sinners** without our aid, but, "in order for us to develop a **character** like **Christ's,** we must share in His **work**" (**THE DESIRE OF AGES, P. 142).**

"Those who would be **overcomers** must be drawn **out of themselves;** and the _only thing_ which will accomplish this great work, is to become *intensely* interested in the **salvation of others"** (**FUNDAMENTALS OF CHRISTIAN EDUCATION, P. 207**).

The Center of **Sin** *is* "*i*"
The Center of **Pride** *is* "*i*"
The Center of **Lucifer** *is* "*i*"

Repeatedly, we have seen **complacent Christians revived** as they have become actively **involved in witnessing.** The more you love Jesus, the more you desire to share His love with others. And the more you share His love, the more you will experience that love yourself.

Growing Christians are:

- witnessing
- faith sharing and
- active

03 | **Evangelism opens the channels of the heart to receive the refreshing rivers of the Spirit.**

Do you long for a **spiritual revival** in your own life?
Do you long to see your local **church revived**?
Here is God's promise.

"But **you shall receive power** when the Holy Spirit has come upon you; and **you shall be witnesses** to Me in Jerusalem, and in all Judea and Samaria, and to the end of the earth" **(ACTS 1:8).**

The **outpouring of the Spirit** in its **fullness** comes to empower us to become effective witnesses. The purpose of the mighty manifestation of God's Spirit on His last-day church is to enable it to **take the gospel to the world.**

Why would God **pour out His Spirit** for **witnessing** if we were not witnessing?

Why should God equip us by the power of the Spirit to witness, if we have no interest in witnessing?

"The great **outpouring of the Spirit of God,** which lightens the whole earth with his glory, will not come until we have an enlightened people, that know by experience what it means to be **laborers together with God.** When we have entire, whole-hearted consecration to the service of Christ, God will recognize the fact by an **outpouring of his Spirit without measure;** but this **will not be** while the **largest portion** of the **church** are not **laborers** together with God" (THE REVIEW AND HERALD, JULY 21, 1896).

What is the largest portion of the church?

The largest portion is at least **51 percent.**

When God's church heeds **God's command** to "Go and preach" or share the gospel, He will honor their commitment by the **outpouring of the Spirit.**

04 | Evangelism brings joy to God's heart.

LUKE 15:7: "I say to you that likewise there will be more joy in heaven over one sinner who repents than over ninety-nine just persons who need no repentance."

Do you think **God ever cries** as He looks at the pain in our world? **I think He does.**
Has anyone ever said to you, **"How is your day going?"**
What if you asked God this morning, **"God, how is Your day going?"** How would He respond? What would He say?
He might say,
"My child, My day is **going rough.**
"I attended thousands of **funerals** today, and I will attend thousands tomorrow.
"I witnessed all the **suffering** of the world today and I will witness it tomorrow.
"**But** there is something that **brings Me incredible joy** in the midst of a world of sorrow.

- "When My **people share My love with others,** My heart thrills through and through with joy.
- "When My **people reach out in loving ministry** as channels of My grace, **_all heaven rejoices_.**"

05 | Evangelism puts you in the center of God's activities.

- Peter on Pentecost was in the center of God's activities.
- Philip witnessing to the Ethiopian eunuch was in the center of God's activity.
- Paul preaching at Ephesus was at the center of God's activity.

When you give a **Bible study,** you are at the **center** of God's activity.
When you **pray** with someone in need, you are at the **center** of God's activity.
When you **distribute literature,** you are at the **center** of God's activity.
When you **visit** a former church member, you are in the **center** of God's activity.
When you stand before an audience **preaching** God's last-day message, you are in the **center** of God's activity.

WHY EVANGELISM? • 15

God is working to save lost people!

There is **no greater joy** for any Christian than to work where God is working.

There is **no greater satisfaction** for any believer than to cooperate with God in saving lost people.

06 | **Evangelism is God's means of unifying His church.**

There are some who say, "We **can't do evangelism because** the church isn't unified. Let's wait for the church to unite and then reach out to the community.

The **unity** of **the church** is related to the **mission** of the church.

Evangelism fosters, stimulates, and **promotes unity.** Leading up to Pentecost, the disciples sought God for power to reach the world with the gospel. It was this sense of mission, this sense of purpose which united them.

- **ACTS 1:14:** "These all continued with **one accord in prayer** and supplication, with the women and Mary the mother of Jesus, and with His brothers." What were the disciples praying about? They were praying for the power to reach the world our Lord had promised in **ACTS 1:8.**

- **ACTS 2:1–3:** "When the Day of Pentecost had fully come, they were **all with one accord** in one place. And suddenly there came **a sound from heaven, as of a rushing mighty wind,** and it filled the whole house where they were sitting. Then there appeared to them divided tongues, as of fire, and one sat upon each of them." The **power to witness** was **poured out** upon disciples who were **longing to share** the grace of God with others.

Placing priority on mission is Heaven's means of unifying God's church. The mission to take the gospel to the entire world consumed the disciples. They were passionate about fulfilling Christ's command, "Go into all the world." They put aside their petty differences. They surrendered their cherished ideas. They broke down all barriers between them and focused on the one thing that really mattered, saving souls for Christ's kingdom.

07 | **Evangelism gives me a reason for living and fulfills the meaning of my existence.**

Jesus stated it powerfully in **MATTHEW 16:25:**

"For whoever desires to save his life will lose it, but whoever loses his life for My sake will find it."

When Jesus speaks of **losing one's life,** He is speaking of **losing it in service.** "Losing" it for others' sake.

We find our lives when we give them away in service. The super abundant life **(JOHN**

10:10) Jesus promises comes to those who unite with the Master in **soul-winning ministry.** There is **no greater joy.** There is **no higher privilege.**

> **Birds** were made to **fly.**
> **Fish** were made to **swim** and
> **We** were made to **know God** and **share a knowledge of His love** with the people around us. The prophet Isaiah states it succinctly:

> "This people I have formed for Myself; they shall declare My praise" **(ISAIAH 43:21).**

> **The essence of life,** the meaning of our existence **is to share His praise, His grace, His glory** with others.

08 | Evangelism is God's means of finishing His work so the sleeping saints can go home.

In the well-known chapter on **faith, HEBREWS 11,** the apostle Paul concluded the passage with these words.

> "And all these, having obtained a good testimony through faith, did not **receive the promise**" **(HEBREWS 11:39).**

The worthies of faith down through the ages have not received the promise of Jesus' return. **When Jesus comes,** we will **be reunited** with **believers** from **all ages.**

- Symbolically, they **cry out** from their graves **for God's work on earth to be finished.**
- The **testimony** of their lives cheers us on.
- Their **faithfulness inspires** us to cooperate with God in the finishing of His work in this generation.

> **HEBREWS 11 concludes,** "God having provided something better for us, that they should not be made perfect apart from us" **(VERSE 40).**

- The **Old Testament heroes** of faith **wait in their graves.**
  - Abraham, Isaac, Jacob, Isaiah, Jeremiah, and the *Old Testament* worthies are sleeping until the gospel is preached to all the world.
- The **New Testament heroes** of faith **wait in their graves.**
  - Peter, James, John, Paul, and the *New Testament* faithful are sleeping until the gospel is preached to all the world.
- The **Waldenses,** Huss, Jerome, Luther, Wesley, William Miller sleep in their graves until the gospel is preached to all the world.

- **Ellen White** and **early Adventist pioneers** sleep in their graves until the gospel is preached to all the world. They **all await the proclamation of the gospel in this generation.**
- You may have a father, mother, brother, sister, friend, or relative who died in Jesus. They are sleeping in Jesus, **waiting for the finishing of the work in this generation.**

Jesus longs to come. He wants to return much more than we can imagine. In fact, Jesus wants to come more than we want Him to come. **His desire** to come and take us home is even **greater than our desire** to go home and be with Him forever.

Why doesn't He come?

There is **somebody** near you who is **not ready.**

There is some family member, some neighbor, some working associate, some acquaintance who **is waiting for you to witness to them.**

Jesus is "long-suffering." He suffers long with the pain of this world. He is "not willing that any should perish but that all should come to repentance" **(2 PETER 3:9).**

Will you rise to the challenge?

Will you commit your life to sharing His love?

Will you tell Him just now you want to make soul winning and evangelism the priority of your life?

Welcome to the greatest adventure of your life!

EVANGELISM!

CHAPTER 2

ESSENTIAL ELEMENTS FOR SUCCESSFUL PUBLIC EVANGELISM

Evangelism is the dynamic **heartbeat** of the **New Testament church.** The book of Acts is alive with thrilling, soul-winning stories.

On the Day of **Pentecost, three thousand** were **baptized.** A few months later, the church grew to at least **five thousand** men, not counting women and children.

Many church growth thinkers have concluded that the Christian **church numbered** between **fifteen and twenty thousand believers shortly after Pentecost (ACTS 4:4, 5:15).** The record states, "And believers were increasingly added to the Lord, multitudes of both men and women" (ACTS 5:14). **The gospel spread rapidly throughout Palestine, Asia, Europe, and even reached into faraway Africa.** "Therefore those who were scattered went everywhere preaching the word" (ACTS 8:4) and "the gospel . . . was preached to every creature under heaven" (COLOSSIANS 1:23).

What an **evangelistic explosion**! The New Testament church was a mighty force for God. Why? How could these believers **accomplish so much** in such a **short time**? What can we learn from the experience of the early church?

- Once thing is for certain, **the time was right.** Jesus had ascended to heaven and poured out heaven's most precious and powerful gift, the Holy Spirit. What the disciples accomplished in Acts was not merely because they used the right methods. It was because they were filled with the Holy Spirit. The Holy Spirit made the methods they used effective.
- The **Holy Spirit empowered their witness.** We do discover, though, in the disciples' ministry as recorded in Acts, some very basic evangelistic principles that when empowered by the Holy Spirit produce amazing results.

These **eternal evangelistic principles** bridge cultural barriers and ensure success in soul winning.
- The disciples were focused on mission.
- Their central objective was winning the lost to Christ.
- They had a passion for soul winning.
- They were committed to evangelism.

A careful study of the **book of Acts reveals** the **reasons** for the **disciples' success** in reaching the lost. It details God-given, **heaven-ordained principles for evangelistic success.**

Successful soul winners and growing churches understand these **<u>universal principles</u>** and they follow them. They bridge cultures. They are effective in large cities, small towns, and country villages.

If you follow **"the biblical principles to successful evangelism,"** God will empower your witness and give you results for His kingdom.

These **principles** or **"keys"** are a **master strategy** for growing churches. There is a difference between a principle and a method. A divine principle is eternal in time and universal in application. It applies at all times in all places. Methods that are successful in one place may not be successful in other places. Methods that were successful one hundred years ago may be irrelevant today, but the principles in the book of Acts reflecting the Spirit-led ministry of the disciples truly are eternal in time and universal in application.

They are **biblical, Christ-centered principles** that are essential if we want true lasting **success** in **public evangelism.**

ELEMENT #1—A Solid Foundation

FOLLOW *"THE FIVE KEYS TO SUCCESSFUL EVANGELISM"*

The *"Five Keys to Successful Evangelism"* are the **solid foundation** that true evangelism is built on. When these Christ-centered, biblical **principles are implemented** in a local congregation, the church will grow.

 ## KEY #1—SPIRITUAL REVIVAL

The New Testament church experienced a genuine revival through the outpouring of the Holy Spirit.

Spiritual revival sets the **tone** for **public evangelism.** Before God can do something through us, He must do something in us. Before God can do something with us, He must do something for us. We will **never reach a lost world** for Christ with the gospel **unless** that **gospel has changed our own lives.**

A live church will grow. A dead church won't. The church in the book of Acts was alive in the Spirit.
- **Without** the **power of the Holy Spirit,** very little is accomplished.
- **Without** the **power of the Holy Spirit,** witnessing is ineffective.
- **Without** the **power of the Holy Spirit,** evangelistic preaching is unable to touch hearts and change lives. Unless the Holy Spirit moves upon the hearts of the congregation, people may understand truth but they will not be transformed by truth and act upon it.

God is waiting to pour out His Holy Spirit on His church today.
New Testament believers were filled with the Spirit. The promise of the Spirit is for the church today just as much as it was for the New Testament church. God's promise knows no limitation. "**The lapse of time** has **wrought no change in Christ's parting promise to send the Holy Spirit** as His representative. It is **not because of any restriction** on the part of God that the riches of His grace do not flow

earthward to men. **If the fulfillment of the promise is not seen as it might be, it is because the promise is not appreciated as it should be.** If all were **willing, all would be filled with the Spirit"** (THE ACTS OF THE APOSTLES, P. 50). Our Lord promised:

"If you then, being evil, know how to give good gifts to your children, how much more will your heavenly Father give the **Holy Spirit** to those who **ask** Him!" (LUKE 11:13).

"Our heavenly Father is more willing to give His Holy Spirit to them that ask Him, than are earthly parents to give good gifts to their children" (SELECTED MESSAGES, BK. 1, P. 121).

God moves in a special way **when God's people pray.** His power is poured out in answer to earnest intercession. The disciples saturated their lives with prayer (ACTS 1:14; 2:42; 4:31; 6:4; 12:5).

"**Prayer** and **faith** will do what no power on earth can accomplish" (THE MINISTRY OF HEALING, P. 509).

Praying churches are growing churches!

Witnessing is the **natural result** of a converted heart. An experience with Jesus leads to the desire to share Jesus.

TO HAVE A SUCCESSFUL PRAYER MINISTRY:
- Select a **prayer coordinator and assistant.**
- Recruit prayer **group members.**
- Commit to **meet to pray** regularly.
- Pray for **specific names.**
- Pray for the **evangelist, the musicians, the staff, and those participating in the meetings.**

Practical ideas to start a prayer ministry in your church:

There are three methods we have found extremely successful in mobilizing our members to pray.

01 | **Prayer Lists**

Encourage each member to develop a **prayer list of three to five people** who are potential candidates for the kingdom of God. Intercede for each one each day. Jesus prayed for Peter by name and He invites us to enter into this ministry of intercession with Him. **Prayerfully read the passages** below and **ask God to deepen your commitment to pray for others.**

> **LUKE 22:31, 32:** "Simon, Simon! Indeed, Satan has asked for you. . . . But I have prayed for you."
> **MATTHEW 7:7:** "Ask, and it will be given to you."
> **1 JOHN 5:14–17:** "This is the confidence that we have in Him, if we ask anything according to His will, He hears us."
> **JOB 16:21:** "Oh, that one might plead for a man with God."
> **JAMES 5:16:** "The effective, fervent prayer of a righteous man avails much."

"**Ministering angels** are waiting about the throne to instantly obey the mandate of Jesus Christ to answer every prayer offered in earnest, living faith" (SELECTED MESSAGES, BK. 2, P. 377).

"**Souls are to be sought for, prayed for, labored for.** Earnest **appeals** are to be **made,** fervent **prayers offered.** Our tame, lifeless prayers need to be changed to **petitions of intense earnestness**" (GOSPEL WORKERS, P. 144).

`02` Prayer Bands

Set aside specific times for **groups of two to four** to **pray** for **specific people** before and after church or during midweek prayer services. Continue these prayer services throughout your evangelistic series.

"Why do not **two or three meet** together **and plead** with God for the salvation of some special one, and then for still another?" (TESTIMONIES, VOL. 7, P. 21).

God's last-day messenger encourages God's last-day people that there is special power in united prayer.

"We are encouraged to **pray for success,** and we are given the divine assurance that our prayers will be heard and 'if two of you shall agree on earth as touching anything that they shall ask, it shall be done for them of My Father which is in heaven. **For where two or three are gathered together in My name, there am I in the midst of them.'** 'Ask of Me, and I will answer your requests.'

"The **promise is made on condition** that the **united prayers** of God's people are offered, and in answer to these prayers there may be expected a **power greater than** that which comes in answer to **private prayer.** The power given will be proportionate to the unity of the members and their love for God and for one another" (CENTRAL ADVANCE, FEB. 25, 1903).

Prayed-for evangelistic meetings are far more effective than meetings where prayer is spasmodic and lackadaisical. When church members pray, the advertising, the visitation, the sermons, and the appeals are all more effective.

03 | Prayer Walking

- One week before the evangelistic meetings, walk the territory where the handbills will be distributed. Pray for the people who will receive them.
- You may want to set aside a **revival weekend** with emphasis on the Holy Spirit or set aside **ten days of prayer** immediately before your evangelistic series.

There are **three main characteristics of revival:**

1. **Prayer**
2. **Bible Study**
3. **Service**

All great revivals throughout history have been characterized by a **study** of and the **proclamation of God's Word.** The psalmist prayed, "**Revive me** according to Your word." The apostle Peter informs us that we are "born again" through the word, and James adds that the **"implanted word" can save your souls,** while Paul declares that the "word of God is living and powerful" **(PSALM 119:154; 1 PETER 1:23; JAMES 1:21; HEBREWS 4:12).** The disciples filled their minds with the words of Christ. They saturated their minds with Scripture.

Combining **prayer and Bible study** and at times reading God's Word with a prayerful heart and a meditative spirit opens our hearts to the deep ministry of the Holy Spirit in revival.

Prayer and Bible study will make a dramatic difference in the success of public evangelism and they lead to a desire to be actively involved in witnessing.

 # KEY #2—TRAINING AND EQUIPPING

Spiritual renewal leads to the desire to share our newly found experience with Jesus, with others. When we discover a deeper, new, refreshing **spiritual life,** our natural **desire is to witness.** Peter declared,

> "For we **cannot but speak** the things which **we have seen** and **heard**"(ACTS 4:20). Paul adds, "So, as much as is in me, I am **ready to preach** the gospel to you who are in Rome also" **(ROMANS 1:15).**

One of the corresponding results of **revival is the desire to witness.**
Spiritually revived church members long to find the best opportunities **to serve Jesus.** They are eager to discover their spiritual gifts and become equipped to serve the Master.

"***Every church member*** should be engaged in some line of **service for the Master. . . . Many** would be **willing to work *if*** they were **taught how to begin.** They **need** to be **instructed** and **encouraged.**

"***Every church*** should be a training school for Christian workers. Its members should be taught how to

- give Bible readings,
- how to conduct and teach Sabbath-school classes,
- how best to help the poor and to care for the sick,
- how to work for the unconverted.
- There should be ***schools of health,***
- ***cooking schools,*** and
- ***classes in*** various lines of Christian help work.

"There should **not only** be **teaching,** but **actual work** under experienced instructors. Let the **teachers lead the way** in working among the people, and others, uniting with them, will learn from their example" (THE MINISTRY OF HEALING, P. 149).

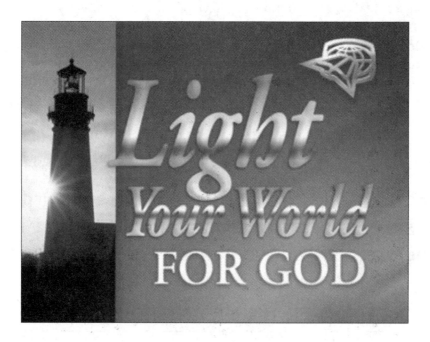

Every place in the world where churches are **growing,** lay people are **actively involved** in service. **Evangelism is the work of the entire church,** not just a few specialists. It is a process, not an event. It is a way of life in growing churches. It was a way of life for the early church and must be for the church today if we are going to reach God's ideal.

If church members were **involved nine months to a year before** the **public evangelistic meetings** begin, the church would explode in growth.

Hundreds would **attend** our **evangelistic meetings *if*** pastors placed priority on equipping their members for service and church members were actively involved.

Seven Effective Principles Pastors Can Use to Train and Equip Lay Members

Scriptural principles of training and equipping are found in the life of Jesus and the ministry of the apostle Paul.

01 | SELECTION

Jesus preached to the multitudes, ministered to the masses, but **spent most of His time equipping His disciples** to carry on His work after His death, resurrection, and ascension to heaven. Jesus recognized that unless He placed priority on training His disciples, His own ministry would not be as fruitful. He carefully selected those who would be future leaders in the church.

> "Now it came to pass in those days that He went out to the mountain **to pray,** and _**continued**_ **all night in prayer** to God. And when it was day, He **called His disciples** to Himself; and from them **He chose twelve whom He also names apostles**" **(LUKE 6:12, 13).**

After praying all night, **Jesus selected His disciples.** He chose them to carry on the work of proclaiming Him as the Christ, the true Messiah.

> "For the **carrying on of His work, Christ** _**did not choose**_ the **learning** or **eloquence** of the Jewish Sanhedrin or the power of Rome. Passing by the self-righteous Jewish teachers, the **Master Worker chose humble, unlearned men** to proclaim the truths that were to move the world. These men He **purposed to train and educate** as the **leaders** of His church. They in turn were to **educate others** and **send them out** with the gospel message. That they might have **success** in their work they were to be given the **power** of the **Holy Spirit.** Not by human might or human wisdom was the gospel to be proclaimed, but by the **power of God**" **(THE ACTS OF THE APOSTLES, P. 17).**

After selecting Timothy, the apostle Paul counseled his young disciple with these words: "And the things that you have heard from me among many witnesses, commit these to faithful men who will be able to teach others also" **(2 TIMOTHY 2:2).**

- Begin to pray about those you can disciple and train for evangelistic leadership in your church.

- Select them prayerfully.
- Invite them to be part of a small training group for a specific aspect of soul-winning ministry.

Paul outlined **the job description of all church leaders** in this powerful passage:

> **"And He Himself gave some to be apostles, some prophets, some evangelists, and some pastors and teachers, for the equipping of the saints for the work of ministry, for the edifying of the body of Christ"** (EPHESIANS 4:11, 12).

The phrase "pastors and teachers" is better translated as "pastor/teachers." The pastor is a God-ordained teacher to **equip believers** (members) for their **work of ministry** or service in the community.

02 | ASSOCIATION

Jesus taught the disciples to minister by **taking them with Him** on His missionary journeys. As they **watched Him** minister, they learned to minister. As they **watched Him heal** the sick, deliver the possessed, and relieve the oppressed, they understood the nature of His mission. As the disciples **listened to Jesus preach,** they learned to preach. **Watching the Master** Soul Winner, **they became soul winners** themselves. Here are Jesus' own words to His disciples:

> "Then He said to them, 'Follow Me, and I will make you fishers of men' " (MATTHEW 4:19).

Principles we can learn from Jesus' ministry and how can we apply them

1. **Soul winning** is more **caught than taught.** If you want to train soul winners, **take them with you** to watch you do it.
2. Different personalities have different gifts. Help your members discover their unique, God-given gifts and **equip them to serve** in harmony with the gifts God has given them.
3. There is no substitute for **active field labor.**

Applying Jesus' Soul-Winning Techniques

As you develop an outreach program in your local congregation, prayerfully
- **Choose leaders** who can lead out in the different ministries you are establishing.
- **Develop a number of training** modules to equip these leaders for service.
- **Investigate the very best possible training** for these potential leaders.
- **Provide them the resources** necessary to do the job. Leaders lead, but they do not do everything.
- **Use your teaching gifts to teach** in the ministry area of your expertise and get others to teach in areas where you may not be as comfortable. You may feel prepared to teach a class in giving Bible studies and taking members out with you, but you may feel ill equipped to teach members how to become effective health ministry leaders.

You need not teach every outreach leadership training class, but you must manage and oversee it.

03 | OBSERVATION

John's Gospel reveals an interesting insight into Jesus' discipleship methods. As Jesus observed two men following Him with keen interest in every word He spoke, He sensed the Holy Spirit working upon their hearts. He took the opportunity to disciple them. Notice His strategy.

> "Then Jesus turned, and seeing them following, said to them, '**What do you seek?**' They said to Him, 'Rabbi' (which is to say, when translated, Teacher), 'where are You staying?' " **(JOHN 1:38, 39).**

He said to them, *"Come and see."* They came and saw where He was staying, and remained with Him that day (now it was about the tenth hour). Jesus invited these followers to witness His life and ministry for themselves. **Successful ministry models provide opportunities for observation of effective methods.** People learn both in the classroom and by personally witnessing service opportunities. We learn largely by observing and doing.

- Invite your lay leaders to **observe** you giving a Bible study.
- Give the members in your class on small group leadership an opportunity to **observe** your Small Group Bible Study seminar.
- Give lay members an opportunity to **participate** with you in a health outreach seminar.

Jesus modeled ministry for His disciples and they learned by observation, by watching Him do it.

04 | EXPLANATION

Jesus often gathered His disciples together in private meetings and **explained the meaning of His words.** He **shared** the deeper meaning of His ministry methods. **He explained** to His disciples what ministry was all about and how to be successful witnesses. **Soul-winning pastors** carefully **share with their church leaders** the great **principles of witness** and **outreach.** They delegate responsibilities and clearly explain the ministry plan.

> "**Well-defined plans** should be freely presented to all whom they may concern, and it should be ascertained that they are **understood.** Then **require** of all those who are at the head of the various departments to cooperate in the **execution** of these plans. If this sure and radical method is properly adopted and followed up with interest and good will, it will avoid much work being done without any definite object, much useless friction" **(EVANGELISM, P. 94).**

As you train lay people for service, it is essential that you **spend time answering their questions,** outlining their responsibilities, and coordinating a plan of action.

05 | IMPLEMENTATION

Someone has said, "All the **talking about walking does not make up for one good walk**." All the certificates on the wall do not make a good soul winner. There comes a point where soul winners launch out into the deep. After spending time training His disciples, Jesus sent them out to witness.

"Then Jesus said to them again, 'Peace to you! As the Father has sent Me, I also send you' " (JOHN 20:21).

> "After these things **the Lord** appointed seventy others also, and **sent them two by two** before His face **into every city** and place where He Himself was about to go" (LUKE 10:1).

> "**Love and loyalty** to Christ are the spring of all true service. In the heart touched by His love there is begotten a desire to work for Him. Let this desire be encouraged and rightly guided. Whether in the home, the neighborhood, or the school, the presence of the poor, the afflicted, the ignorant, or the unfortunate should be regarded, not as a misfortune, but as affording precious opportunity for service. In this work, as in every other, **skill is gained in the work itself**. It is by training in the common duties of life and in ministry to the needy and suffering that efficiency is assured. Without this the best-meant efforts are often useless and even harmful. **It is in the water**, not on the land, **that men learn to swim**" (THE ADVENTIST HOME, P. 490).

Jesus' principles applied

1. **Prayerfully select** your ministry leaders.
2. **Organize** your ministry teams.
3. **Train and equip** your teams for service.
4. **Develop** a plan of action and explain responsibilities.
5. **Supply** the materials necessary for the ministry.
6. **Implement** your plan by launching your ministry.

06 | EXAMINATION AND EVALUATION

After **Jesus sent out the Seventy** as recorded in Luke 10 verse 1, they returned to report on what had happened in their ministry and to **evaluate their methods and results** (LUKE 10:1, 18–20). Jesus used these occasions to instruct His disciples in how to minister more effectively and to encourage them in their work. These two vital principles of examination and accountability are found throughout the New Testament.

> "But let **each one examine** his own work, and then he will have rejoicing in himself alone, and not in another" (GALATIANS 6:4).

> "According to the grace of God, which was given to me, as a wise master builder **I have laid the foundation,** and **another builds on it.** But let each one **take heed** [examine] how he builds on it" (1 CORINTHIANS 3:10).

"After a long time the lord of those servants came and **settled accounts with them**" (MATTHEW 25:19).

Without **regular ministry meetings,** members often become discouraged and drop out of their chosen ministry. Meetings at least **monthly** or at times every other week provide encouragement and further instruction.

- **Set aside specific times** to follow up with your ministry groups. It's important for lay members to **meet together** with the pastor or leader of a certain ministry and **give reports** on what is happening in their sphere of outreach.
- If this is not done, very little will be accomplished. Ministry members will tend to become discouraged and drop out.
- Ministry meetings are a **time to examine** and **evaluate** what we have or have not done and how to do it more effectively.
- Ministry meetings are **times to encourage and instruct.**

07 | CELEBRATION—REJOICING

All of **heaven rejoices** when people are won to Christ's kingdom and so should we. As we testify of God's goodness and power, others are encouraged by those testimony times. Take advantage of the personal ministry times in church to report on what God is doing through the varying ministries of the church. **Affirm** those involved and **encourage** them to give their testimony on how God is using them. **Plan a fellowship meal** for particular ministry groups and let them **report** on the blessings of God on their ministry. The power of an effective testimony of what God has done and is doing through one's life is incredibly motivating.

"I say to you that likewise there will be **more joy** in heaven **over one sinner who repents** than over ninety-nine just persons who need no repentance" (LUKE 15:7).

"**The LORD** your God in your midst, the Mighty One, **will save;** He will <u>**rejoice**</u> over you with gladness, He will quiet you with His love, He will <u>**rejoice** over you</u> with singing" (ZEPHANIAH 3:17).

- **Celebrate** what God has accomplished in your ministries.
- **Celebrate** what God has done for your community.
- **Celebrate** the baptism of new believers won to Christ through the ministry groups.

As you celebrate and rejoice over what God has done for you and your members, you will find a closeness and unity with one another.

Practical Ways to Equip Your Church for Outreach Ministry

01 | ## Equip church members to work on an updated pastor's interest file:

- Seek names from every source possible
- Develop a computerized interest file. (For more information, see **LIGHT YOUR WORLD FOR GOD, PP. 124–126.**)
- Mail quarterly to the interest file to cultivate the interests.
- Generally **25 percent of the interest file will respond** to an offer for a series of Bible guides, a spiritual book, a seminar, or the evangelistic meetings within a twelve-month time frame.

02 | ## Equip church members how to conduct an active visitation program.

Someone has said "**Successful evangelism depends** on three things, **Visit, Visit,** and **Visit** some more."

When Paul discussed His work at Ephesus with the elders of the church there, he reminded them that he proclaimed the Word of God to them both publically and from house to house **(ACTS 20:20)**. He wrote to the church at Galatia that there were some people that he must share God's Word "privately" with or his preaching would be "in vain" **(GALATIANS 2:2)**. Ellen White highlights this truth in this powerful statement.

"There are numbers of families who will **never be reached** by the truth of God's Word **unless** the stewards of the manifold grace of Christ **enter their homes,** and by earnest ministry, sanctified by the endorsement of the Holy Spirit, break down the barriers and enter the hearts of the people. As the people see that these workers are messengers of mercy, the ministers of grace, they are ready to listen to the words spoken by them" **(EVANGELISM, P. 158).**

<u>Visit</u> everyone on the pastor's updated **interest file.**
<u>Visit</u> all **former** and **inactive Seventh-day Adventists.**
<u>Visit</u> all **media interests.**
<u>Visit</u> children, youth, and **spouses of church members** who have not committed their lives to Christ.

People are won to Christ in the context of warm, friendly relationships. Visitation enables us to make friends so we can develop Christian friends who become Seventh-day Adventist Christian friends.

03 | ## Teach church members to organize a literature ministry.

Truth-filled **literature sows seeds for God's eternal harvest.** The **purpose of literature ministry** is to **develop interests and advertise** upcoming community outreach programs. An organized literature distribution program conducted systematically will continually discover new interests for church programs. It will keep a steady stream of people flowing into community outreach programs and to develop a continuing stream of new interests:

A. Literature teams divide up the territory and **systematically pass out:**

- Bible **enrollment cards**
- Bible study **seminar flyers**
- Health Expo and **cooking school brochures**
- **Archaeology seminar brochures**
- **Evangelistic** meeting **handbills, doorknockers, posters,** etc.

God will lead seeking people to **read a piece of literature** and their whole lives will be changed. Before your literature teams embark on their missionary journey, God is preparing the minds of people to receive the truth-filled literature they will distribute. The Holy Spirit goes ahead of them to open minds to divine truth and develop receptivity for eternal things.

> "**Publications must be multiplied,** and **scattered** like the leaves of autumn. These silent messengers are **enlightening and molding** the minds of **thousands** in every country and in every clime" **(THE REVIEW AND HERALD, NOV. 21, 1878).**

"To give *all nations* the message of warning,—this is to be the object of our efforts. A way will be prepared for the faithful worker to labor at all times and seasons for the conversion of souls. **Upon all who have received the word of God there rests the burden of doing this work.** From city to city, and from country to country, they are to **carry the publications** containing the promise of the Saviour's soon coming. These **publications are to be translated into every language;** for to all the world the gospel is to be preached. To every worker Christ promises the divine efficiency that will make his labors a success" **(THE REVIEW AND HERALD, FEB. 9, 1905).**

B. Have quarterly **systematic mailings** to the interest file. See interest file letters on page 194–197.

- These mailings will develop interests for Bible studies.
- The **literature ministry** team that is **formed** during the community outreach phase can also do the weekly mailings during the evangelistic meetings.

04 | Equip church members how to be lay Bible instructors.

The **most effective way** to **train** lay **Bible instructors** is **on-the-job training.**

Jesus trained His disciples by taking them with Him on His evangelistic journeys. As a pastor or a church officer experienced in giving Bible studies, choose a church member who has potential as a lay Bible instructor and take him or her with you. Let him or her **observe** how you do it. **Explain how to use the Bible study lessons** and the best approaches. Encourage each of your experienced lay leaders to train someone else.

- Encourage **each lay Bible instructor** to have at least **one Bible study** prior to the evangelistic meetings.
- There are many **methods of Bible study.**
  - **One-to-one** Bible studies
  - Bible studies through **correspondence**
  - Bible studies through **audio and videotape** ministry
- See *Light Your World for God* manual for more information on training and equipping.

05 | Train church members how to conduct "home Bible study groups."

Here is a possibility that we have used effectively and may work nicely for you. We have discovered that **small home Bible study groups** are **one of the most effective ways to develop interests for a major reaping series.** Although there are many possibilities of study for these small groups, we especially like the *Unsealing Daniel's Mysteries* lessons. The lessons highlight **three major themes in Daniel.**

- **The character of God**
- **Godly character qualities**
- **Last-day events**

We have regularly organized **twenty-five to seventy-five of these groups, meeting three to four months before our evangelistic meetings.** Here is how you can begin:

- **Choose four to six church members** to form a small group.
- **Meet** with the groups and review the *Unsealing Daniel's Mysteries* material.
- **Instruct** your groups to meet together to pray and bond as a group at least three weeks before they have their first meeting with their guests.
- **Encourage** each one of them to invite **a non-Adventist friend to join** them for this series of Bible studies focusing on the book of Daniel.
- **Provide** each group with **two hundred** *Unsealing Daniel's Mysteries* invitational **brochures,** a set of **videos,** and four **color lessons** for each participant.
- The groups should plan to meet once a week for **twelve weeks** before your evangelistic series.
- **Encourage** all members of the small groups to attend **the evangelistic series** and provide a reserved seat ticket to the evangelistic meetings for each attendee.

06 | Equip church members how to conduct community health programs.

In an increasing secular society, health ministry is an "entering wedge" to open hearts and minds to the gospel. Cast the gospel net broadly. **Jesus met the felt needs of people** to open their hearts to spiritual realities. In

- JOHN CHAPTER 2, Jesus met social needs at the wedding feast at Cana of Galilee.
- JOHN 3, in His discussion with Nicodemus, Jesus appealed to the rabbi's deeper spiritual nature.
- JOHN 4, Jesus met the emotional needs of the Samaritan woman by offering her that which truly satisfies—the water of life.

- **JOHN 5,** Jesus met the physical needs of a man afflicted for thirty eight years at the Pool of Bethesda.
- **JOHN 6,** He fed the five thousand. It is no wonder that the crowds wanted to make Him King. He had so identified with them and met their needs that they wanted Him to be their Leader forever.

People's hearts and minds will be open to the gospel when, like Jesus, your church is actively involved meeting community needs through:

- **Health fairs, blood-pressure screenings, health expos**
- **Stop smoking plans**
- **Cooking schools and nutrition demonstrations**
- **Weight management** programs
- **Stress management** seminars
- **Wellness seminars, Creation health** seminars
- **Family** life programs
- **A host of other felt-need** programs

There will be plenty of interested people for the evangelistic meetings because their prejudice has been broken down and they are now interested in hearing God's Word.

> "**Nothing will open doors for the truth like evangelistic medical missionary work.** This will find access to hearts and minds, and will be a means of converting many to the truth. . . .
>
> "Doors that have been closed to him who merely preaches the gospel will be opened to the intelligent medical missionary. God reaches hearts through the relief of physical suffering" (**EVANGELISM, P. 513**).

Trained and equipped church members organized into small missionary groups in various ministries will make an impact on their communities.

 # KEY #3—COMMUNITY OUTREACH

The biblical model of the church is God's people, the body of Christ, equipped to serve, using their God-given gifts to meet needs everywhere in Jesus' name.

Pastors of growing churches place emphasis on equipping their members to use their gifts in service through a variety of ministries. Christ's method of loving service is the key to all successful evangelism.

> "**Christ's method alone will give true success in reaching the people. The Saviour mingled with men as one who desired their good. He showed His sympathy for them, ministered to their needs, and won their confidence. Then He bade them, 'Follow Me'** " (**THE MINISTRY OF HEALING, P. 143**).

The more church members catch this vision of ministry, the more their commitment, and the more the church will grow. People are attracted to the church through two entities, its people and its programs. It is very simple. The **fewer** the **programs** you conduct, the **fewer** the **interests** you will develop. Programs or ministries are the vehicles God uses to touch lives.

Don't misunderstand, **we are not suggesting that programs alone win people to Jesus.** Let's make it clear. Community outreach programs never won anyone to Christ. <u>**People win people**</u> to Jesus. Our Lord uses people not programs. But the more programs, the more opportunity to contact more people.

We recommend that each church set a **goal** to have **three times its active membership** attending felt-need, small-group, or Bible-study community outreach programs each year. Reach out into your community through Bible-based and felt-need health programs three to six months before you evangelistic meetings and watch what God does.

> The **role** of the **pastor** is **to lead** his people into **spiritual renewal, equip** them for service, and **unleash them** through a variety of ministries/**community outreach** initiatives to touch lives for the kingdom.

But the goal of all of this community activity is to influence people for God's kingdom. One way to do this is to **invite them to public evangelistic meetings.**

Practical Ways of Transitioning From Community Outreach Programs to the Evangelistic Meetings

- Use the **pre-registration form** on page 205 (have a sample).
- Be sure every Bible instructor **signs up** their Bible studies for the evangelistic meetings.
- **Pre-register** all those attending the **home Bible seminars.**
- Pass out the **pre-registration form** at the **archaeology seminar.**
- Have the **pre-registration forms** and the evangelistic handbills at the **health expo.** You can use these in the **Trust in Divine Power** section of the booth.
- Be sure the handbills and the **pre-registration forms** are distributed the last two weeks of the **cooking school.** Mention the **Revelation of Hope** evangelistic meetings publicly in the cooking school and sign people up.
- **Collect** the pre-registration forms right there at the nutrition class.
- **Encourage** each church member to **pre-register** their **friends** and **neighbors** for the **evangelistic meetings.**

Remember, there is **no substitute for personal relationships.** Community outreach programs provide the church with an opportunity to meet needs and build relationships. **Friends inviting friends** is the **most effective** form of **evangelistic advertising.**

An active community outreach program will give success to public evangelism!

KEY #4—PUBLIC EVANGELISM

When **interest** in the **gospel** is **developed** through Bible studies and felt-need programs, **reaping logically follows.** The gospel seed has been sown and it is now **time to reap** the **harvest.** God promises to grant a harvest through biblical preaching and public evangelism. The preached Word transforms lives. The preached Word touches hearts and is an instrument of conversion in God's hands.

Paul describes the power of evangelistic preaching this way, "For the message of the cross is foolishness to those who are perishing, but to us who are being saved it **is the power of God. . . .** It pleased God through the foolishness of the message preached to save those who believe" **(1 CORINTHIANS 1:18, 21).** For the apostle Paul, the preached Word was life transformational. It changed lives. It delivered men and women from hopelessness and despair. The book of Acts clearly demonstrates the **priority the disciples placed on evangelistic preaching.** It mentions their preaching over twenty times in passages like these:

"And when they had prayed, the place where they were assembled together was shaken; and they were all filled with the Holy Spirit, and **they spoke the word of God with boldness"** (ACTS 4:31).

"Therefore those who were scattered went **everywhere preaching the word"** (ACTS 8:4).

"We sought to go to Macedonia, concluding that the Lord had called us to **preach the gospel** to them" (ACTS 16:10).

"**Evangelistic work, opening the Scriptures** to others, warning men and women of what is coming upon the world, **is to occupy more and still more of the time of God's servants"** (THE REVIEW AND HERALD, AUG. 2, 1906).

This **entire manual** will outline the steps necessary to have a successful public evangelistic series. We will focus especially on **Key #4—Public Evangelism.**

In this manual, we fully explain how

- **to organize** for a public evangelistic meeting, the committees necessary for a smooth functioning series,
- **effective advertising,**
- **preparing your budget,**
- **preaching powerful sermons,**
- **the art of visitation,**
- **how to make appeals and answer objections,**
- **how to prepare candidates for baptism, and**
- **how to nurture and follow up** with new converts. We have included a number of **forms in the appendix** that you can photocopy and reproduce for your series.

Public evangelism is the heartbeat of the church today!

KEY #5—NURTURE AND FOLLOW-UP

Nurture and follow-up was a significant part of the disciples' evangelistic strategy. When people accepted Christ, understood His Word, and were baptized, they were integrated into a nurturing body of believers.

The book of Acts describes their experience in these words:

> **"And they continued steadfastly in the apostles' doctrine and fellowship, in the breaking of bread, and in prayers"** (ACTS 2:42).

Note: A more detailed study of the "Five Keys to Successful Evangelism" can be found in *Light Your World for God* training manual.

The **"Five Keys to Successful Evangelism"** are the **foundation** for a **successful evangelistic series.** They provide a solid foundation to build upon.

EVANGELISM MAY BE LIKENED TO THE BUILDING OF A HOUSE

If we compare an evangelistic series to building a house—we might call it in biblical terms **"The Household of Faith"**—we might say we need **four elements.**

1. **A Solid Foundation**—The **Five Keys** to Successful Evangelism
2. **A Master Plan**—An evangelistic countdown **calendar**
3. **Top-Quality Supplies**—field-tested **materials**
4. **Efficient Builders**—**Pastors** and **laity**

Now let's pause for a moment and consider the importance of developing a MASTER PLAN.

The Master Plan = Evangelistic Countdown Calendar

A **builder** always consults **architectural drawings** when building a house. In the same way, pastors and lay members doing **public evangelism** need a **master plan** in order to have **success.** This master plan is structured around the "Five Keys to Successful Evangelism."

ELEMENT #2—A Master Plan

THE PREPARATION OF AN EVANGELISTIC COUNTDOWN CALENDAR

This **OVERALL STRATEGY** with each specific activity is placed in a **calendar** and serves as the **master plan** for the entire **evangelistic program.** It outlines all the specific activities that take place over a twelve- to eighteen-month period. Preparing an evangelistic calendar is crucial. It is not possible to do effective evangelism without detailed plans. All **major activities** are placed **on the calendar.**

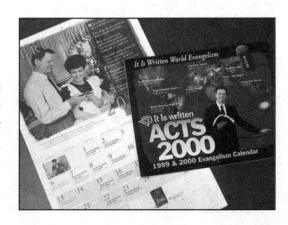

Start at the **point** of the **evangelistic series** and **work backwards. Begin** with the date of the **opening night of your evangelistic series** and begin your planning events at least nine months to a year in advance. For those programs that you want to end just before the evangelistic meetings, begin to count back from the opening night's meeting.

For example:

If you are beginning an evangelistic **series in October, count back nine months** to January to plan a major **evangelistic rally** and launch your prayer ministry.

Set the date for your evangelistic meetings first. Next, plan

- Your **revival dates,**
- Your **equipping and training seminars,**
- Your **community outreach activities,**
- Leading up to your **public evangelistic meetings,** and
- Your **nurture events.**

Once you have **The Plans** and **The Foundation,** you are ready to build. But you must have "**good materials.**"

TOP-QUALITY Supplies = Good Field-Tested Materials

It is best to **use field-tested materials,** which have been used to impact thousands of lives. These **time-tested materials** will make a difference in your evangelism too. Here is a **list of materials** we have found helpful.

ELEMENT #3—Top-Quality Materials

USE FIELD-TESTED MATERIALS

In order to have real success in public evangelism, it is imperative to conduct **multiple seed-sowing activities.** Praying people who are praying for the outpouring of the Holy Spirit will make a dramatic difference. Having a solid preparation program is absolutely essential. Choosing the right preparation programs and materials is very important. Use programs and materials that have been **field tested by others.** You want the assurance that the materials you use will work because they have been used many times in the past.

01 | BIBLE STUDIES

It is not necessary to write your own set of Bible studies. There are many good, solid, proven sets of studies that have been field tested. Be sure to choose a series of Bible studies that is **simple, clear, and a straight chain of Bible truth based on the commandments of God and the testimony of Jesus.** This is very important. Ellen White writes:

"God is leading out a people and establishing them on the one great platform of faith **'the commandments of God and the testimony of Jesus.** He has given His people a straight chain of Bible truth, clear and connected. This truth is of heavenly origin and has been searched for as for hidden treasure. It has been dug out through careful searching of the Scriptures and through much prayer" **(TESTIMONIES, VOL. 3, P. 447).**

Bible Study Interest Cards

Although there are quite a variety of **Bible study interest cards** available, we recommend either the **"Jesus Cards"** or the **"Prophetic Beast"** cards by **Color Press,** as a mass mail piece or a hand distribution item for your literature teams. These **Bible study interest cards** will provide a steady stream of good interests for your Bible study program.

Search for Certainty Bible lessons

- The *Search for Certainty* lessons are **a set of thirty fully illustrated, four-color, Christ-centered Bible lessons** used by lay Bible instructors to teach the full message to their Bible students. They **cover all the major topics in Scripture.**
- The *Search for Certainty* Bible lessons present each Bible truth as a **link in a connected chain.** The lessons are systematically arranged. One lesson flows logically into the next.
- The *Search for Certainty* lessons have transitions from one text to another.
- The *Search for Certainty* lessons have an appeal at the end of each topic, giving the Bible student an opportunity to make a decision.
- **There is a list of all the *Search for Certainty* lessons on page 203 in the appendix under "Essential Supplies for a Public Evangelistic Campaign."**

Bible Study Program

The **Bible study program** may **start small,** but it will build as time goes on.

- **Select two to four** people and train them to give Bible studies. These small numbers will grow.
- Before the evangelistic meetings begin, most **lay Bible instructors will have at least one contact** to invite to the meetings.
- **Providing** your Bible instructors with **field-tested materials** is vitally important.

02 | ## Home Bible Seminars—*Unsealing Daniel's Mysteries*

- *Unsealing Daniel's Mysteries* is a series of **twelve dynamic, life-changing lessons on each chapter of Daniel. Each lesson stresses the practical aspects of Daniel's teaching against the backdrop of last-day events.**

The lessons and accompanying DVDs are designed to:

- **Deepen** your **faith, encourage faithfulness, and enhance devotional life.**
- These DVDs, videos, and lessons have been **used by thousands** across North America. Pastors and lay members have found the material **excellent for small groups** to **develop interests** about three months before public evangelistic meetings.
- A large number attending *Unsealing Daniel's Mysteries* will **transfer** into the evangelistic meeting.

03 | Biblical Archaeology Program—*Ancient Discoveries*

This newly developed, **fully illustrated series** with accompanying **study guides** and **DVDs** regularly draws large audiences preliminary to a public series of evangelistic meetings. You have a choice of either conducting the series yourself with the **PowerPoint graphics** or using the DVDs for the main presentation and then **reviewing** the **material** presented via the written material.

The *Ancient Discoveries* **Archaeology Seminar** is an excellent approach for **small house meetings** as well. The topics include:

- Amazing Discoveries in Egypt
- Fantastic Finds
- A Journey to Iraq
- Jesus and the Smoldering Middle East
- Israel: Land of Promise
- A Journey to the Isle of Patmos
- Revelation's Seven Churches

04 | Felt-Need Programs

Health Expo

If you have a number of **health professionals** in your church, you may desire to conduct a **health expo.** The health expo consists of:

- Varying **stations emphasizing** the **essentials of health.**
- Each station is manned by a **health volunteer** who **explains** that **aspect of health** as visitors visit each booth routinely.
- A variety of **health-screening tests** are given.
- There is also a **computerized health age** appraisal available.

Each **panel** for the health expo has been prepared by health experts and is **scientifically sound** as well as **artistically attractive.**

There is a new **wellness magazine** designed especially to be distributed at health expos and health fairs **by Pacific Press.** It is inexpensive and covers the essential principles of good health as outlined below.

- **W—Water**
- **E—Exercise**
- **L—Love for God**—Trust in Divine Power
- **L—Lifestyle**—Temperance
- **N—Nutrition**
- **E—Environment**—Air
- **S—Sunshine**
- **S—Sleep**—Rest

Cooking School

The *Natural Lifestyle Cooking* school is a **seven-night event** covering:
- **Bread-making made easy**
- **Making breakfast a better meal**
- **Meal balancing**
- **The advantages of a plant-based diet**
- **Simple healthful suppers**
- **Holidays and special occasions**
- **Simple healthful desserts**

There are **DVDs** and a **workbook** with scientific nutritional lessons **and** a beautiful, four-color *Natural Lifestyle Cooking* cookbook.

There are also **advertising** materials for the *Natural Lifestyle Cooking* nutrition classes. A sample of the brochure is on page 31. An electronic brochure is available also. There are also flyers, bulletin inserts, and radio spots.

Once you have a **master plan** (the evangelistic calendar), a **solid foundation** (The Five Keys to Successful Evangelism), and **top-quality supplies** (field-tested materials), the next is **efficient builders** (pastors and laity) working together.

Church members **praying, planning,** and **working together** with their pastors **spells evangelistic success**.

ELEMENT #4—Builders
Putting Forth Faithful Effort

A house will never get built if you don't have **faithful workers.** Someone has to lay the foundation, pour the concrete, frame the house, put the roof on, and work on all the details of the inside. A house does not get built by itself. It is similar in public evangelism. **Jesus uses people.** The **Holy Spirit blesses the efforts of committed Christians.**

Someone has to do the work faithfully. God blesses what we do, not what we wish to do or never do. God rewards our humble efforts when we labor for Him. Success in evangelism is a combination of divine power and human effort. Our Lord promises,

"Whatever a man **sows,** that he will also **reap**" (GALATIANS 6:7).

It is not any one thing that makes evangelism successful. It is a combination of many things.

Some people have asked, "Why are some evangelistic meetings more **successful than others?**" **Success** comes by **tending to the little things;** by not giving up when you feel like giving up and it looks like few people are interested. It takes many streams to make a mighty river. **Evangelistic activities often start out small and keep building.** The Holy Spirit will bless the literature we distribute, the small groups we conduct, the visits we make, the Bible studies we give, the health programs we conduct, and the evangelistic sermons we preach. Here is an example of what could happen if church members worked together in evangelistic activities.

> **Imagine** what might happen if the members of **your church** were **actively involved** in **distributing** literature, **mailing** to the interest file, **visiting** former Adventists, **giving Bible studies, conducting** home Bible seminars, **reaching out** to the community through a variety of **health seminars,** and bathing all these activities in **earnest intercessory prayer.**
>
> Can you catch a glimpse of what might happen if these interests were **pre-registered** for your church's evangelistic meetings? The **church** or **auditorium** would be **full every night** with interested people.

Many little things make a big difference! Remember:

Large evangelistic **results come** as a unified, Spirit-filled team of pastors and lay people are **willing** to faithfully persevere in the **little things that make a big difference.**

"He who is **faithful** in what is **least** is **faithful** also in **much;** and he who is unjust in what is least is unjust also in much" (LUKE 16:10).

In Luke 19:17, Jesus' words are very penetrating and powerful!

"And he said to him, '**Well done,** good servant; because you **were faithful** in a **very little, have authority** over ten cities.' "

If pastors, evangelists, and lay members are not willing to **faithfully preach to a few** in **small campaigns,** God will not give us the opportunity or responsibility of **preaching in large campaigns.** This concept is confirmed by the prophet of God in the book *Evangelism.*

> "**This work in God's service**, to meet the moral darkness, **requires self-denial, toil**, and **persevering effort**, and **earnest faith**."

> "Many **flatter** themselves that they **could do great things** if they only had the **opportunity**, but something has always prevented them; Providence has hedged their way in so that they could not do what they desired to do."

> "We expect **no great opportunity will meet us** on the road, but by prompt and vigorous action we **must seize the opportunities, make opportunities and master difficulties**" (EVANGELISM, P. 647).

As we enter into the work of **public evangelism,** there will be **difficulties** and **challenges,** but as we faithfully take on these difficulties, God will bless in unusual ways. **He will powerfully bless our humblest efforts and give us unusual results.** We will see miraculous conversions. Hearts will be touched and lives will be changed. We will see some results here but **in eternity we will see the full result of our labors.** Heaven will be wonderful because we will see how God used even our smallest, sincerest efforts for the glory of His kingdom.

If you are <u>too big</u> to do the <u>small things,</u> then you are <u>too small</u> for God to give you <u>big results.</u> Pastors and laity should unite in cooperating in these **four elements:**

- **Following the "Five Keys to Successful Evangelism"**
- **Planning an evangelistic calendar**
- **Using fField-tested materials**
- **Putting forth faithful effort**

There will be a great harvest of souls!
God has promised it and you can count on it!

CHAPTER 3

HOW TO INCREASE YOUR EVANGELISTIC AUDIENCE FROM PRE-WORK

Evangelism is a **process** not an **event.** It is part of an ongoing, **continuing ministry** in local congregations to **win souls** for Christ.

It does not begin or end with public evangelistic meetings. If the **church** has little burden for souls and is **complacent about winning the lost,** the efforts of the most outstanding evangelist will produce few results.

Ellen White makes it plain in this thought-provoking statement:

"A serious and perhaps **unsuspected hindrance** to the **success** of the truth is to be found in our **churches** themselves. . . . For this reason the **labor** of our most able ministers has been at times **productive of little good.** The very best sermons may be preached, the message may be just what the people need, and yet no souls be gained as sheaves to present to Christ.

"In laboring where there are already some in the faith, the minister should at first seek not so much to convert unbelievers, as to train the **church-members** for acceptable co-operation. Let him labor for them individually, endeavoring to arouse them to seek for a **deeper experience** themselves and to **work for others**" **(GOSPEL WORKERS, P. 196).**

This is exactly what Jesus did. Certainly, we cannot improve on the Master's methods. **Jesus spent three and a half years training the disciples to be effective soul winners.** The apostle Paul spent a year and a half in Ephesus teaching the gospel and evangelistic principles in the school of Tyrannus. He counseled his young colleague Timothy to be ready to preach the gospel, "in season and out of season." In other words, **be continuously sharing the message of Jesus** and His truth with people around you daily **(2 TIMOTHY 4:2).**

Evangelism is a **systematic process** of **sowing** and **reaping, equipping** and **sharing, personal visitation** and **public evangelistic** meetings. Here is a formula for successful evangelism.

50 percent Pre-Campaign Preparation
20 percent Public Evangelism
30 percent Preservation—Nurture and Follow-up

The **promise** of God is sure!

> "Do not be deceived, God is not mocked; for whatever a **man sows,** that **he will** also **reap**" (GALATIANS 6:7).

In both the natural and spiritual world, there are **laws** of the **harvest.** One of the most basic is simply this, "If you want to have a harvest, it is necessary to **sow** the seed." No **farmer** expects God to work a miracle and germinate seed that he has not sown.

- The only **prayers** God can bless for souls are prayers we offer.
- The only **visits** God can bless are the ones we make.
- The only **literature** God can bless is literature we distribute.
- The only **Bible studies** God can bless are the ones we give.
- The only **health programs** God can bless are the ones we conduct.
- The only **Bible seminars** God can bless are the ones we hold.
- The only **evangelistic meetings** God can bless are the ones we conduct.

It is presumptuous to believe we can have a great harvest without adequate **effort** in **sowing** the seed of God's Word. In fact, it is in the **process** of **sowing** that our own **hearts are watered** by the Holy Spirit and prepared for the harvest. As we **participate** with Christ in touching the lives of others with the gospel, the **Holy Spirit transforms** our own hearts, **making** our **churches centers** of His healing grace.

When a church organizes **prayer bands, visits interests, conducts** multifaceted **health programs,** gives **Bible studies,** conducts **Bible seminars,** and **then** follows up with **evangelistic meetings,** there **will be a harvest.** God Himself promises it. A church that is actively reaching out to win souls for Christ is a church that God will bless with converts for the kingdom of God.

In this section, we will specifically emphasize **pre-campaign preparation.** Here are the goals of pre-campaign preparation:

Goals for pre-campaign preparation

1. **To lead** as many church members as possible into a deep spiritual commitment to share Jesus and His end-time message.
2. **To organize** the church into small intercessory prayer groups.
3. **To equip** church members to make effective visits for Christ, build relationships, and share God's Word.
4. **To equip** church members in specific areas of community outreach to meet physical, mental, and spiritual needs.
5. **To develop** as many interests as possible preliminary to the public evangelistic meetings through personal visitation and community outreach programs.

6. **To teach** church members how to **pre-enroll** their **contacts** through special **reserved seat tickets** and the evangelistic brochure.

7. **To pre-register** as many guests as possible for the opening night of the **Revelation of Hope** evangelistic meetings.

Steps in Building Attendance for the Revelation of Hope Evangelistic Meetings

01 | Invite all those attending each community outreach program to your Revelation of Hope evangelistic meetings.

- The relationships you develop in the varied seminars provide opportunities for you to **encourage people to attend** the **evangelistic meetings.**

Have **evangelistic handbills** and **reserved seat tickets** printed and ready to pass out at all the community outreach programs. Let us give you a few examples of how to transition from community outreach felt-need classes to the evangelistic series.

Natural Lifestyle Cooking Classes

At the cooking school or health programs, you can **say** something like this:

"Many of you have told us how thrilled you have been as you have **attended the *Natural Lifestyle Cooking* classes** for the past seven weeks. You have been thankful for the principles you have been learning that will help you to live seven to ten years longer.

"Since this has been a **health seminar,** we primarily shared health principles. Although documented scientific studies have shown that you can live longer if you follow these principles, we would like to give you much more.

"There will be **another seminar following this one** that will reveal divine principles from the Bible of how you can live a hundred million years longer or **how you can live forever.**

"This **biblically based seminar** answers the deepest questions of the human heart. It focuses on the Bible's last book—**Revelation.**

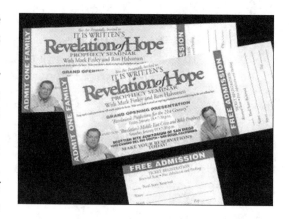

"We would like to invite you to this seminar called **Revelation of Hope.** Our ushers have a brochure for the Revelation of Hope series and reserved seat tickets for each of you."

At this point, **we pass out the evangelistic handbill** along **with the pre-registration card.** We review the handbill and summarize a few of the highlights of the seminar and review the first few nights' topics. Then make comments something like this:

"If you would **like to attend** this seminar, just **fill out the pre-registration card** for a reserved seat. Give it to the usher at the door as you go out this evening. We **look forward to seeing you** again at the next exciting seminar on Bible prophecy."

02 | Invite all small group home Bible study seminar attendees to the evangelistic series.

- Recently, we have had outstanding success in developing interests in the *Unsealing Daniel's Mysteries* home Bible study seminar and then **bridging** them to our **Revelation of Hope** evangelistic series.

Hundreds of **lay people** are finding new success in witnessing. As in the New Testament model, they are **opening their homes** as centers of evangelism.

- The apostle Paul invited interested people to his rented home in Rome and shared Bible truth with them in small groups. One of Paul's fellow workers, Archippus, led out in a **small house group Bible study,** which grew into a church **(PHILEMON 2).**
- The **disciples ministered from house to house** and shared God's Word to small groups of people **(ACTS 20:20).**
- Nympha **developed a house group** in Laodicea **(COLOSSIANS 4:15).**
- New Testament **believers invited their friends into their homes** to share Jesus' love and study God's Word.

In our post-modern twenty-first-century culture, **home Bible study groups are still an effective way to win people for God's kingdom.** As church members pray for specific people, invite their friends and neighbors to their homes, and share God's Word, home Bible study groups become the bridge to the public evangelistic meeting.

Unsealing Daniel's Mysteries Bible studies can be used for this home seminar.

As we discussed in chapter 2, *Unsealing Daniel's Mysteries* **is a twelve-session DVD or video series** focusing especially on the prophecies of Daniel. This seminar **covers every chapter** in the book of Daniel and emphasizes specifically:

- The **character qualities** necessary to thrive in these tumultuous times.
- The great **end-time prophecies of Daniel.**

- The sovereignty, power, and wisdom of God.

Each chapter is **fully illustrated** with **graphics, prophetic images, charts,** and **diagrams.**

Friends and neighbors are **invited** to come and **view** one **video** or **DVD** presentation a week for **twelve weeks.** Each program is correlated with an *Unsealing Daniel's Mysteries* **lesson.** The individual attending the small group meeting completes the lesson at home that week.

As each session begins, the **Bible lesson is reviewed,** summarizing the previous week's topic. The next *Unsealing Daniel's Mysteries* DVD or video is shown.

This unique approach enables individuals in the small home group to become acquainted with essentials of Bible prophecy and practical godliness. This enables them to have a basic grasp of Bible truth before the evangelistic meetings and **prepares them to make decisions in the meetings. The relationships built** in the context of a home setting **provide the basis for confidence in the spiritual integrity of the host of the Bible study and the church members attending.**

Invite every participant in the home Bible seminars to the evangelistic meetings.

- **Give** them a **handbill** and a pre-registration card.
- Have them **sign up** for a reserved seat.
- **Collect** their **pre-registration** card.
- **Send** them a **confirmation letter.**
- **Offer** to **go with them** to the **evangelistic meeting.**

03 | Invite all Bible study contacts to the evangelistic meetings.

One of the **best sources of interest** for evangelistic meetings is **Bible study contacts.** As lay people study the Bible with newly interested persons, public evangelistic meetings are the arena of truth in which Bible study contacts make decisions. **Personal Bible study ministry and public evangelistic proclamation blend to give soul winners their greatest success.**

Without personal work, public evangelism produces meager results.

Without public evangelism, personal Bible study ministry lacks the forum for the greatest number of decisions. **Personal and public witnessing efforts blended** together produce an abundant harvest for the Master.

(For more information on a **weekly witnessing program** called **Soup and Salvation,** see chapter 9 in the book *Light Your World for God.*)

How to increase the possibility of your Bible study contacts coming to the evangelistic meetings:

- **Give** each Bible student **a handbill** and tell them about the **Revelation of Hope** meetings.
- Offer to provide transportation for them to the meetings.
- If they have not completed the **Bible lessons,** tell them they can **continue** during the series **through the Bible school.**

NOTE: We use the same set of *Search for Certainty* lessons at the **evangelistic meetings** in our **Bible school** to enable the people who have not completed their lessons in the home studies to continue studying the lessons and complete them during the evangelistic meetings.

04 | Invite former Seventh-day Adventists.

Most cities have a significant share of former Seventh-day Adventists. Usually, there are many former Seventh-day Adventists in the pastor's updated interest file. Develop a plan **to visit former Seventh-day Adventists** with the express purpose of **developing relationships with them.** People may argue with our doctrines, debate about what is wrong with the church, and feel angry or deeply hurt over how they have been treated, but **most people respond to kindness.**

NOTE: Remember **former Adventists need love, understanding,** and **compassion.** Ministry among former Adventists is a long-term commitment. Usually, you will need to **visit more than once,** although there are times that the Holy Spirit has been mightily working on the hearts of former Adventists, preparing the way for your visit, and **you will find them open to returning to Christ and His church very quickly.**

Here are a few general principles in working with former Adventists.

- It may take weeks of visitation until you build a sufficient **level of confidence** where former Adventists trust you enough to open their hearts regarding their inner struggles.
- Make a **long-term commitment** to develop meaningful relationships with former Adventists. **Don't** be concerned about **urging them to return to the church** on your first visit. Former Adventists often are looking for the love the church preaches to be translated into action in the lives of the members.
- When they see **"love in action,"** the Spirit will touch their hearts and **lead them back to the church** that has loved them in spite of their mistakes, and they will respond to an approach which acknowledges the church's mistakes and is not overly defensive.

05 | Invite friends, neighbors, and working associates.

Give your friends, neighbors, and working associates an opportunity to attend the evangelistic series by **inviting them personally** to the meetings. Many will respond, if we only ask. I am intrigued by this statement in *The Acts of the Apostles:* "**There are many who are reading the Scriptures who cannot understand their true import. All over the world men and women are looking wistfully to heaven.** Prayers and tears and inquiries go up from souls longing for light, for grace, for the Holy Spirit. **Many are on the verge of the kingdom, waiting only to be gathered in**" **(P. 109)**. You may have colleagues at work who are praying for someone to share God's truth with them.

- You may have **neighbors** whose hearts are open to the ministry of the Holy Spirit now.
- You may have **family members** who would respond to an invitation to attend one of the church's felt-needs seminars or evangelistic meetings, if you only asked. I am reminded of the apostle Paul's statement, "I am **not ashamed of the gospel** of Christ" **(ROMANS 1:16)**. It is my prayer that **we, too, will have the courage to share our faith with those around us.**

06 | Invite contacts from your literature distribution program.

Rather than spasmodically scatter literature all over town. Why not try something different. **Visit a specific territory with literature** at least once a month. Make a long-term commitment to your specific territory. **Get to know** the people who live in these neighborhoods. **Pray** for them. **Develop** positive relationships. **Invite** them to felt-needs seminars through the year. Bring an inspirational book, a DVD, or a Christian music CD as a gift for Christmas. Personally get to know people in your territory by name. As you go door-to-door visiting interested people and distributing literature, **include a handbill advertising the evangelistic series.** Invite your contacts personally, give them a handbill and pray that the Holy Spirit will move upon their hearts.

07 | Personally invite all those on the pastor's interest list through a phone call, a letter, or a visit.

The **pastor's interest list** is one of the **most productive** tools that we have to acquire, cultivate, and nurture interests. A current interest list can be a gold mine for soul-winning results. **Every name is a sacred trust.** As you carefully develop your interest list and organize it thoroughly, remember the names you are processing are people for whom Christ died. I am reminded of this penetrating statement:

"At the foot of the cross, remembering that **for one sinner Christ would have laid down His life**, you may **estimate the value of a soul**" **(CHRIST'S OBJECT LESSONS, P. 197).**

Cultivate the interest list by mailing systematic letters before the evangelistic meetings begin. Typically, we like to **mail a letter each quarter to all the interests on the interest list.**

- The **first** letter of the new year offers them a **free book.**
- The **second** invites them to take a series of the *Search for Certainty* lessons.

- The **third** invites them to a **felt-needs seminar**.
- The **fourth** invites them to **attend the evangelistic meetings.** You can find a copy of these letters on pages 194–197. You may want to call people on the interest list as well as personally visit them at least once a year.

08 | Invite all Bible students enrolled in the Bible Correspondence School to attend the evangelistic meetings.

Review the list of your correspondence students and check what lessons they have completed and visit them. When you visit them:

- **Offer** them an inspirational book.
- **Ask** them how they are enjoying the lessons.
- **Answer** any questions they might have.
- **Offer** to pray with them.
- At times, we have used the telephone quite effectively to **call** all of the media interests and attendees of past community outreach seminars to invite them to our evangelistic meetings. Of course, we
- **Follow up with a special letter of invitation to the evangelistic meetings.** If your members have Bible studies already from the interest list, encourage them to **give each Bible student a handbill and reserved seat ticket** for the Revelation of Hope evangelistic meetings.

09 | Mail a handbill and a letter of invitation to all media interests.

Most of the main media ministries like *Voice of Prophecy, It Is Written, Breath of Life,* and *Amazing Facts* will mail a letter of invitation to interests who are watching their broadcasts in your area. You will need to contact each media ministry individually to discover how best to access their interest list.

Guests will show up at your evangelistic meeting with the letter in their hands explaining that they got a special invitation from the speaker of *Voice of Prophecy, It Is Written, Breath of Life,* or *Amazing Facts.*

10 | Hand-deliver an evangelistic invitation to personal friends and relatives.

Ask yourself this **question: Who** of my closest friends or family members, who do not know Jesus' truth for these last days, may respond to an invitation to the **Revelation of Hope** series? **Invite** them to the meetings.

Remember that **God has placed "eternity" in every person's heart (**ECCLESIASTES

3:11) and **Jesus is the "light"** that lights every person born into this world **(JOHN 1:9).**

The Holy Spirit is at work in hearts all around us, and as we extend the invitation, **we often will be surprised at who responds.**

11 | ## Pass out a Revelation of Hope handbill along with a pre-registration form on Sabbath morning.

We usually **pass out evangelistic handbills and reserved seat ticket forms** at least three times, starting three weeks before the evangelistic meetings begin. There will be church members who are impressed by the Holy Spirit to invite their families, friends, and working associates. In one evangelistic meeting a number of years ago, when I appealed to members to invite their relatives who may not know Jesus and His end-time truth, a local elder requested around twenty reserved seat ticket forms. He then invited all of his family members including his wife, sons, daughters-in-law, and grandchildren. At the end of the series, we baptized most of his family. As we inspire our members to invite people, God will do some amazing things.

12 | ## Invite all those who have been a part of your lending library "CD/DVD ministry."

Some church members have been actively distributing **CDs and DVDs** to many of their potential interests. About **two weeks before** the evangelistic series begins, take a **handbill to each** one of those **contacts.**

The goal is to **fill** at least half of whatever evangelistic **auditorium** you have from the **pre-work.** Then let God take care of **filling the second half** by blessing the **advertising brochure** exceedingly abundantly above all you could ask or think.

We have seen Him do that in the past and He will do it again. As we **sow the seed** and actively **cooperate with God** in the pre-work, He will bless the evangelistic advertising in remarkable ways.

What **good news**! As we cooperate with God in reaching out to the lost, He will give us a harvest. As we commit ourselves to His work, He **guarantees** us **results.** The scripture is very plain in this matter.

"Those who **sow** in **tears** shall **reap** in **joy.** He who **continually goes forth** weeping, bearing seed for sowing, **shall doubtless come again** with rejoicing, **bringing his sheaves** with him" **(PSALM 126:5, 6).**

Inspire your church to **be actively involved in pre-work** and you **will _increase_** your **evangelistic audience**!

Follow the simple but effective Spirit-inspired **principles** in this chapter and **watch what God does through you and your members.**

CHAPTER 4

PLANNING THE EVANGELISTIC BUDGET

Conducting a successful evangelistic campaign necessitates careful **financial planning.** The **most important dollar spent** is the **dollar to win souls** for Christ. Our Lord can work miracles to multiply the effectiveness of our funds as He did the loaves and the fishes. He never runs out of resources. **Heaven's bank is never empty.** Hudson Taylor, the great pioneer missionary to China, put it this way: **"God's work done God's way will never lack God's supply."** George Mueller, founder of multiple orphanages in England, carried on a faith ministry for decades and believed that, "God **is well able to supply all of our needs."** He, of course, was paraphrasing PHILIPPIANS 4:19: "For my God shall supply all your needs." Although God will supply all of the finances we need, we do not have one dollar to waste. William Carey, called the father of modern missions, stated, **"Attempt great things for God, expect great things from God."** Look at these encouraging statements, assuring us that when we do soul winning, the funds will come in:

"As men and women are brought into the truth in the cities, the **means will begin to come in.** As surely as **honest souls** will be **converted, their means** will be **consecrated** to the **Lord's service,** and we shall see an **increase** of our **resources"** (EVANGELISM, P. 89).

"Shall we not **advance in faith,** just as if we had thousands of dollars? We do not have half faith enough. Let us act our part in **warning these cities.** The warning message must come to the people who are ready to perish, unwarned, unsaved. How can we delay? **As we advance,** the **means will come.** But we must **advance** by faith, **trusting** in the Lord God of Israel" (EVANGELISM, P. 62).

It is **not** the **size** of your **budget** that will **determine** the **success** of your **evangelistic meeting,** but the **commitment of your members to invite** their friends, neighbors, and working associates, the number of interests your church generates through interpersonal relationships and community events before the meetings, and **how** you **allocate** the **resources you have.** Money used wisely goes much further than money which is thoughtlessly or carelessly spent.

Here are some **principles** to keep in mind when you are **planning your budget. Divide your budget into three parts to be spent over a nine-month period on pre-work, the evangelistic meetings, and follow-up.**

Pre-work—30 percent of the budget

Spend **30 percent** of the budget on pre-work. This is a good use of your evangelistic dollars, since many of the individuals that you work with before the evangelistic meetings begin will be the **first fruits** in your **baptisms.**

We have found through the years that the **best spent money** on pre-work is by conducting the following five programs:

- **Personal Bible studies**
- **Home Bible study groups**
- **Archaeology seminars**
- **Health ministry (health expos, vegetarian cooking schools, weight management, wellness programs, etc.)**
- **Literature outreach**

Remember: Many **pre-programs** are **self-supporting.** The **cooking school** is a good example. With a modest charge, you can **pay for** the **printing of the advertising brochures** if they are hand distributed and given out by church members to their contacts. A modest registration fee will also pay for the **materials, food supplies,** and **samples.**

Often you can get **news articles,** free television, and radio announcements or interviews, since your cooking school classes are a free community service.

Evangelistic meetings—50 percent of the budget

Spend approximately **50 percent** of your total budget on evangelistic **advertising materials, such as lecture outlines, Bible lessons, books, and, if necessary, auditorium rental.** If you do not get people out to the meetings, it is **difficult** to win them for Christ. Advertising is basic, but it is extremely important. It does not substitute for biblical preaching, but you cannot preach to people if they are not there. The following is a list of possible advertising methods:

- **Evangelistic handbills**
- **Posters**
- **Newspaper ads**
- **Radio and TV ads**
- **Electronic handbills and Facebook advertising**
- **Billboards**
- **Flyers**

Once people attend your meetings, nothing will continue to **build** your **attendance** like **biblical preaching.** Powerful preaching will bring people back night after night. God has ordained preaching as a vehicle to save men and women. When a church prays and a Spirit-anointed evangelist preaches, **God guarantees success.**

> "Those who **sow** in tears *shall reap* in joy. He who **continually goes forth weeping,** bearing seed for **sowing, shall doubtless** come again with **rejoicing, bringing** his sheaves with him" **(PSALM 126:5, 6).**

However, there are some things we can do to **maintain and build attendance** during the evangelistic campaign. It is wise to save some of your budget to provide worthwhile **incentives** for people who attend the meetings.

Be sure to budget adequate funds for literature. This includes the cost for the following gifts:

- Lecture magazines
- Gift Bibles
- Gift books

- Gift pictures
- CDs or DVDs

"Very much more can be **accomplished** by the living preacher with the **circulation of papers and tracts** than by the preaching of the word alone without the publications. . . . Many minds can be **reached in no other way**.

"Here is **true missionary work** in which labor and means can be invested with the **best results**" (LIFE SKETCHES, P. 217).

Children's meetings

- Provide a budget for the children's meetings supplies.

Office and record-keeping supplies

To operate a **well-organized campaign** means that there will be some expenses for **office supplies.**

- Ticket books or scanner cards and envelopes
- Decision cards
- Paper for visitation cards, alphabetical list, etc.
- Labels and postage for weekly mailings
- Miscellaneous supplies—rubber bands, paper clips, etc.
- Offering envelopes

Note: The **larger** the **campaign,** the **more you will spend** in this area, but we have found that you will **receive it all back** with the amount of **offerings** the people give. There will also be supplies left over from previous campaigns. These can be used in another campaign.

Nurture and follow-up—20 pecent of the budget

Someone has said, **"In authentic, biblical evangelism, we do not dip them and drop them, we immerse them and instruct them."** Save some of your evangelistic budget to provide books such as *Studying Together* and *What the Bible Says About* to new converts. We regularly enroll our new converts in a weekly Bible study class and encourage them to attend our Sabbath morning new believers' class.

EVANGELISTIC BUDGET PLANNER

EXPENSES

Pre-Campaign Expenses

Interest file mailings

Your costs will be based on the number of letters you mail
and what you offer those who respond to your mailings.

Bible Studies

Interest file development (mailings, postage, etc.)

Bible enrollment card

Bible study lessons

Home Bible Seminars (*Unsealing Daniel's Mysteries*)

Brochures (for hand distribution)

DVDs and lessons

Archaeology Program

Brochures

Outline summaries

Health Expo

Health panels on "New Start"

Advertising

Literature

Cooking School

Brochures

Natural Lifestyle cookbooks

Natural Lifestyle workbooks

Food samples

Note: Although the *Natural Lifestyle Cooking* seminar is **typically self-supporting,** you should **budget the expenses listed above and offset them with a modest registration fee.**

Total Pre-Campaign Expenses

CAMPAIGN EXPENSES

Auditorium Rental (Most campaigns can be held in the churches.)

Advertising

Handbills (Printing)

Handbills (Postage and labeling)   _____

Posters   _____

Newspaper ads   _____

Personal invitation letters   _____

Radio and television ads (use with extra budget)   _____

Meeting Expenses

Literature (Bibles, books, etc.)   _____

Office and record-keeping supplies   _____

Total Meeting Expenses   _____

INCOME

Pre-campaign offering   _____

Local church subsidy   _____

Campaign offering   _____

Follow-up offering   _____

TOTAL INCOME   _____

Total Expenses   _____

Minus Total Income   _____

BALANCE (Conference subsidy requested)   _____

"**The means in our possession** may not seem to be sufficient for the work; but if we will **move forward in faith,** believing in the all-sufficient power of God, **abundant resources will open before us**. If the work be of God, **He Himself will provide the means for its accomplishment.** He will reward honest, simple reliance upon Him. The little that is wisely and economically used in the service of the Lord of heaven will increase in the very act of imparting. In the hand of Christ the small supply of food remained undiminished until the famished multitude were satisfied. **If we go to the Source of all strength,** with our hands of faith outstretched to receive, **we shall be sustained in our work,** even under the most forbidding circumstances, and shall be enabled to give to others the bread of life" **(THE DESIRE OF AGES, P. 371).**

CHAPTER 5

ADVERTISING THAT DRAWS A CROWD

There is **no single method** of **advertising alone** that will **draw large crowds** to public evangelistic meetings. **Effective evangelistic advertising** is a must if you are going to have an outstanding audience. **Use every method** possible to inform people about the meetings. **Repetition** through using as many as possible of the methods of advertising suggested here will increase the results.

> "We must take every justifiable means of bringing the light before the people. Let the **press** be **utilized,** and let **every advertising agency** be **employed** that will call attention to the work. This should not be regarded as nonessential" (TESTIMONIES, VOL. 6, PP. 36, 37).

INEXPENSIVE METHODS OF ADVERTISING THAT ARE VERY EFFECTIVE

01 | Personal invitations

Personal invitations by church members are of course the **most effective** method of advertising.

- Provide your church members with Revelation of Hope **handbills** and pre-registration **reserved seat ticket** forms at least two weeks before the meetings begin.
- Encourage them to **enroll t**heir friends and working associates and **return** the completed stubs to the pre-registration coordinator.

When the **Holy Spirit is powerfully moving** in a congregation, the **church members often take the initiative to personally invite their friends,** relatives, and working associates to the evangelistic series.

02 | Letters mailed to personal contacts

- **Mailing** a **letter** along with a **handbill to every person on the church interest list** is an inexpensive and very effective method of advertising. These invitations should be mailed or delivered at least **ten days before** the meetings begin.

03	**Weekly evangelistic letters**

- Once the series begins, **weekly evangelistic mailings** consistently remind people of the meetings and **motivate** them to regularly attend. They help to keep the attendance **consistent** and draw some people back to the meetings who otherwise would have dropped out. You will find a sample letter in the appendix on page 197.

How to Increase Your Attendance for the Evangelistic Meetings Through Public Advertising

Methods of mass advertising

Mass advertising depends largely on the budget you have to spend. We can be thankful that the **Holy Spirit directs** our advertising. God guides people who are seeking truth to the evangelistic meetings through the advertising brochures. In every community, God creates **receptivity** in the minds of the people. These people respond to mass advertising.

Ellen White expands on this thought in her book *The Acts of the Apostles.*

"All over the **world** men and women are looking wistfully to heaven. Prayers and tears and inquiries go up from souls longing for light, for grace, for the Holy Spirit. **Many** are on the verge of the kingdom, **waiting only** to be **gathered in**" (P. 109).

As **truth seekers receive a handbill** on the prophetic book of Revelation in the mail or from a friend, many are impressed to attend to the meetings. It is Heaven's desire to link up the praying, seeking people who are longing for truth with witnessing Christians.

01	**Handbills**

Things to do that will increase results from the handbill
- Use an **800 number** on the handbill.
- Use telephone operators effectively by having them **pre-register** callers.
- Have telephone operators send a **confirmation letter** to everyone who registers.

Ordering and cost:

- Order your handbills a minimum of **three months before** the evangelistic meetings begin.
- In figuring your **cost** for mailing handbills, you must figure in the cost of the **handbill**, the **addressing,** and the **postage.**

Mailing:

- **Mail** your handbills only within a **twenty to thirty minute driving radius of the meeting place.** If you are in a major city, concentrate them around your auditorium.

Delivery:

- The **in-home delivery** of handbills for evangelistic meetings should be done one week prior to the opening night meeting.
- **Call** your **post office** two days before the handbills are to be delivered to be sure they have received the handbills and plan to begin delivery on the appropriate date.
- Ask a few **church members in the target area** to **call you** as soon as they have received their handbill in the mail.

Results:

- As a rule of thumb, **one to three people** attend the meeting per **one thousand handbills** mailed.
- **Thirty thousand handbills mailed** can attract as many as thirty to ninety people, depending on the city and part of the country.
- The results of the mass mailed handbills will be greater if you place a phone number on the handbill where the person can **pre-register.**
- Remember, if you place a phone number on the handbill, plan to have the **phone staffed** daily, twenty-four hours per day if possible. If total twenty-four-hour coverage is not possible, plan to have phone operators available at least from 8:00 A.M.–5:00 P.M.

02 | Electronic handbills

- **Electronic handbills** are a **creative way** of inviting many people to the evangelistic meetings through e-mail.

"If a press can be secured to be worked during the meeting, **printing leaflets, notices,** and **papers** for distribution, it will have a telling influence" (TESTIMONIES, VOL. 6, P. 36).

03 | Posters

Posters in strategic places

- **Two to three hundred posters in strategic places** reinforce the advertising at least two weeks before the evangelistic meetings and serve as a constant reminder during the meetings.
- Put up your **posters two weeks before the meetings** begin and keep them up throughout the entire meeting.
- Put the **dates of the entire meetings on all posters,** especially if you plan on keeping the posters up the whole time during the series.
- Place your **posters in a concentrated area.** Two hundred posters in a ten-block radius around the hall will draw more people than scattering them all over town.

Small flyers

- These small flyers can be used in **doctors' offices, hospitals, Laundromats,** etc.

Doorknockers

- **Doorknockers** are very easy for church members to distribute. Thousands of door knockers can be **placed on doors** in **apartments, condos,** and **private homes.**

Newspaper advertisements

- **One large ad** is generally far more successful than several small block ads or a single column ad. If you can only afford one large ad, run it five days before opening night when your handbills are being delivered. We prefer ads on the right-hand side of pages 3, 5, 7, or the back page of the newspaper if it is available.
- If your budget allows, **place ads**:
  - Five days, three days, one day before the opening night
  - The **morning** of the **opening night**
  - The **middle** of the **first week** of the meetings
- When possible, include a phone number for people to call and **pre-register** them for reserved seats.
- Do not advertise on the church page if you possibly can avoid it. The **bottom** of **page 3** is the **prime spot.**
- If you are running several ads, ask for the combination rate. Also ask for the church rate and compare rates.

Radio and television interest lists

- *It Is Written, Voice of Prophecy, Breath of Life,* and *La Voz* have **computerized mailing lists** with thousands of names of interested people.
- *Voice of Prophecy* and *It Is Written* ministry **will mail** your **handbill** with a **letter** from the speaker-director for the cost of the postage. There is no charge for printing the letters or stuffing the letters and handbills. If sufficient advance notice is given, the names and addresses are also available on a green bar list. This service request must be placed **four to six weeks** in advance to the mailing.

Radio spots

- Run **fifty to one hundred** spots from Monday morning through Friday at 5:00 P.M. of opening night.
- Be sure to begin your radio spots the day the handbills are delivered.
- Place radio spots for **two or three days** total. It's more effective to have **fifteen to twenty spot announcements** a day for five days than five a day for nine days.

Television spots

Television spots are one of the **most productive,** yet the most costly, forms of advertising, although we have recently had good success with local cable television announcements at a much lower cost than national network television, which is extremely expensive.

- To be effective, the **minimum** media saturation is between **thirty-four to thirty-eight**

spots in the **five-day period** preliminary to the meetings. Plan your TV spot announcements to be aired at the same time when the handbills are being delivered by the post office. Unless you can **afford** these many spots, it is **not advisable** to use them.

- If you use TV, be sure to **include a phone number for pre-registration** to help people crystallize their decision to attend the meetings.
- **Remember the principle of repletion. It's more effective to have fifteen spots on a day for three days than five a day for nine days.**

Web site

With the extensive use of **computers** and social media, one of the best and most profitable types of advertising for the Revelation of Hope evangelistic series (or whatever series you present) is through a **Web site.** We have had hundreds **pre-registered** through this means. **On an average, 30 percent of our pre-registrations for our evangelistic meetings are coming via our Web page.**

- **Set up a Web site** for your evangelistic campaign.
- **Print** the **Web site address** on every piece of **advertising** that goes out for the evangelistic campaign.
  - **Handbills**
  - **Posters**
  - **Doorknockers**
  - **Post cards**
  - **Newspaper ads**
  - **Radio spots**
  - **Television spots**
- Give people an opportunity to **pre-register** for the series on the Web site.

Note important principles:

- Plan to have your **advertising all hit** on **one day.** This gives a much greater impact.
- **Save some of your budget** to provide a worthwhile **incentive** for people to attend the meetings. This is one of your greatest means of building and sustaining your attendance. For example:
  - **Offer** the New King James **Bible** if an individual attends for eighteen nights.
  - **Offer** a **book** when they attend for three important subjects, such as the law, the Sabbath, and the change of the Sabbath.
  - **Offer** a **picture** for each one who brings a guest and give the picture to the guest as well.

As you **implement** many of these **advertising techniques,** God will bless you and **people will come** to your evangelistic meetings. Take **advantage of every opportunity** to build your evangelistic audience. Do everything you can to get people out to the evangelistic meetings on opening night. As the famed evangelist Dwight L. Moody once said, **"We should pray as if everything depended on God and work as if everything depended on us."** John Bunyan added, "You can do a lot more after you pray but nothing until you pray." God will multiply your efforts and do what we cannot do.

Watch and you will see God work miracles!

CHAPTER 6

ORGANIZING THE CHURCH FOR PUBLIC EVANGELISM

The more thoroughly organized your church is the more the Holy Spirit can work through you to produce outstanding results for the kingdom of God. Organization is like the rails a train travels on. The rails do not carry you to your destination but you cannot get there without them. Organization does not give you success, God does, but if you are disorganized, you will limit what God can do in your evangelistic series. For an **evangelistic series** to be **successful,** the church must be thoroughly **organized.** Ellen White makes this point clear in the book *Evangelism*. Heaven's counsel is just as relevant today as when it was written.

> "It is essential to **labor with order,** following an **organized plan** and a definite object. . . .
> "Well-defined plans should be freely presented to all whom they may concern, and it should be ascertained that they are understood. Then require of all those who are at the head of the **various departments** to cooperate in the execution of these plans" **(P. 94).**

The First Three Steps in Organizing for an Evangelistic Series Are:

- **Choose** a campaign **coordinator.**
- **Choose chairpersons for your specific committees.**
- **Establish** your evangelistic **committees.**

Your chairpersons should be chosen at least **four months prior** to the opening of the **campaign** so that the committees can function in an orderly manner.

Involving the church members in the campaign has huge benefits.
Membership involvement:
- **Builds solid attendance** as members participate in the meetings.
- **Stimulates members to invite** their **friends** and **neighbors.** If they are not involved, they will not invite people as readily.
- **Provides church members with the joy of service.**
- **Enhances their relationship with Christ.**
- **Creates an environment for members to build friendships with guests attending the meetings. Friendships** made at the meetings **help solidify new converts.**

COMMITTEES AND THEIR RESPONSIBILITIES

The **committees** we have suggested **are essential for the ongoing success of a public evangelistic**

campaign. Creating and establishing these committees will also provide a strong base of support for your meetings.

The **coordinators** are **chosen by** the **pastors.** Church members will sign up for the various committees.

EVANGELISTIC CAMPAIGN ORGANIZATION

- **Campaign coordinator**
- **Associate coordinator**
- **Treasurer**
- **Pre-Registration coordinator**
- **Materials coordinator**
- **Visitation coordinator**
- **Platform coordinator**
- **Committees coordinator**

CAMPAIGN COORDINATOR (Pastor)

The campaign **coordinator** is responsible for the **successful organization** of the campaign. He/she is responsible for the organization of the entire campaign. Each committee chairperson ultimately reports to the campaign coordinator. The chairman of each committee is responsible for organizing his/her staff and fulfilling their specific task while the campaign coordinator oversees all campaign operations.

ASSOCIATE COORDINATOR (Local church leader)

The associate coordinator **assists** the **coordinator** in the responsibilities of the campaign, especially working with the heads of the varying committees to be sure their areas are functioning smoothly.

TREASURER

The treasurer of the campaign is usually the church treasurer. His/her responsibilities are as follows:
- Work with the coordinator in **developing a budget** for the campaign.
- Set up an **evangelistic account.**
- **Receive** and **count** the **offering** each week from the campaign.
- **Pay** all campaign **bills.**

PRE-REGISTRATION COORDINATOR

The pre-registration process ensures the local church of a successful series of meetings by building attendance previous to the public advertising through the ongoing ministry of the local congregation in its personal contacts, seminars, and outreach activities.

- The pre-registration coordinator is responsible for **collecting** all the pre-registrations from the different preparation programs. **Pre-registration cards may be used in the following ways:**
- **ON SABBATH IN CHURCH**—Pre-registration cards should be given out to every church member on Sabbath giving them an opportunity to register for the Revelation

of Hope evangelistic meetings. There may be non-Adventist visitors in the congregation who will register along with the church members.

- **AT ALL PREPARATION PROGRAMS**—Pre-registration cards should be given out at all preparation programs, such as *Unsealing Daniel's Mysteries,* health programs, family programs, etc.
- **PERSONALLY DELIVERED**—Pre-registration cards should be given to all Bible study contacts, friends of the church, and former Seventh-day Adventists.
- **HANDBILLS SENT TO NAMES ON THE INTEREST LIST**—Handbills and a letter of invitation along with the pre-registration cards should be sent to all interests on the pastor's interest list.
- **SENT TO MEDIA INTERESTS**—Handbills will be sent with a letter from the Revelation of Hope speaker to all the media interests. The pre-registration coordinator should fill out the media center interest form with appropriate zip codes and mail it to the media center.

Note: A week before the evangelistic meetings, a confirmation letter with a brochure of the meetings is sent to all those who have pre-registered.

MATERIALS COORDINATOR

- The materials coordinator is responsible for **ordering all materials and books** needed during the evangelistic meetings.
- He/she is responsible for **keeping track of the inventory,** making sure there are always adequate supplies of lecture magazines, books, decision cards, or any other materials used during the campaign.
- He/she is responsible for **counting out any materials** needed by the hosts and hostesses to distribute at the door.
- He/she is responsible for making sure that ushers have decision **cards and pencils** ahead of time and they are counted out by rows so they can be distributed quickly and efficiently.
- He/she is responsible for having enough **offering buckets and envelopes** for the entire campaign.

VISITATION COORDINATOR

Visitation is essential to the success of the meetings. The preaching of God's Word raises **questions** in the minds of many who are attending the meetings and hearing the end-time truths of God's Word for the very first time. Obstacles to decisions will arise. Barriers against accepting the truth may loom in their minds. Without **adequate visitation,** which lovingly **answers** these **questions** and leads men and women to **decisions** on the truths presented, the preaching of the Word will be less effective.

- Without **systematic visitation,** many will drop out of the meetings.
- **Weekly visitation** during the evangelistic meetings **keeps people coming.**
- Visitation **answers** their **questions,** leads them to decisions, and maximizes the effectiveness of the spoken Word.

The **pastor or the campaign coordinator** usually **leads** out in the **visitation,** coordinating the visitation team and working closely with the records committee to acquire all names of the guests attending the meetings.

The visitation coordinator:

- **Organizes the visitation teams**—The teams are made up of either pastors or lay people who will visit the non-Adventist guests who are regularly attending the evangelistic meetings.
- **Gets names from the records committee**—An accurate record of everyone attending the evangelistic meetings is kept by the record keeping committee. There will be a visitation card for every non–Seventh-day Adventist guest. Each visitor (worker) will get an updated record after each meeting.
- **Coordinates a regular, systematic visitation program**—It is extremely important for the success of the campaign to follow the visitation program outlined on pages 184, 185.

Note: Visitation is so important that there is one whole chapter in the manual discussing visitation.

The section in the manual titled, "Evangelistic Visitation" provides an outline of the visits each week to the guests attending the evangelistic series. It describes:

- **Who to visit**
- **When to visit**
- **How to visit**

PLATFORM COORDINATOR

The **platform chairman organizes the program each evening.**

- Checks with the evangelist regarding the evening **announcements.**
- Appoints someone to have **prayer.**
- Coordinates with the **musicians** regarding the evening's musical selections.

The main function of the **platform chairman** is to **keep the program flowing smoothly,** creating a positive atmosphere for the preaching of God's Word.

The **platform coordinator** is **responsible** for:

- **Meeting with all participants** in the evening program at least twenty minutes before the program begins to review the order of service and individual evening assignments.
- **Placing the necessary schedules, gift books, and Bible on the podium** for the announcement period.
- **Reviewing the announcements** with the evangelist.
- **Informing the special music participants** where their part comes in the program.
- **Leading out in** a **prayer** session before the meeting begins with the all platform participants.

MUSIC COORDINATOR

The **music coordinator is responsible for all music** during the campaign. This includes the following:

- Arranging for an **organist or pianist** each evening.
- Providing for **background music** as people enter and leave the meetings.
- Arranging for **special music** including **all appeal songs.**
- Organizing **special musical programs on select nights,** preliminary to the evangelistic meetings.

- **Working closely with the evangelist** to carefully plan the music to coordinate with the evening's topic.

COMMITTEES COORDINATOR

The committees' coordinator is responsible for the successful organization of the campaign. He/she is responsible for the **organization of all the committees.** The chairman of each committee is responsible for organizing his/her staff and fulfilling their specific task.

The **following are necessary committees** for a successful campaign.

They are filled by church members as they sign up Sabbath morning.

We have provided an enlistment form on pages 199, 200 to be passed out in your church. The leaders of each of these committees are either chosen by the church board or individually selected by the pastor.

- **Prayer coordinator**
- **Ushers**
- **Hosts and hostesses**
- **Registration personnel**
- **Attendance record personnel**
- **Bible school**
- **Parking attendants**
- **Children's meetings and babysitting**
- **Resource center (materials sold)**
- **Decoration committee**
- **Transportation committee**

COMMITTEE JOB DESCRIPTIONS

PRAYER COORDINATOR

The prayer committee coordinator is responsible for enlisting church members who intercede with God for people coming to the evangelistic series.

Prayer groups will:

- **Pray daily** for the evangelistic meetings.
- **Pray before the meeting** each evening.
  - We suggest that prayer groups meet at least thirty minutes before the meeting in a designated room and pray for specific people coming to the evangelistic meetings. Once the meeting begins, we invite all prayer group members into the meeting to pray for the evangelist as he/she preaches and for specific interests who are being prompted by the Holy Spirit to make decisions. We want everyone to receive the **blessing** of being in the **meeting**.

Here is the copy for a prayer commitment card we have found helpful:

Believing that we are living in the days of earth's final harvest, and that the work of God on earth can never be finished until each of us consecrate ourselves to God for service and be filled with the mighty outpouring of the Holy Spirit, **I am willing and committed to pray for the following specific names:**

1.

2.

3.

4.

5.

I **will pray** for the **evangelistic meetings** and **intercede** for the **guests** that are attending.

"For the LORD will not forsake His people, for His great name's sake, because it has pleased the LORD to make you His people. Moreover, as for me, far be it from me that I should **sin** against the LORD **in ceasing to pray for you;** but I will teach you the good and the right way. Only fear the LORD, and serve Him in truth with all your heart; for consider what great things He has done for you" **(1 SAMUEL 12:22–24).**

Ellen White encourages us to pray for souls in these words:

"Church members, let the light shine forth. Let your **voices be heard** in humble **prayer. . . .** Your voice, your influence, your time—all these are **gifts** from God and are to be **used in winning souls to Christ**" **(TESTIMONIES, VOL. 9, P. 38).**

One of the most important things that you can do is to organize prayer groups. Without the work of the Holy Spirit, very little will happen.

- **Prayed-for advertising** is more effective than non-prayed-for advertising.
- **Spirit-filled music** transforms lives when a mere performance may inspire people but leave them unchanged.
- **The best sermons preached** without the accompanying power of the Holy Spirit are powerless.

Even when there is a large attendance, there will be few decisions without the moving of the Holy Spirit. This is why Ellen White gives this counsel to churches conducting public evangelistic meetings:

" 'Let the **believers** living near the place where you are holding meetings, **share** the **burden of the work.** They should feel it a duty and privilege to help **make** the **meetings** a **success.** God is pleased by efforts to set them at work. He desires every church member to labor as His helping hand, seeking by loving ministry to win souls to Christ.' . . .

". . . The **blessing** of the Lord **will come** to the **church members** who thus **participate in the work,** gathering in **small groups daily** to **pray** for its **success**" **(EVANGELISM, P. 111).**

Remember:

"It is part of God's plan to grant us, in answer to the **prayer of faith,** that which He would not bestow did we not thus ask" **(THE GREAT CONTROVERSY, P. 525).**

USHERS

RESPONSIBILITIES OF USHERS

There should be **two ushers** for every **twenty-five people** attending the meetings each evening. It is important to assign your ushers to the same section of the auditorium each evening so they can become acquainted with the guests that are attending. People tend to sit in the same place every night and one of the major responsibilities of the ushers is to get acquainted with people in their section.

The **head usher** or his **assistant** will need to be **available every night** throughout the campaign. Without this consistency, the ushering system will break down.

- All ushers should be at the auditorium **forty-five minutes before the meeting begins.** At least **one hour before on opening night.**
- Make sure all **seats for ushers** are marked **"Reserved"** well in advance We typically reserve the end seats at either side of the rows every three to four rows.
- Keep a supply of the nightly schedule sheets and extra registration envelopes and scanner cards for anyone who might have missed them.
- Once a week, pass out **offering envelopes.** These should all be counted out ahead of time based on the number of people seated in a row. For example, if there are twelve people in a row, the usher simply hands a stack of twelve envelopes to the person sitting in the aisle seat and asks that individual to pass the envelopes down the row.
- Once a week, **collect the offering.** Plain buckets should be acquired ahead of time. Ushers pass the bucket on one side and collect it on the other. One bucket per row will help this process to go very quickly.
  - The offering will then be given to the head usher, counted, and then given to the treasurer. **For safety and the integrity of the process, we always have two people count the offering** and sign for the amount that is received before they give the offering to the treasurer.
- Pass out **decision cards.** Decision cards must be counted by rows and passed out quickly and quietly when the evangelist calls for them.
- All ushers should keep a **supply of pencils** in their pockets so that if the guests need a pencil to fill out their decision card they are readily available.
- **Keep alert** for minor things that may arise during the meeting.
- Help **clean up** after the meetings. Arrange chairs and pick up any materials left behind, etc.
- **Dress neatly and attractively.** Some visitors will form their opinions of the program by the caliber of dress of the personnel. A dress shirt and tie is appropriate.

HOSTS AND HOSTESSES

HOSTS' AND HOSTESSES' RESPONSIBILITIES

The **hosts and hostesses** are **responsible for creating a positive atmosphere** as people enter the meeting. They are the first ones the visitors meet. It is extremely important that they radiate a positive cheerful attitude as they greet the visitors. A **warm, friendly smile** enables our guests to feel welcome and comfortable. A positive, cheerful atmosphere helps them feel they made the right decision by coming to the meeting.

Two hosts or hostesses are needed **for every door** where people can enter or exit.

- All hosts and hostesses should **be at the auditorium forty-five minutes before** the meeting begins. At least **one hour before on opening night.**

- All hosts and hostesses should be wearing a **name badge.** The head host or hostess is responsible for obtaining the name badges, putting the names on them, and distributing them to the hosts and hostesses.
- **Greet** people at the door with a warm welcome.
- **Give** every person attending a **registration envelope** on opening night. Each evening after the opening night, hosts and hostesses will direct new people to the registration table to register if they missed the opening night registration.
- Be alert to all **visitors with children,** directing them to the children's meetings.
- The hosts and hostesses should be aware of the **seating balance** in the auditorium. After the auditorium is almost full, they should direct people to the ushers to help them find empty seats.
- The hosts and hostesses should **dress neatly and attractively,** representing the high standards of Christ and His church. Often guests form their impressions of the program by the dress of the staff. Modest skirts and blouses or dresses are appropriate for ladies, while jackets and ties are in order for men.
- Get **lecture summaries** corresponding to the evening's lecture from the materials coordinator and distribute them to each attendee as they leave the meetings.

REGISTRATION PERSONNEL

The registration personnel are in constant **contact** with the **attendees.** Choose people who are cheerful, positive, organized, and accommodating.

There should be **two to three people** taking care of the **new registration table** each evening. One table will usually be enough to accommodate the new registrations each evening. On the nights that the attendance incentives are given out, you will need an additional table.

Responsibilities:
- **Set up:** Set up the registration table each evening with the supplies.
- **Serve at the table each evening.**

SUPPLIES:
- **Registration table:** Set up a skirted eight-foot table in the lobby or some place where people enter the auditorium.
- **Registration forms—Scanning system:** Registration envelopes with scanning card (All envelopes are given out in numerical order.)
- **Registration forms—Ticket system:** Ticket books (All new ticket books are given out in numerical order.)
- **Pens**
- **Lecture magazines—**There needs to be an ample supply of lecture magazines. We usually sell these lecture magazines to people who miss previous meetings or to those who desire extra copies.
- **Gift books—**When people attend a specific number of evenings, they will receive gift books or incentives for their attendance. They receive these books at the registration table.
- **Gift Bibles—**When people attend eighteen nights, they are given a Bible or some other extra special gift.
- **Computerized alphabetical list/attendance list:** The registration table coordinator will receive from the record keeping coordinator a list of all attendees with their

attendance records to confirm who is entitled to what incentive gifts. (This is supplied by the record keeping personnel.) You will also have an updated record of how many nights each person has attended the meetings.

- **Computerized gift list**—There will be an updated list each night listing the names of the people who are eligible for gifts.
- **Lecture schedule sheets**—There should always be a supply of the Revelation of Hope schedule sheet at the registration table. Every new person who registers should be given one.
- **Gift pictures:** A **large unframed picture** is given to everyone who attends twenty-four nights. A **small unframed picture** is given to everyone who brings a guest as well as the guest.
- **Framed pictures:** The framed pictures will be on display at the registration table for new guests to see.

ATTENDANCE RECORDS AND PERSONNEL

It is vital to **keep accurate records.** The ticket book and scanner card systems are not only a great asset in keeping accurate records but also are very valuable to the person attending the meetings because they **receive** a **free** copy of the **lecture** for each evening they attend. The tickets or scanner cards are also used as an **attendance incentive, so attendees can** receive free books as they come each evening. This enables those attending the meetings to continue growing spiritually as they read additional material or listen to CDs. The individual only fills his/her name in one time. Once they have registered, they turn in the numbered ticket that corresponds to that evening or scan their card as they enter the meeting. Since record keeping is so important for both the evangelist and the attendees, we will explain the system in detail in an entire chapter on pages 117–122.

BIBLE SCHOOL

Jesus says in **MATTHEW 28:19, 20,**

> "**Go** therefore and **make disciples** of all the nations, **baptizing them** in the name of the Father and of the Son and of the Holy Spirit, **teaching them** to observe all things that I have commanded you; and lo, I am with you always, even to the end of the age."

Setting up a Bible school during the evangelistic meetings is one way to **reinforce the messages** that the individual is hearing from the evangelist each evening. The lessons will answer questions the person has from the presentations they have heard. Many people who begin to study the lessons in the Bible school will continue with the Bible lessons after the evangelistic meetings have finished. As they discover new Bible truths, many will accept Christ and the message of the three angels of Revelation. Since the Bible school is so important, we have an entire chapter on it. See chapter 12 on pages 139–144.

PARKING ATTENDANTS

The parking attendants provide both guidance and security for individuals arriving and departing the meetings. They are responsible for the general safety of the exterior of the church or auditorium. The parking attendants should have **flashlights** to direct the cars.

Responsibilities:

- Parking attendants should **be visible** to approaching drivers to direct them to the correct parking location.
- **Church members** should be directed to the **less desirable locations,** leaving the better lighted and more easily accessible parking spots for guests.
- There should be some **handicapped parking** available and attendants ready to assist any handicapped individuals or senior citizens needing assistance.
- Several **umbrellas** should be available to escort drivers to and from autos on rainy evenings.

CHILDREN'S MEETINGS

Children's meetings are **imperative** if young adults are going to attend the lecture series consistently.

> Jesus always provided for the children. He is still drawing the children today. He bids us, "Let the little children come to Me, and do not forbid them; for of such is the kingdom of heaven" **(MATTHEW 19:14).**

This statement in the book *Evangelism* under the section "Children's Meetings in Evangelistic Efforts" encourages us to conduct children's meetings in our evangelistic meetings today.

> "**Meetings for the children should be held,** not merely to educate and entertain them, but that **they may be converted.** And this will come to pass. If we exercise faith in God we shall be enabled to point them to the Lamb of God, which taketh away the sin of the world" **(P. 582).**

We have discovered through personal experience that it works best if you separate **children into** at least **two groups.**

- Birth to four years—**Babysitting**
- Five to eleven—**Children's meetings**

Birth to Four Years

This is a very important part of the evangelistic meetings, since many of the people who come to a public evangelistic meeting are people with young children and babies. If you do not provide for them, you will have many parents who will not be able to attend.

This is basically a **babysitting service.** Be sure to select responsible , qualified adults to care for this age group. As the children come, place a name tag on each of them. You will need some baby furniture to take care of their needs, such as cribs, car beds, or play pens and some toys for the three- and four-year-olds. You can get the young people of the church to assist with this service. Many of them will be delighted to serve this way.

Basic Supplies Needed to Run a Successful Nursery

- Name tags for each child
- Disposable diapers
- Wipes

- Stuffed animals
- Toys for infants
- Rocking chair for those who need to be rocked to sleep

Steps in organizing children's meetings—Ages five to eleven

Select Leaders

Select five leaders, one for each night of the evangelistic series. Each leader continues his/her program on that given night they have been assigned throughout the campaign. This gives continuity to the program. The children begin to identify with the same people. This also enables these leaders to attend some of the evangelistic series, since they are leading out in the children's meeting only one night each week.

The **leader is responsible** for **everything** that takes place on that evening from start to finish. The leader makes sure they have someone to:

- **Lead out in the Bible story**
- **Tell the continued story**
- **Give the nature nugget/health nugget or the character development story**
- **Take charge of the crafts**

The leaders themselves may be some of the best storytellers, therefore, they can tell the Bible story or the continued story if they desire to or they can delegate it to someone else. Their **main responsibility** is to see that the **program runs smoothly** and **efficiently** each evening.

Sample Children's Meeting Program Schedule

7:15—WELCOME AND REGISTER CHILDREN

7:30—SINGING AND PRAYER

7:45—CONTINUED STORY

- The continued story summarizes an entire book.
- This is done in approximately one week, telling a portion of the book each evening for five nights.
- Leaving off at a point of heightened interest will continue to draw the children back.

8:00—BIBLE STORY

- Bible stories from Genesis to Revelation are chosen. These are taken from the three-year Sabbath School cycle series.
- Starting from the beginning story, Creation, stories are continued in order throughout the entire cycle ending with the last story in Revelation, which is about heaven.
- Each Bible story is to be organized with each leader, so the same story is not repeated.

8:30—NATURE STORY, HEALTH NUGGET, or CHARACTER DEVELOPMENT STORY

This section features either nature, health, or character development.

- Nature stories along with felts can be purchased from your local ABCs.
- Principles of health, emphasizing the importance of water, fresh air, exercise, sunshine, nutrition, temperance, rest, positive relationships, and trust in God. There is an entire series on health in felts.

- Character development stories can be used from Uncle Arthur's *Bedtime Stories* books.

8:40—CRAFTS

Use a simple craft each evening, something the child can take home.

RESOURCE CENTER—(SALES)

Sales of materials are provided for the attendees at the evangelistic meeting so that each attendee will have the opportunity to reinforce the messages they have been hearing with truth-filled literature. The resource center gives the guests attending an opportunity to build their spiritual library.

Personnel involved have the following responsibilities:

- Determine what materials, such **as books, magazines, audio tapes, DVDs, videos, music, pictures,** etc., are going to be sold.
- **Order** all materials.
- **Set up tables** and **display** of all sales items.
- Get cash **boxes, change, receipt books,** and bags.
- **Serve** at the sales table selling materials.

Note: We usually record new CDs from the current messages presented each evening and duplicate from the master CD or DVD and sell them at the sales table.

DECORATION COMMITTEE

The decoration committee decorates the platform for the evangelistic series.

TRANSPORTATION COMMITTEE

Some campaigns require extra transportation to and from the meetings. Therefore, the following are the responsibilities of the transportation committee.

- **Determine** what the transportation needs are.
- **Work** within the budget that has been allocated.
- **Acquire** buses or vans that will care for your needs.
- **Determine** the transportation route and schedule.
- **Communicate** with the pastors regarding the transportation schedule.

Throughout the New Testament, there is an emphasis on organization.

- In Acts 7, deacons were chosen to relieve the disciples of certain responsibilities so they could focus on "prayer and to the ministry of the word" (ACTS 6:4).
- In 1 CORINTHIANS 12, the apostle Paul describes the gifts of the Spirit that God has given to build up His church.

When the **church of Christ harmoniously works together,** with each member using their unique gifts, cooperating in loving ministry and joyous service, the **Holy Spirit will be poured out** abundantly and a rich harvest of souls won to Christ.

CHAPTER 7

PREACHING POWERFUL SERMONS

In every generation, God has **used preaching to win the lost.** He has raised up men and women as well as young people to **powerfully proclaim** His message of **truth.**

The apostle Peter's preaching on the Day of **Pentecost** resulted in three thousand baptized in a day. Paul's **evangelistic preaching** in Asia Minor **resulted in new churches** in Ephesus, Colossae, Philippi, and Galatia.

Throughout the book of **Acts,** powerful **biblical preaching** resulted in believers being added to the church. Luke's account tells us that

> **"believers were** increasingly **added** to the Lord, multitudes of both men and women" **(ACTS 5:14).**

The New Testament believers were **passionate about sharing** the gospel.

> "They did not cease **teaching** and **preaching Jesus** as the Christ" **(ACTS 5:42).**

> "Therefore those who were scattered went everywhere preaching the word" **(ACTS 8:4).**

Once again at the end time, God is raising up a generation of pastors and **lay people** who are powerfully **preaching His Word.**

Thousands of **young people** are **joining** this **army of preachers.** These Spirit-anointed men and women of truth are being used of God to win tens of thousands.

There is a new urgency gripping God's people today. They are responding to God's call. They are sharing God's last-day truths in homes, churches, and public auditoriums.

Ellen White underscores the importance and significance of preaching the great truths of the Bible in this crisis hour.

> "We are living in the **close** of this **earth's history.** . . . **Prophecy** is fulfilling. Soon **Christ will come** with power and great glory. We have **no time to lose.** Let the **message sound forth** in earnest words of warning" **(EVANGELISM, P. 217).**

> "The time has come when the message of Christ's **soon** coming is to **sound throughout the world"** **(TESTIMONIES, VOL. 9, P. 24).**

> "In every land we are to **herald** the **second coming** of Christ, in the **language of the revelator** proclaiming: 'Behold, He cometh with clouds; and** every eye shall see Him' " **(TESTIMONIES, VOL. 8, P. 116).**

> ## There are three key points to keep in mind in powerful evangelistic preaching.

3 Key Points in Evangelistic Preaching

 ## KEY #1: *The Message*—What you preach

"God has given us a message"—the three angels' messages

God's message in the Bible's last book, **Revelation, speaks** to **this generation** with penetrating urgency. It is a call to prepare for the coming of Christ.

This message is **as important** for our day as **Noah's message** was for His day. Noah's message prepared a sin-polluted world for destruction by water. All who chose to could enter the ark.

Revelation's message is a **message of deliverance** for men and women in a world soon to be destroyed by fire. All who choose to can respond to the "everlasting gospel" and enter the ark of safety and be saved.

Powerful **evangelistic preaching** unfolds God's last-day message outlined in Revelation. It is an urgent end-time appeal.

It **reveals truth** in the face of falsehood and calls for eternal decisions.

It is not a tame, lifeless, status quo message. Just as God sent a message through John the Baptist to prepare the world for the first coming of Jesus, He is sending a message to the world through the preaching of the three angels' messages to prepare a world for the second coming of Jesus.

> "In a special sense **Seventh-day Adventists** have been **set** in the world as watchmen and **light bearers.** To them has been entrusted the last warning for a perishing world. On them is shining wonderful light from the word of God. They **have been given** a work of the most solemn import—the **proclamation** of the **first, second,** and the **third angels' messages.** There is no other work of so great **importance.** They are to allow **nothing else to absorb their attention**" (TESTIMONIES, VOL. 9, P. 19).

God's last-day message is based on His Word. The apostle Paul's counsel to his young friend Timothy certainly applies to preachers today.

> "**Preach the word!** Be ready in season and out of season. Convince, rebuke, exhort, with all longsuffering and teaching" (2 TIMOTHY 4:2).
>
> "Be diligent to present yourself approved to God, a worker who does not need to be ashamed, rightly dividing the word of truth" (2 TIMOTHY 2:15).

In all biblical evangelism, the Word of God is central. The **power is not** in our **eloquence,** our **rhetoric,** our **persuasiveness,** our **charisma,** or our **ability.** It **is in the Word of God.** The evangelist may influence people's thinking but only God can change their hearts. Only the Holy Spirit can work the miracle of **conversion in their lives.** The same Holy Spirit who inspired the Bible in the first place accompanies the **preaching of God's Word, impresses** the truths of God's Word on inquiring minds, and **empowers** those who hear to follow God's Word.

James urges New Testament Christians to receive the "implanted word, which is able to save your souls" **(JAMES 1:21).** Peter declares that believers are "born again, . . . through the word of God" **(1 PETER 1:23).** Paul adds that "the **word of God is living and powerful**" **(HEBREWS 4:12).** Jesus proclaims that all the Scriptures "testify" of Him **(JOHN 5:39).** The **Bible is the foundation** of all evangelism and Jesus is the center of every Bible doctrine.

Christis is the center of all doctrine!

Uplift Jesus as the **center** of all **doctrine.** Doctrine without Christ is merely lifeless dogma. Jesus makes every Bible truth come alive. **Jesus is the main theme of every Bible doctrine.** He is the **"blessed hope"** of the Second Advent. He is the **"Giver"** of the divine law. He is the Christ who conquered the grave and raised the dead. He is the Creator of our bodies and the Lord of the Sabbath. He is the **dying Lamb** and the **living Priest** in heaven's sanctuary. **He is the center of all our hopes** and the fulfillment of all of our dreams. **Without Him evangelistic preaching is powerless.** When **Christ** is the **center** of every **doctrine, evangelistic preaching is dynamic, alive, and powerful.**

Seven key principles to keep in mind as you unfold the three angels' messages

01 | **Present the saving power of Jesus in each message.**

"But as many as received Him, to them He **gave the right** to become children of God" **(JOHN 1:12).**

"In whom we have redemption through His blood, the **forgiveness of sins**" **(COLOSSIANS 1:14).**

- **Present Christ**, His divinity, His life, His death, His resurrection, His high priestly ministry, and His soon return.
- **Focus on Christ's power to change lives.** Never preach a sermon without pointing to Jesus as the Divine Source of all spiritual power.

"Tell the story of His life of self-denial and sacrifice, His humiliation and death, His resurrection and ascension, His intercession for sinners in the courts above" (GOSPEL WORKERS, P. 154).

"Of all professing Christians, **Seventh-day Adventists** should be **foremost in uplifting Christ** before the world" (GOSPEL WORKERS, P. 156).

02 | Emphasize the practical application of each Bible truth.

Show how the **biblical truth** you are sharing **can change** the life of the person listening. For example:

- How will your **message bring hope** to a discouraged widow?
- **Encouragement** to a struggling teenager?
- **Strength** to an addicted alcoholic?
- **Peace** to a devastated divorcée?
- How will your message on the Second Coming give **courage** to a stressed-out mother?
- How will your message on the Sabbath give **peace** to an overworked businessman?
- How will your message on the 2,300-day prophecy give **hope** to college students who feel they have been treated unjustly?

Think through every message and practically apply it to the hearts of your listeners.

03 | Weave the second coming of Christ into each message.

The urgency of our times demands it. The **second coming of Christ speaks with new relevance** to a society caught in the grip of economic catastrophes, social chaos, natural disasters, and international conflicts. Our world is looking for hope and ultimately there is nothing more hopeful than the blessed hope of Christ's return.

04 | Make appeals in each presentation.

Remember the **destiny of souls hangs in the balance.** There are people in every meeting on the verge of the kingdom. The Holy Spirit is impressing them to make eternal decisions. **Appeals provide the Holy Spirit an opportunity to work more powerfully on people's minds** to prompt them to make a decision.

05 | Preach each subject in the order given in the schedule at the end of this chapter.

Each message is like a link in a **connected chain.** One builds upon another. The pieces in the **puzzle of truth** fit together to form a magnificent picture of God's loving character.

06 | **Present the major testing truths on the nights you will have the largest audience.**

As you think through the nights you will conduct your meetings, be sure to **preach the most important messages** when you have the **most people in attendance.**

07 | **Constantly refer your audience to God's Word. Read the texts from the screen. It is God's Word that changes lives, not our words.**

 KEY#2: *Proclamation of the Message*—How you preach

Preaching is not devoid of our **personalities.** What we say is deeply entwined with who we are. Phillips Brooks, the great nineteenth-century American preacher, once said, **"Preaching is God's truth through human personality."** The apostle Paul says, "We have this treasure in earthen vessels" (2 CORINTHIANS 4:7). Since we are custodians of divine grace and stewards of divine truth, let's **present that grace and truth as clearly and convincingly as possible.** Writing of Jesus' presentation of truth, Ellen White shares this powerful insight:

> "His blessings He presents in the most alluring terms. He is not content merely to announce these blessings; He presents them in the most attractive way, to excite a desire to possess them. So His servants are to present the riches of the glory of the unspeakable Gift. The wonderful love of Christ will melt and subdue hearts, when the mere reiteration of doctrines would accomplish nothing" (THE DESIRE OF AGES, P. 826).

KEY POINTS

 #1 | **Preaching the Message**

Points of Preaching Style to Consider

Your preaching style will make a dramatic difference whether people will **accept or reject the message** you preach.

There are **three aspects of effective preaching.** They are:

- **Logos**
- **Pathos**
- **Ethos**

Let's define each one and discover how they apply to effective preaching.

Logos—Has to do with the <u>content</u> of <u>what you preach</u>.

In every sermon, **the message** must be solidly **supported with Bible texts. It must be clear. If truth is not clear, the listeners will not accept it.**

Pathos—Has to do with the <u>passion</u> with which <u>you preach</u>.

Do you **communicate** the message with spirited **conviction**?

Can the audience tell **you believe** what you are preaching?

Does your audience sense that **you believe** you **have an urgent message** of extreme importance to deliver?

If you don't preach like you believe it, they will not believe it.

The story is told of a preacher who was one day talking to an actor and asked the question,

> "Why are the theaters packed and the churches empty? Why do people **flock to hear you** and **I struggle to get a few to come** to hear me?" The actor responded, "It is quite simple. We on the stage take things that are imaginary and make them real, you in the pulpit take things that are real and make them imaginary."

One of the best compliments anyone can give you is that you **preached like you learned it yesterday and could not wait to tell it today.**

Ethos—Has to do with your <u>likability</u>.

Does the audience **trust you**?

Do they have **confidence in you?**

Have you **bonded with the audience**?

Ethos occurs when the audience sits back and says, **"I like that preacher."** Before the meeting begins, visit people who come to the auditorium early.

- Get to **know them** by name.
- Ask them questions about their family, their work, their interests, and hobbies.
- Show a genuine interest in others. If they share needs, offer to pray with them right there.
- After you are through preaching, **go to the door** and **greet** those who have attended your meetings and thank them for coming.

As you develop relationships with those coming to your meetings, they will accept your preaching more readily.

Here is a list of five things to concentrate on in your preaching.

- **Pronounce** each word **distinctly.**
- Maintain **eye contact** with the audience.

- Concentrate on developing a **pleasantness** in your **voice** and in the way you **look.**
- **Avoid criticizing** any individual or group.
- **Present** what the **Bible** says and expose error by presenting the truth.

"The **preaching** of the **word** should appeal to **the intellect** and should impart knowledge, but it should do more than this. The minister's utterances, to be effectual, must reach the hearts of his hearers" **(GOSPEL WORKERS, P. 152).**

#2 Illustrating the Message

How to Make the Preached Message More Effective

Using **visual aids** can be very effective in holding your audience's attention each evening. Research indicates that when we see, hear, repeat, and then write what we hear, retention, comprehension, and commitment skyrocket. Studies reveal we **remember only 15–20 percent of what we hear** but up to **70 percent of what we see.**

Perhaps this is why Jesus tied His teachings to common scenes familiar to His hearers that they saw every day. Visual illustrations of truth rivet it in the mind of the listener.

The prophet Habakkuk instructs us to **clearly illustrate truth** at the end time. "Write the vision and make it plain on tablets, that he may run who needs it. For the vision is yet for an appointed time; but at the end it will speak, and it will not lie" **(HABAKKUK 2:2, 3).**

The prophet's point is clear. **Illustrate what you are saying** so those listening can plainly understand it.

"The **use of charts** is most **effective** in explaining the prophecies relating to the past, the present, and the future. But we are to make our work as simple and inexpensive as possible" **(EVANGELISM, P. 203).**

"By the **use** of **charts, symbols,** and **representations** of various kinds, the minister can make the truth stand out clearly and distinctly. This is a help, and in harmony with the Word of God" **(EVANGELISM, P. 206).**

Today there are **outstanding graphics to illustrate each message** clearly.

It is extremely effective to use visual aids and computer graphics to illustrate truth. Every sermon in the **Revelation of Hope** series is **fully illustrated with four-color graphics.** Many of the sermons include video footage as well.

Advantages and Disadvantages of Using Graphics

Presenters' advantages of using graphics:

- **Graphics provide** the audience with the **opportunity to see** as well as hear the message. This double impact reinforces the truth they are hearing.
- **Graphics help** the presenter to **stay focused** on the topic by providing an outline for the sermon. The **Revelation of Hope** series provides the complete text in addition to the graphics.

Christ's coming will be a literal event.

- **Graphics give** the presenter **confidence,** since the majority of the material is on the screen.
- **Graphics focus** the attention of the audience **on the truths** of Scripture, not on the presenter.
- **Graphics assist** the presenter in **engaging the audience.** As the audience participates by reading from the screen, the truth of God's Word is reinforced in the mind.
- **Graphics enable** the presenter to **hold the attention** of their audience better.
- **Graphics help** people who are new to the Bible **not to feel embarrassed** because they cannot find the texts in the Bible.

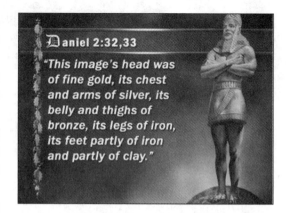

Daniel 2:32,33

"This image's head was of fine gold, its chest and arms of silver, its belly and thighs of bronze, its legs of iron, its feet partly of iron and partly of clay."

Presenters' disadvantages of using graphics:
- The presenter **may spend less time in preparation** and **depend too much** on the graphics.
- Since the lights are out, it may be **more difficult to make eye contact** and **determine the audience response.**
- **If the technology fails** or there is a power outage, the presenter dependent on his/her graphics may be unable to present.
- Since the presenter is using graphics on the screen, **the audience may never learn to study God's Word** for themselves.

Overcoming the disadvantages of using graphics:

Review the sermon several times before the presentation.

Practice the presentation out loud. It is often helpful to review the sermon in the setting that you will preach it in. This will give you a sense of confidence with the message and familiarity with the surroundings.

Make an outline of your complete sermon in advance so that if you have technical difficulties you can preach your sermon from your notes. You should always have a copy of the printed sermon with the graphics to fall back on.

Audience's disadvantages of viewing graphics:

There is a danger that people attending evangelistic meetings where graphics are used exclusively may **not become acquainted with** their **Bibles.**

Overcoming the disadvantages of graphics:
- Operate a full-fledged **Bible school** (See chapter 12, "Conducting a Bible School.")
- Give a **free lecture magazine** or outline of the texts each evening.
- Have a **question-and-answer period** at least twice a week as a special feature for twenty minutes, answering questions directly from the Bible.

#3 | **How to Reinforce the Message**

Reinforcing the Message With a Question-and-Answer Period

The **question-and-answer** period is of great value in teaching truth in a series of evangelistic meetings. Let's look at some of the **reasons** to **conduct a question-and-answer period** in the campaign.

> "The **best work** you can do is to **teach,** to **educate.** Whenever you can find an opportunity to do so, sit down with some family, and **let them ask questions.** Then **answer them** patiently, humbly. **Continue** this work **in connection with your** more **public efforts**" **(GOSPEL WORKERS, P. 193).**

This statement applies in both our personal work and our public meetings. Providing an opportunity to **ask questions** by the use of a **question box** helps the audience feel more a part of the meetings.

REASONS WHY THE QUESTION-AND-ANSWER PERIOD IS SO VALUABLE

Reason #1

The question-and-answer period allows the evangelist to review **the message and fill in gaps** people may have in their understanding of truth.

Reason #2

The question-and-answer period enables the evangelist to **build credibility** by answering questions from the Bible.

Reason #3

The question-and-answer period allows the evangelist the **opportunity to present new information** not covered in the public meeting.

Reason #4

The question-and-answer period gives the evangelist an opportunity to **repeat** the **truth** a second time.

Reason #5

The question-and-answer period can often **clear up** many **objections** that arise after new truth is presented.

Reason #6

The question-and-answer period gives people biblical **help on the practical points** they struggle with, such as Sabbath keeping, smoking, Christian standards, etc.

Reason #7

The question-and-answer period allows the evangelist to **concentrate on particular points** that may need special attention.

Reason #8

The question-and-answer period stimulates an interest in the **upcoming subjects.**

Reason #9

The question-and-answer period adds **interest in the meetings** and keeps people coming back. They want to be at the meeting when their question is answered.

Reason #10

The question-and-answer period gives the audience an opportunity to feel like they are a **part of the meetings.**

As the meetings progress into the second week, we normally schedule a **fifteen minute question-and-answer** period at least twice per week.

Reinforcing the Message With Literature

When evangelistic messages are preached, Satan will suggest doubts in the minds of your audience. He will raise questions. **If these questions are not answered, they become obstacles to a decision for truth.** The evil one will try misrepresenting your words.

What can be done to counteract Satan's strategy? We have been given specific counsel in the Spirit of Prophecy.

When the evangelist **reinforces the presentations with literature** and places each **sermon in print, the results are far greater.** Prepare the text of your message or at least a sermon outline to distribute to your audience each evening. This will give them an opportunity to review the nightly messages. Here is a fascinating reference on Satan's tactics:

> "When a **discourse** is **given,** the people may listen with interest, but it is all strange and new to them, and Satan is ready to suggest to their minds many things that are not true. He will seek to pervert and misrepresent the speaker's words. **What shall we do?**
>
> "**The discourses** presenting the reasons of our faith **should be published in little leaflets, and circulated as widely as possible. . . .**
>
> ". . . Thus the **falsehoods** and **misrepresentations** which the enemy of truth constantly tries to keep in circulation would be revealed in their true character, and the people would have an opportunity of **knowing** just **what the minister said**" (EVANGELISM, PP. 159, 160).

- Give a **free lecture outline** each evening to everyone who attends the meeting.
- Anyone who misses the meeting can **purchase the presentations** for a minimal fee.
- **Provide reading material** on the topic presented each evening. This will anchor your audience solidly in the truth of God's Word. When they hear truth, they may believe it, but **when they read it, they understand why it is so important.** Reading

the messages fixes them in their minds. It makes them personal. Reading internalizes the truth. Printed messages provide interested people opportunity to study the topics more thoroughly. As they study truth for themselves, they personalize it and own it.

 ## KEY #3: *Order of the Messages*—When you preach

Preaching powerful sermons is **like building** a house. There is a certain order in the construction of a house. You don't put the roof on before you build the foundation. You don't put the windows in before you frame the house. Evangelistic preaching is similar. There is a **proper order to be followed in the construction of the temple of truth.**

The **sequence of subjects** during an evangelistic campaign is **extremely important.** The **subjects should be arranged in the order that will produce the best results.**

When a series of public evangelistic meetings are presented, the **sermons should be arranged** so that one topic logically follows another. God's **message should be unfolded gradually** so that the listeners will gladly choose to leave their former beliefs and enter into this beautiful new truth. **Each subject is like a link in a connected chain.** One topic rightly presented leads into the next.

Every pastor or lay evangelist should **study how to arrange** his/her **subjects** in the best possible order.

You may be wondering, "**Does it really make any difference what order the subjects are in?** People will accept the truth regardless of the order." To some degree they may, however, we would maintain a much larger attendance until the close of the meetings and there would be much **greater results** if we wisely **planned** the **order of subjects.** We will also lose many people unnecessarily if testing truth is presented to quickly.

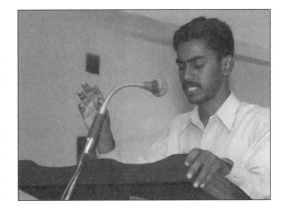

The **order of topics** should be planned in such a way as to cover the **major truths of doctrine** on the nights that draw the **largest audience.** There are certain nights that tend to be larger than others. **Major truths** should be presented on those nights.

GUIDING PRINCIPLES IN THE ORDER OF SUBJECTS FOR EVANGELISTIC SERMONS

A. | **The evangelistic lectures should cover all the essential doctrines of Scripture.**

- The opening presentations should be attractive and pleasing subjects of a **non-controversial** nature that will win the confidence of the people.
- While focusing on the great prophetic themes, it is wise in the early meetings to preach on **Jesus** the only Savior, the **divinity of Christ,** the **atoning power** of the blood of Christ, **salvation** by grace, the **second coming** of Christ, etc. This will silence the critics who think that Adventists do not preach Christ or believe in salvation by grace.

Ellen White confirms this:

> "In laboring in a new field, **do not think it your duty to say** at once to the people, **We are Seventh-day Adventists;** we believe that the seventh day is the Sabbath; we believe in the non-immortality of the soul. This would often erect a formidable **barrier** between you and those you wish to reach. **Speak** to them, as you have opportunity, **upon points of doctrine** on **which you can agree.** Dwell on the necessity of practical godliness. **Give** them **evidence** that **you are a Christian,** desiring peace, and that you love their souls. Let them see that you are conscientious. Thus you will gain their confidence; and there will be time enough for doctrines. Let the heart be won, the soil prepared, and then sow the seed, **presenting in love the truth** as it is in Jesus" **(GOSPEL WORKERS, PP. 119, 120).**

> "I have **been shown** that our **ministers go too rapidly through** their **subjects** and **bring the most objectionable features** of our faith **too early** into their effort. There are truths that will not involve so great a cross, that should be kept before their minds, day after day and even weeks before the Sabbath and immortality questions are entered upon. Then you **gain** the **confidence** of the people as being men who have clear, forcible arguments, and they think you understand the Scriptures. When **once** the **confidence** of the people **is gained,** then it is **time** enough **to introduce** publicly the Sabbath and immortality questions.
> "But men who are **not wise advance these questions too soon,** and thus **close the ears of the people,** when **with greater care** and more faith and aptness and wisdom **they could have carried them along step by step** through the important events in the prophecies and in dwelling upon practical subjects in the teachings of Christ" **(EVANGELISM, PP. 246, 247).**

B. The subjects should be so arranged that the entire series will unfold the special message of Revelation 14 as God's present truth for this present time.

It takes the preaching of this special message **to make solid and genuine Seventh-day Adventists.** The *three angels' messages* **capture the attention** of the members of other **churches** as well as the **unchurched.**

No one else is **preaching** the *three angels' messages* except Seventh-day Adventists.

C. The subjects should be arranged in a connected order so that the whole series fits together like links in a chain.

The audience should be **led along each meeting gradually, tactfully,** step by step, to the full acceptance of the three angels' messages.

> "God is leading out a people and establishing them upon the one great platform of faith, the commandments of God and the testimony of Jesus. He has given His people

a **straight chain of Bible truth, clear and connected.** This truth is of heavenly origin and has been searched for as for hidden treasure. It has been dug out through careful searching of the Scriptures and through much prayer" (TESTIMONIES, VOL. 3, P. 447).

Any attempt to **present the message** of the Seventh-day Adventist Church **outside** of the setting **of the three angels' messages** is to **separate** it **from** its real source of **power.**

"**Separate the Sabbath** from the messages, and it **loses its power;** but **when connected** with the message of the third angel, **a power attends it which convicts unbelievers and infidels,** and brings them out with strength to stand, to live, grow, and flourish in the Lord" (TESTIMONIES, VOL. 1, P. 337).

Place your sermons in "blocks" with a common theme.
<u>Block preaching</u> is **arranging** the **topics** so a **common theme** is **covered** on a **series** of **consecutive nights.**
Block preaching will **reinforce** the same subjects, preaching them on consecutive nights. If a person misses one night, they will still receive the general thrust of the topic the next evening. We have listed a common order of subjects below. **This order is not locked in stone and never changed.** There are times when we adjust it some due to the location and the times of our meetings, but it is a general outline of topics presented systematically.

REVELATION OF HOPE ORDER OF SUBJECTS

Sermon Titles, Topics, Preaching Goals, and Appeals

01 | Revelation's Predictions for the Twenty-First Century

- Topic—**Overview of Revelation**
- Preaching Goal—**To introduce Revelation as God's hopeful answer to our world's overwhelming problems.**
- Appeal—**To trust a God who is powerful enough to solve the world's problems when He returns in glory.**

02 | Revelation's Biggest Surprise

- Topic—**Daniel 2**

- Preaching Goal—**To present God's outline of the future**
- Appeal—**Specific hand-raising**

03 | Revelation's Greatest End-Time Signs

- Topic—**Signs of the Second Coming of Christ**
- Preaching Goal—**To present the urgency of the signs of Christ's coming**
- Appeal—**Specific hand-raising**

04 | Revelation's Star Wars—Battle Behind the Throne

- Topic—**Origin of Evil**
- Preaching Goal—**To lead to commitment to Christ in light of the great controversy**
- Appeal—**Prayer call**

05 | Revelation's Peacemaker

- Topic—**Salvation**
- Preaching Goal—**To present Christ as the world's only hope and true Savior**
- Appeal—**Response card**

06 | Revelation's Power Line—Secret of a Whole New Life

- Topic—**The Divinity of Christ**
- Preaching Goal—**To present Jesus as the Messiah of prophecy and Changer of hearts**
- Appeal—**Response card**

07 | Revelation's Most Amazing Prophecy

- Topic—**The Three Angels' Messages**
- Preaching Goal—**To introduce God's urgent end-time message**
- Appeal—**Hand-raising**

08 | Revelation Reveals How Jesus Will Come

- Topic—**The Manner of Christ's Coming**
- Preaching Goal—**To clearly reveal the manner of Christ's second coming in light of counterfeit movements**
- Appeal—**Specific hand-raising**

09 | Revelation Predicts the Time of the End

- Topic—**2,300-Day Prophecy**

- Preaching Goal—**To trace prophetic history through the 2,300-day prophecy and reveal that since 1844 we have been living in God's judgment hour.**
- Appeal—**Prayer appeal**

10 | Revelation's Answer to Crime, Lawlessness, and Terrorism

- Topic—**The Law**
- Preaching Goal—**To reveal that God's love always leads to obedience**
- Appeal—**Hand-raising**

11 | Revelation's Eternal Sign

- Topic—**The Sabbath**
- Preaching Goal—**To present the Bible Sabbath as God's sign of loyalty**
- Appeal—**Hand-raising**

12 | Revelation Exposes History's Greatest Hoax

- Topic—**The Change of the Sabbath**
- Preaching Goal—**To unfold the truth of Daniel 7 regarding a union of church and state in the early centuries to change the Bible Sabbath**
- Appeal—**Response card**

13 | Revelation Unmasks the Cult Deception

- Topic—**Cults**
- Preaching Goal—**To present the Bible as the foundation of all truth**
- Appeal—**Specific hand-raising call**

14 | Revelation Reveals Deadly Delusions

- Topic—**The State of the Dead**
- Preaching Goal—**To present the Bible truth regarding death and the hope of the resurrection**
- Appeal—**Specific hand-raising appeal**

15 | Revelation's Seven Last Plagues Unleashed

- Topic—**Seven Last Plagues**
- Preaching Goal—**To reveal Jesus' love in the midst of the plagues**
- Appeal—**A kneeling call for earnest prayer to be ready for the coming of Jesus**

16 | Revelation's 1,000 Years of Peace

- Topic—**The Millennium**
- Preaching Goal—**To present the Bible truth regarding the millennium and appeal for decisions for eternity**
- Appeal—**Altar call for prayer to be on Christ's side**

17 | Revelation's Lake of Fire

- Topic—**Hell**
- Preaching Goal—**To present the Bible truth regarding hell and the destruction of the wicked**
- Appeal—**Hand-raising**

18 | Revelation's New Life for a New Millennium

- Topic—**Baptism**
- Preaching Goal—**To present Bible truth regarding baptism and appeal for baptism**
- Appeal—**Combination call—response card/altar call**

19 | The Revelation Lifestyle

- Topic—**Health**
- Preaching Goal—**To present the Bible truth about health and appeal to present the body as God's temple**
- Appeal—**Response card**

20 | Revelation's Four Horsemen Galloping Across the Sky

- Topic—**Why So Many Denominations?**
- Preaching Goal—**To present truth regarding apostasy in the church and restoration of truth**
- Appeal—**Hand-raising**

21 | Revelation's Last Appeal

- Topic—**The Holy Spirit and the Unpardonable Sin**
- Preaching Goal—**To appeal to each listener to follow all truth the Spirit reveals**
- Appeal—**Kneeling call**

22 | Revelation's Mark of the Beast Exposed

- Topic—**The Mark of the Beast**
- Preaching Goal—**To clearly reveal the issues in the coming crisis over the Bible Sabbath**
- Appeal—**Response card**

23 | Revelation Describes the United States in Prophecy

- Topic—**The United States in Bible Prophecy**
- Preaching Goal—**To clearly reveal the United States in Bible prophecy and the coming religious liberty crisis**
- Appeal—**Hand-raising**

24 | Revelation's Spiritual Revolution for a New Millennium

- Topic—**The True Church**
- Preaching Goal—**To clearly reveal God's true church as outlined in Revelation 12 and 14**
- Appeal –**A card call or altar call to be part of God's true church today**

25 | Revelation's Prophetic Movement at the End Time

- Topic—**The Gift of Prophecy**
- Preaching Goal—**To identify the tests of a true prophet and unfold God's plan for the gift of prophecy to His last-day church**
- Appeal—**Hand-raising**

26 | Revelation Reveals the Ultimate Answer to Life's Greatest Problems

- Topic—**Revelation 10**
- Preaching Goal—**To reveal how God has raised up His end-time church out of the disappointment of 1844**
- Appeal—**Hand-raising**

27 | Revelation's World of Tomorrow

- Topic—**Heaven**
- Preaching Goal—**To present the joy of heaven**
- Appeal—**Altar call**

The Power and Privilege of Preaching

It is amazing but still true. God has chosen to **use preaching to win the lost** to His kingdom. What is still more amazing is that He allows us to do it. He could have chosen the angels. He didn't. **He chose us.** Wonder of all wonders, God uses frail, weak, powerless human beings to preach His eternal, end-time message to a dying world.

There can be no greater privilege. There is no higher calling. **Will you accept His personal invitation** today **to become a powerful preacher** for the kingdom? You will find no greater joy and no deeper satisfaction.

One day in a land called heaven and a time called **eternity,** you will meet men and women, boys and girls that you have labored for.

1. They have sat in your audience, **heard your preaching,**

2. **Responded to** your **appeals,** and **accepted** your invitation.
3. Now they **are redeemed** to live together with Jesus through all eternity.

There is **nothing more important in life** than letting God's love and truth flow through us to **win others** for His kingdom.

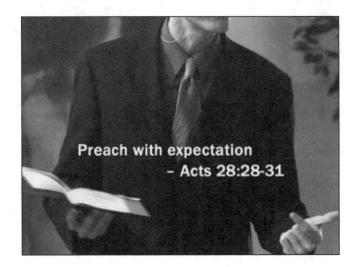

May you be a mighty preacher of His Word!

CHAPTER 8

EVANGELISTIC MUSIC

Music is a vital part of the evangelistic meeting. Often during our evangelistic meetings, we have witnessed the moving of the Holy Spirit during appeal songs. People who have been informed through the preached Word but not moved to action are **touched by a song and make their decision for Christ.** On one occasion in our evangelistic series in a meeting on the second coming of Christ, a young man sat in the meeting moved but undecided. As one of our musicians began to **sing a powerful song on the nearness of Christ's return,** he could hold back no longer and **fully committed his life to Jesus.** Charles Spurgeon once urged young preachers to never forget that "a sinner has a heart as well as a head." God has made us emotional beings. Although our emotions should never replace reason in the decision-making process, they do have a part to play. **Biblical, Christ-centered moving music touches the depths of our beings and prompts us to action.** Effective evangelists use all God-given means to lead people to Jesus. When used properly, **music can be one of the most effective means** of **impressing truth** upon the **heart.** This is born out in the writings of Ellen White.

 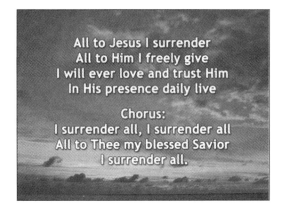

"**Song** is one of the **most effective means** of **impressing spiritual truth** upon the **heart.** Often by the **words of sacred song,** the springs of **penitence** and **faith** have been unsealed" **(THE REVIEW AND HERALD, JUNE 6, 1912).**

Lucifer, one of the greatest musicians the universe has ever known, **waged war against God.**
- Satan knows a great deal about music.
- Satan knows how to manipulate minds and enslave our souls through music.
- Satan knows exactly how to **mix theologically sound words with worldly music** and he knows how to **distort biblical truth in a song and blend it with wonderful music.**

"Adam and Eve assured the angels that they should never transgress the express command of God, for it was their highest pleasure to do His will. The **angels united with Adam and Eve** in holy strains of **harmonious music,** and as their **songs** pealed forth from blissful Eden, Satan heard the sound of their strains of **joyful adoration** to the Father and Son. And as **Satan heard it** his envy, hatred, and malignity increased, and he expressed his anxiety to his followers to incite them (Adam and Eve) to disobedience and at once bring down the wrath of God upon them and **change their songs of praise to hatred** and **curses to their Maker**" (THE STORY OF REDEMPTION, P. 31).

There is power in music. It may be from the **words** or it may come from the **music itself.** Satan knows the power of music and he uses it to his advantage. Let's look at some biblical guidelines of uplifting, inspiring music.

Music in the Old Testament:

In the Old Testament, **singing** was a **regular part of religious worship.** In Exodus, the children of Israel **sang** about their **personal experience** through **song. Israel's music reflected their unique faith journey. Many of the psalms of David were songs of his experience.**

Just as the children of Israel journeyed to the Promised Land through the wilderness and were **cheered by the music** of sacred song, God longs for His children today to be cheered as they **sing of His greatness as He leads them to the heavenly Canaan. Israel's music was the music of a unique people led miraculously by God.**

Repeating words in song is a most effective way of fixing words into our memory.

The **song of Moses** was repeated to all Israel and formed the basis for a song which was sung often. **Moses presented the truth to the Israelites through the melody of song.** This was a way of impressing the truth of God upon the whole nation. It was a **sermon.**

> "**This was the wisdom** of Moses **to present the truth** to them [the children of Israel] **in song,** that in strains of melody they should become familiar with them, and **be impressed upon the minds** of the whole nation, young and old. It was important for the children to learn the song; for this would speak to them, to war, to restrain, to reprove, and encourage. **It was a continual sermon**" (EVANGELISM, P. 496).

Imagine Moses singing with one group of Israelites praising God for His deliverance over the Egyptians and Miriam with another group responding in song.

> "Then Moses and the children of Israel sang their song to the LORD, and spoke, saying:
> '**I will sing to the LORD,**
> **For He has triumphed gloriously!**
> The horse and its rider
> He has thrown into the sea!
> The LORD is my strength and song,
> And He has become my salvation;
> He is my God, and I will praise Him;
> My father's God and I will exalt Him....'
>
> "And Miriam answered them:
> '**Sing to the LORD,**

For He has triumphed gloriously!
The horse and its rider
He has thrown into the sea!' "
(EXODUS 15:1–21).

In the Old Testament, we discover this critically important principle regarding music—**music is a teaching tool to communicate truth as well as a vehicle to praise God.**

How does this principle apply to evangelistic music?

- All songs chosen must compliment the message of the evening and be both inspirational and powerfully communicate biblical truth in a compelling way.

Many of David's psalms were sung by the people on their journeys to the national altar at the annual feasts. The influence of song prepared them for worship at these feasts. **Here is another vital principle in evangelistic music: the songs must prepare hearts for the preached Word.**

There are key thoughts to keep in mind when planning evangelistic music.

 # KEY THOUGHT #1—A CONSECRATED HEART

"Give Glory to God"

Spirit-filled evangelistic music is all about God, not the performer. Its purpose is to bring glory to God.

The psalmist said it well, "I will sing of mercy and justice; to You, O LORD, I will sing praises" **(PSALM 101:1).**

Music was made for a holy purpose. It is to lift the thoughts to that which is pure, noble, and elevating. It is to give gratitude to God for what He has done in our lives.

"What a **contrast** between the **ancient custom** and the **uses** to which **music** is **now** too often devoted! **How many employ this gift to exalt self, instead of using it to Glorify God!**" (PATRIARCHS AND PROPHETS, P. 594).

Music is God's chosen method of praise. God gave us the gift of music because He knew praising Him in song brings us one of life's greatest joys.

Satan wants us to bring praise and attention to ourselves rather than God. We are instructed to "Glory in His holy name;

"Let the hearts of those rejoice who seek the LORD!" **(1 CHRONICLES 16:10).**

This is, of course, the true purpose of all evangelistic music. Music flowing from a **consecrated heart desiring to praise God** has a **greater spiritual impact** on an evangelistic audience than the most professional music from someone who merely wants to draw attention to themselves.

A musician with a consecrated heart has the supreme desire to give **glory to God,** not to glorify self.

The question is, "Who does my music give glory to, the performer or God?"

Music done as a performance is dramatically different than music done as a ministry. There is a dramatic **difference between inspiration and performance** in the work of evangelism. Although the following statement applies to the speaker of the Word, it can certainly be applied to evangelistic music.

"The **work** in the **large cities** is to be done after Christ's order, **not** after the order of a **theatrical performance.** It is **not a theatrical performance that glorifies God,** but the **presentation** of the **truth** in the love of Christ" (EVANGELISM, P. 206).

The question is, "Who does my music center around, the performer or God?"

Satan's heart was "lifted up" because of his beauty (EZEKIEL 28:17). Unfortunately, the problem of pride plagues people today.

The spirit of exalting one's self is a significant factor in the secular music industry and it can even creep into the church. Pride caused Satan to fall. Isaiah describes Lucifer's heart:

"How you are fallen from heaven,
O Lucifer, son of the morning!
How you are cut down to the ground,
You who weakened the nations!
For you have said in your heart:
'**I will** ascend into heaven,
I will exalt my throne above the stars of God;
I will also sit on the mount of the congregation
On the farthest sides of the north;
I will ascend above the heights of the clouds,
I will be like the Most High' " (ISAIAH 14:12-14).

Beware if the **music** promotes or **exalts the person** or his/her gifts. We were **created to glorify God,** not self. When the temptation comes to promote the person rather than God, remember the fall of Lucifer.

"**Praise no man;** flatter no man; and permit no man to praise or flatter you. Satan will do enough of this work. **Lose sight of the instrument,** and think of Jesus. Praise the Lord. Give glory to God. **Make melody** to God in your hearts" (EVANGELISM, P. 630).

Secure musicians to sing in your evangelistic meetings **who have a consecrated heart and desire to glorify God through their music. If their lifestyle off the stage,** outside of the meetings, **does not glorify God, neither will their music.**

KEY THOUGHT #2—APPROPRIATE DRESS

The **dress of the musician** can have a **greater impact** on the audience **than the song sung.** If the listener is distracted with the dress of the musician rather than the message of the song, the spiritual impact of the music will be lost. Modest dress conceals, while immodest dress reveals. **Modest dress is neat and attractive.** It is neither tight, form fitting, sloppy, or gaudy. There is an old poem that goes something like this, **"Lord, make me a nail upon the wall and let this thing so common and so small be the space to hang a lovely picture of Your face."** The supreme goal of a godly musician with a consecrated heart and modest dress is to be **an ambassador for Jesus in both their demeanor and dress.** It is written of the disciples on the Mount of Transfiguration that they saw no man but "Jesus only." We long for our audiences to see no man but Jesus only through our music and our dress.

The question is, "Who is the focus of attention on, the musician or God?"

KEY THOUGHT #3—MESSAGE-FOCUSED—NOT BEAT- OR RHYTHM-FOCUSED

When the focus of attention is on the **beat or rhythm** of the song **rather than on the message** of the song, the **music appeals** to the **senses** and **emotions** rather than the spiritual faculties. It is **God's desire that our emotions be led by our intellect not our intellect governed by our emotions.** The essence of what it means to be human is our ability to reason and think logically. Satan tries to bypass the mind and appeal directly to the emotions. The messenger of the Lord points this out:

> **"A bedlam of noise shocks** the **senses** and **perverts** that which if conducted aright might be a blessing. The powers of satanic agencies blend with the din and noise, to have a carnival, and this is termed the Holy Spirit's working. . . .
>
> "Those things which have been in the past will be in the future. **Satan will make music a snare** by the way in which it is conducted" **(SELECTED MESSAGES, BK. 2, PP. 36, 37).**

In his book, *The Music of Heaven,* on page 43, John Thurber puts it this way, **"When the beat overshadows the words, or the physical side of music takes precedence over the intellectual, the music is from beneath.** But while there are **natural rhythms** that God built into our lives, some of the music we have today fights with those natural rhythms. Though these **rhythms seem exciting or stimulating, our bodies are somehow disturbed by them.** This is why fish die, sunflowers turn away, and rats become retarded and lose their way in a maze when exposed to certain subversive rhythms. As Christians, we can be sure that **any music which causes such chaos in the world of nature attacks our own mental, physical and/or spiritual health as well."**

The question is, "Does the beat and rhythm overshadow the words?"

KEY THOUGHT #4— THEOLOGICALLY ACCURATE

When the words of the song are theologically inaccurate, they undermine the integrity of the message. A song may be extremely appealing musically. It may be extremely popular with Christian audiences yet at its heart, it may be biblically flawed. As an evangelist, be sure the songs you choose reflect the message you preach or else there will be dissonance in the minds of your audience. The **biblical accuracy of the message of a song is critically important just as is the accuracy of the message you preach.**

- If the sermon is on the **second coming of Christ** and the special music has a **subtle rapture** slant, the audience may be confused.
- If the musician sings a song that communicates that all you have to do is to **"believe"** and you preach on the **need to obey God, doubts may linger in the minds of your listeners.**
- If you preach on the **state of the dead** and the song describes our dead loved ones now rejoicing around the throne of God, beware.

The question is, "Is the song being sung theologically accurate or is it theologically flawed?"

KEY THOUGHT #5—MATCHING THE MESSAGE

When the words of the song are **theologically accurate,** but do not match the message, they **create dissonance** in the minds of the listeners.

The **song** that is sung just **before the message** should inspire the evangelist to preach. The song should also match the message preached. The **appeal song** is a **continuation of the message.** It is to give the evangelist an opportunity to make effective appeals. We have often asked our musicians to let us choose from a selection of three or four songs the very best song to coordinate with the message. Since **music** is not an add-on, but **an integral part of the message,** we are very careful in the selection of the songs to be sure they enhance and enrich the biblical message for the evening.

On page 101, there is a list of possibilities of pre-message songs and appeal songs.

Coordinate all songs sung before and after the sermon with the message preached.

KEY THOUGHT #6—COMMUNICATING THE MESSAGE

Since the **musician communicates visually as well as audibly,** facial expression with a godly smile and eyes wide open make a dramatic difference in the response of the listener. Words clearly sung without the syllables running together impact audiences for the kingdom of God. If the preacher did not distinctly pronounce the words of the sermon and the audience had difficulty understanding them, they would receive little blessing. It is the same with vocal presentations. **The power of the music is in the clarity of the words** indicted by the Holy Spirit through the melody upon the heart.

"The melody of song, poured forth from many hearts in **clear distinct utterance,** is one of God's instrumentalities in the work of saving souls" (**TESTIMONIES, VOL. 5, P. 493**).

 # KEY THOUGHT #7—SING SPIRIT-INSPIRED APPEALS

Being Uninhibited in Spirit-Inspired Appeals

When an appeal song is sung with track music, it severely limits the evangelist's flexibility and his opportunity to cooperate with the Spirit in a call. We prefer to use live accompaniment in our evangelistic **appeal songs.** Have you ever been at an evangelistic meeting when the evangelist had just finished preaching, made his appeal, invited the soloist to sing the appeal song, and the track did not play properly or the wrong track began to play and the soloist had to stop and signal the sound engineers to change the track? The spiritual atmosphere is interrupted and the appeal is much less effective. We like to **coordinate all appeals with the soloist and the pianist** so as an **evangelist, I can talk between the stanzas** to make further appeals.

Songs used in appeals make a dramatic difference.
- **Hearts** are touched.
- **Lives** are changed and
- **Decisions** are made for the kingdom of God.

"There are **few means more effective for fixing His words in memory than repeating them in song.** And such song has wonderful power. It has power to subdue rude and uncultivated natures; power to quicken thought and to awaken sympathy, to promote harmony of action, and to banish the gloom and foreboding that destroy courage and weaken effort" (**EDUCATION, PP. 167, 168**).

Often I have stood on the platform in some grand auditorium, some huge stadium, or local church and watched as the Holy Spirit has moved audiences. I have seen tens of thousands of people come forward to surrender their lives completely to Jesus as they have stood to their feet and sung **simple gospel hymns** such as
- "Just When I Need Him Jesus Is Near"
- "What a Friend We Have in Jesus"
- "Come Every Soul of Sin Oppressed, There Is Mercy With the Lord"

Regularly, after passing out a decision card for people to fill out at their seats on the night of the subject of baptism, once the ushers have collected the cards and are bringing them forward, **I will often invite one of our musicians to begin singing, "I have decided to follow Jesus, no turning back, no turning back."** I will then make an appeal for the people who have checked the cards for baptism to come forward. **As we sing, often hundreds come forward.**

Billy Graham has used the appeal song "Just as I Am" for years. There is a reason he does. It reaches down into the hearts of his audiences and moves them at the point of their deepest needs. You may or may not have a singing evangelist or a soloist available for your meetings. Don't let that trouble you.

- Simply invite the congregation to stand to their feet and **sing a familiar hymn.**
- Put the **words of the song on the screen** and
- **Make your appeal** while the audience is standing.

You will be amazed what God will do. A number of years ago, I was teaching a class on public evangelism to a group of university students. These students would listen to me preach a couple nights a week and preach themselves on the alternate nights in their own evangelistic series. In class, **I discussed the art of making appeals and using simple gospel songs.** I encouraged my students to make an appeal at their very next meeting. It was with some fear and anxiety that they began making appeals. I shall never forget their comments the next day in class. "Pastor, God worked. I was amazed to see the Holy Spirit moving on the audience. People actually came forward." **God will use you, too, as you combine the preached Word with heartfelt gospel music.**

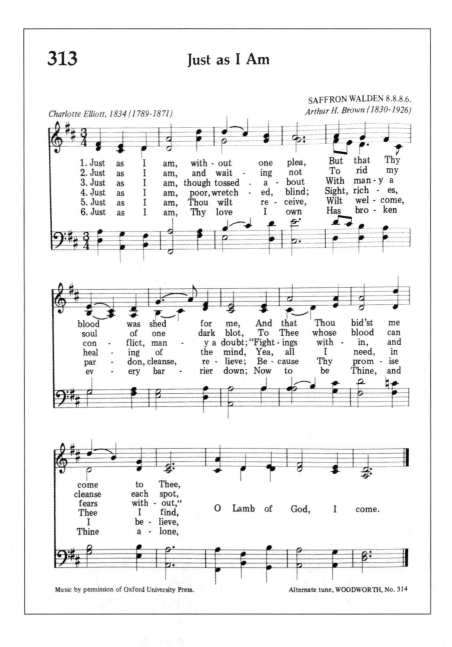

Use simple appeal songs, make appeals and watch what God does.

Prayerfully consider the following references on music as you **plan the music** for your church or evangelistic meetings.

Look at this powerful statement:

"Eternal things have little weight with the youth. **Angels** of God are in **tears** as they write in the roll the words and acts of professed Christians. Angels are hovering around yonder dwelling. The young are there assembled; there is the sound of **vocal** and **instrumental music.** Christians are gathered there, but what is that you hear? It is a **song, a frivolous ditty,** fit for the **dance hall.** Behold the pure angels gather their light closer around them, and **darkness envelops those in that dwelling.** The **angels are moving** from the scene. **Sadness** is upon their countenances. Behold, they are **weeping.** This **I saw repeated a number of times all through** the **ranks of Sabbathkeepers. . . .** Satan has no objection to music if he can make that a channel through which to gain access to the minds of the youth. Anything will suit his purpose that will divert the mind from God and engage the time which should be devoted to His service. He works through the means which will exert the strongest influence to hold the largest numbers in a pleasing infatuation, while they are paralyzed by his power. **When turned to a good account, music is a blessing;** but it is often made one of Satan's most attractive agencies to ensnare souls. **When abused, it leads the unconsecrated to pride, vanity, and folly**" (TESTIMONIES, VOL. 1, PP. 505, 506).

"The things you have described as taking place in Indiana, **the Lord has shown me would take place just before the close of probation.** Every uncouth thing will be demonstrated. There will be **shouting, with drums, music,** and **dancing.** The senses of rational beings will become confused that they cannot be trusted to make right decisions. And this is called the moving of the Holy Spirit.

"**The Holy Spirit never reveals itself in such methods, in such a bedlam of noise.** This is an **invention of Satan** to cover up his ingenious methods for making of none affect the pure, sincere, elevating, ennobling, sanctifying truth for this time. **Better never have the worship of God blended with music** than to use musical instruments to do the work which last January was represented to me would be brought into our camp meetings. **The truth for this time needs nothing of this kind in its work of converting souls.** A **bedlam of noise shocks the senses** and **perverts** that which if conducted aright might be a blessing. The powers of Satan blend with the din and noise, to have a carnival, and **this is termed the Holy Spirit's working**" (SELECTED MESSAGES, BK. 2, P. 36).

CHAPTER 9

BUILDING AND MAINTAINING YOUR AUDIENCE IN PUBLIC EVANGELISTIC MEETINGS

Why does the audience **grow** at some evangelistic meetings and **diminish** at others?

Why do **some evangelists end** their evangelistic meetings **with more** people than they began with and other evangelists **finish theirs** with **significantly less** than they began with?

What is the difference?

The **ongoing ministries of the local church** as well as members inviting their friends to the meetings may bring an audience. **Advertising may swell the opening night attendance** but once people walk through the doors of an evangelistic meeting, **what will keep them coming back night after night**? Let's explore answers to these questions by looking at some practical things you can do to build and maintain your audience.

After **conducting evangelistic meetings** around the **world** for **decades,** we have **discovered some effective** ways to **keep people coming back** night after night to the evangelistic series. In this chapter, we will share what you can do to **grow your audience.** By following these **simple principles,** you will hold your audience and even **see attendance increase.**

The **_methods_** we suggest are **not merely theory.** We have **_tested_** them **thoroughly** in countries around the world.

Sixteen Ways to Build Your Audience in Evangelistic Meetings

01 | Enthusiastic, Biblical Preaching

The **apostle Paul** was one of the **most effective evangelists** of all time. He preached powerful messages in Galatia, Ephesus, Philippi, Corinth, Colossae, and a host of other cities in Asia Minor. At the close of his ministry, he counseled Timothy to **"Preach the word!"** (2 TIMOTHY 4:2). To the church at Corinth, Paul wrote,

"It pleased God **through the foolishness** of the message **preached** to **save** those who **believe**" (1 CORINTHIANS 1:21).

Ellen White adds,

"The creative energy that called the worlds into existence is in the word of God. This **word imparts power;** it begets life. **Every command is a promise;** accepted by the will, received into the soul, **it brings with it the life of the Infinite One.** It **transforms** the nature and **re-creates** the soul in the image of God" (EDUCATION, P. 126).

When **God's Word** is powerfully **proclaimed,** hearts are touched, **lives** are changed, and minds **convicted** of eternal truth.

It is the **preaching of the life-changing Word** that **keeps people coming back** to the meetings night after night. When their hearts are stirred with the Word and their lives changed through the Word, **they will cancel other appointments and re-order their priorities to attend.**

Your audience will grow if you pour yourself into the **biblical message preached each evening.** It is the **biblical content preached** with enthusiasm that will keep people coming back. Many years ago, a **preacher** in England **asked** an **actor** why the **theaters** were **jam packed** and the **churches** were nearly **empty.** The actor responded this way.

> **"We, on the <u>stage</u>, take things that are imaginary and make them real. You <u>preachers</u> take things that are real and make them imaginary."**

The heart of **holding any audience** is a **man or woman of God** with a **message from God pouring** out of his or her **soul for God.** Describing his all-consuming passion for preaching, the apostle Paul declared,

> **"So, as much as is in me, I am ready to preach the gospel to you who are in Rome also"** (ROMANS 1:15).

The apostle **Paul was passionate** about **what he preached.** The gospel mattered to him. He did not take Jesus lightly. Truth mattered. He did not handle the Word of God lightly. The great **English preacher Phillips Brooks** once said,

> **"Preaching is proclaiming God's truth through human personality."**

> When the preacher is on fire for God, people will come to watch the blaze.

Powerful preaching combined with **up-to-date graphics** to illustrate each sermon is a winning combination **to keep your audience coming** each night to your evangelistic meetings. When an enthusiastic biblical preacher illustrates prophetic messages with the **latest computer generated graphics,** the results will be **remarkable.** The audience **will return** nightly to listen to prophetic messages that speak to the needs of their hearts today and give them hope for tomorrow.

God illustrated prophetic truth through the amazing images in the visions of Daniel and Revelation. **Jesus illustrated divine truth in the symbolic imagery of the parables.** By the use of these attention-getting divine depictions, our Lord pictured truth through real life stories.

The Lord instructed the prophet Habakkuk to **"write the vision and make it plain on tablets, that he may run who reads it"** (HABAKKUK 2:2).

> The purpose of all illustrations is to "make truth plain."

Graphics are **not an end in themselves.** They are valuable only as they make divine truth more understandable to the listener.

Using computer graphics holds the attention of the audience, rivets their interest, and keeps them coming back. Ellen White affirms the importance of illustrating our evangelistic presentations.

> "**Instruction** has been **given me** clearly and distinctly that **charts** should be **used** in the **presentation of truth**" (EVANGELISM, P. 203).

> "The use of **charts** is **most effective** in **explaining** the **prophecies** relating to the past, the present, and the future" (IBID.).

> "By the **use of charts, symbols,** and **representations** of various kinds the minister can make the **truth stand out** clearly and distinctly. This is a help, and in harmony with the word of God" (TESTIMONIES, VOL. 9, P. 142).

Ellen White spoke of **the value of charts and life-size images of the prophetic beasts in her day.** If she were alive today, her counsel would be on the value of **using computer graphics,** for they certainly make truth stand out "clearly and distinctly."

02 | Thorough Preparation

There are three things you can do to make your sermons more effective:
- **Prepare** well
- **Review** thoroughly
- **Practice** often

A shoddy, half-prepared delivery is inexcusable. The most effective evangelists **review** their **messages** again and again. Internalize the message by **practicing** it. Set aside an **hour or two** to **review your sermon** just before you present it. Even after **four decades of preaching evangelistic messages hundreds of times, I still arrive at the auditorium two hours early to review my message and practice preaching** it to an empty auditorium. As I preach it in the silence of an empty building, the Holy Spirit often impresses my mind with new thoughts to apply that very night to that very audience. I rarely preach the same message the same way twice. **Let the Holy Spirit burn the truth into your soul.** Let God write it on your mind and preach it with confidence and conviction.

03 | Christ-Centered, Practically Applied Messages

Jesus shares a **powerful secret** of **effective soul winning** when He says,

> "**And I, if I am lifted up from the earth, will draw all peoples to Myself**" (JOHN 12:32).

When Jesus is presented in all of His beauty, **audiences are attracted to Him.** When **Christ** is presented as the **center** of each doctrine, men and woman are charmed by His love. One night I was preaching in a public auditorium in the state of Connecticut and a group of teenagers who were paying little attention to my message began talking quite loudly and distracting those around them. I paused for a moment and began to picture Christ's cruel death on the cross. As I continued to describe Jesus' love and His immense sacrifice in dying for our sins, a hush fell over the audience. These teenagers quieted down and the Holy Spirit spoke to their hearts.

After the apostle Paul struggled to win a few converts in Athens by meeting philosophical arguments with mere logic, he exclaimed to the Corinthian believers,

> **"For I determined not to know anything among you except Jesus Christ and Him crucified"** (1 CORINTHIANS 2:2).

> To the Galatian church, he declared, **"But God forbid that I should boast except in the cross of our Lord Jesus Christ"** (GALATIANS 6:14).

The apostle **Paul uplifted Jesus** and the crowds flocked to hear Him. The cross of Christ has an attractive charm to hold an audience.

> "Let Daniel speak, let Revelation speak, and tell what is truth. But **whatever** phase of the **subject** is presented, **uplift Jesus** as the **center** of **all hope,** 'the Root and the Offspring of David, and the bright and morning Star' " (TESTIMONIES TO MINISTERS, P. 118).

Here is something practical you can do. Review each of your evangelistic sermons and ask these three questions:
1. If I had never accepted Jesus before, **would I accept Him based on this sermon alone**?
2. Is **Jesus** truly the **Center** of this message?
3. What is this message's **central theme** and where is Jesus in this doctrine?

04 | Managing the Meeting Time Well

We live in a hectic, fast-paced society. Your audience will become **bored** if they have to sit through **long preliminaries** and announcements. Ideally, it would be good to **be preaching within fifteen or twenty minutes from the time the meeting begins.** Time is valuable and most people do not want to waste it. They have worked all day, rushed to your meeting, and will get home late only to get up to return to work the next morning. To keep them coming back, the meetings must be worth their while. They must be compelling, thought-provoking, spiritual, up-to-date, and practically helpful. Every part of the program must be thought through. It is **extremely important** to **begin and end** the meeting **on time.**

Here are a few key principles:
- Begin on time.
- Limit the preliminaries.
- Clearly instruct those who make announcements and those who pray to be short and to the point.
- Clearly instruct your musicians to sing and not to give a sermon before their musical item.
- Rehearse with your ushers so they quickly and efficiently distribute materials.

"**Many speakers** waste their time and strength in **long preliminaries** and **excuses.** Some use nearly half an hour in making apologies; thus **time is wasted,** and when they reach their subject and try to fasten the points of truth in the minds of their hearers, the people are wearied out and cannot see their force" **(GOSPEL WORKERS, P. 16).**

Make every minute in your meetings count for the glory of God. Your **audience will continue to come** out night after night if they feel that they are being richly blessed by every part of the program. **Cut out everything that is extraneous** and of little difference and focus on those things that are of eternal consequences.

05 | A Well-Organized Bible School

You will discover some of your **best interests** by **establishing a Bible school** during the evangelistic meetings. (For more information, see the chapter on the Bible School.)
- During the meetings, encourage the audience to **enroll** in the *Search for Certainty* Bible guides.
- The Bible study guides **answer questions** raised by the presentations. They will solidify your audience.
- Encourage the audience to **bring** their **completed Bible study guides back** each evening.
- Offer an **attractive incentive** if they **finish all** of the lessons.
- The **audience participation** will engage them in the meetings and keep them coming back. Their questions will be answered as they do their Bible lessons and they will not develop a resistance to divine truth because they do not have biblical answers. As they study the Bible lessons, they will be eager to learn more and will continue attending the meetings.

06 | A Vibrant Intercessory Prayer Ministry

Prayer creates an **atmosphere** for **God to work.** Angels descend from the realms of glory in response to answered prayer. Describing the warfare between the forces of good and the powers of darkness, the apostle Paul states,

> "**For we do not wrestle against flesh and blood,** but against principalities, against powers, against the rulers of darkness of this age, against spiritual hosts of wickedness in the heavenly places" **(EPHESIANS 6:12).**

We are powerless to fight the enemy on our own. **Evangelism is a declaration of war against Satan.** As long as the **church** of God **is half-awake or sleepy in the trenches,** Satan will leave them alone. But when the **church** rises to its destiny, fulfills its purpose, and becomes **aggressive in soul winning,** the devil is furious.

Prayer gives God permission to work powerfully. As we intercede for others, we are saying, "**God, we cannot reach this person, but You can.**" We are trusting God to do what it is impossible for us to do alone. Ellen White writes that

"**Ministering angels are waiting** about the throne to instantly obey the mandate of Jesus Christ to answer every prayer offered in living faith" (SELECTED MESSAGES, BK. 2, P. 377).

Jesus prayed for Peter **by name** (LUKE 21:31, 32).

Paul prayed for each of the churches he planted **by name** (EPHESIANS 1:16, 17; PHILIPPIANS 1:3, 4; COLOSSIANS 1:3).

Through prayer, God works miracles in the hearts and minds of people attending the meetings. We can recall numerous occasions through the years where our **meetings** were **at a critical juncture.** We had presented the testing truths. The audience was diminishing. Some people were not returning to the meetings. As we besieged heaven, **God turned things around.**

An **organized, diligent prayer effort** is indispensable to building an evangelistic audience. **Evangelistic meetings saturated with prayer** make a **powerful impact** on doubting hearts and questioning minds.

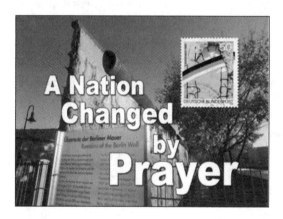

Prayer makes a difference!

Here are some pointers to remember in organizing a mighty intercessory prayer movement:
- **Organize** prayer groups to meet one hour before each meeting.
- **Invite** members of the prayer groups into the meeting to pray silently for the evangelist and the audience while the evangelist is preaching.
- **Distribute** names of your interests to the prayer groups and encourage them to pray for each interest by name.
- As the prayer groups **meet** each evening, share prayer promises from the Bible and writings of Ellen White.
- As the prayer groups meet each evening, **share** answers to prayer.

"**Prayer** and **faith** will accomplish what **no power** on earth can accomplish" (THE MINISTRY OF HEALING, P. 509).

"It is part of God's plan to grant us, in answer to the prayer of faith, that which He would not bestow did we not thus ask" (THE GREAT CONTROVERSY, P. 525).

07 | **A Systematic Visitation Program**

There are few things as **effective as visitation** for **building your attendance.** The difference between many people attending the meetings and dropping out may be a single visit.

Often people coming to the meetings develop questions. As they ask their priest, minister, or religious friends, they often get answers which discourage them from returning to the meetings.

If their questions are not answered in a timely manner, they may develop what is known as *"cognitive dissonance."*

> **Cognitive dissonance** occurs when a person **becomes uncomfortable** with what they are **hearing** because they have unanswered questions.

Questions loom large in their minds. Their conventional beliefs are challenged. Traditions they have believed all of their lives are confronted with God's Word.

If they are **not visited** at the right time, they **will not return** to the meetings. If their **questions** are **not answered,** they will **drop out.** Visitation makes a huge difference. The apostle Paul states,

"And I went up by revelation, and communicated to them that gospel which I preach among the Gentiles, **but privately to those of reputation, lest by any means I might run, or had run, in vain**" (GALATIANS 2:2).

The New Testament church visited house to house (ACTS 20:20).

Here are some practical keys:

- **Develop** an attendance **tracking system.**
- **Use** the "evangelistic tracking" system.
- **Visit** each guest who has attended at least one meeting.
- **Follow** the **guidelines** for visitation outlined in chapter 11.

"Not only is the **truth** to be **presented in public assemblies; house-to-house work is to be done.** Let this work go forward in the name of the Lord" (EVANGELISM, P. 431).

It is the **house-to-house work** and **visitation** that **makes** the **preaching** of the Word **effective.** Home **visitation** builds rapport and keeps people coming back to the meetings. If the **attendance** stays **low,** it is often because **visitation is weak.**

08 | **Response/Decision Cards**

When people check a **decision card** that they would like more information, it is important for the visitor to **supply them with books or literature** that will answer their questions on that subject. **Response cards** provide an **opportunity** for people **to make** a **decision, ask questions, request prayer,** or **request additional literature.** In this way, they feel they are participating in the process. People who are engaged in the process will tend to continue coming to the meetings.

Ancient Discoveries
REVEAL THE FUTURE
Hope Beyond Tomorrow
My Response
❏ I believe Jesus will come literally, personally, visibly and audibly.
❏ I desire to be ready for Jesus' return.
❏ I would like to be baptized soon.
❏ I would like more reading material on Jesus' coming.

Response/decision cards enable the evangelist to have some idea of what the person's attitude is toward truth and provide answers both publically and privately to their questions.

09 | Schedule Sheets

- A **schedule sheet** of the **entire program** is given to each one who attends the meetings. These schedule sheets are given to new attendees throughout the entire series.
- The **audience will be intrigued** by the upcoming topics and anticipate which presentation is coming next. As the evangelist promotes the nightly topics, people have the feeling that they cannot miss a single presentation.
- The **schedule sheets allow** the audience to **"block out time"** for the meetings. Each evening as the **evangelist** enthusiastically **promotes the next night's subject,** people are motivated to attend.
- The schedule sheets also provide "talking points" for the visitors to give to their friends to invite them to attend as well.
- The schedule sheets provide for church members and guests a constant reminder of the meetings.

10 | Reinforcing the Message With Literature

Literature serves an **immense value** throughout the meetings. It is the silent preacher. Well after the evangelist has gone to sleep, the truth-filled literature that you have distributed during the meetings is still speaking to hearts, still informing minds, still answering questions, and still convicting people of divine truth.

When people begin regularly attending your evangelistic meetings, it is generally because they are **serious about knowing truth.** They are going to study the subjects you present thoroughly before making a decision. They will read and research each topic. It is far better for you to **place truth-filled literature in their hands** than have them seek out materials filled with half-truths and falsehoods.

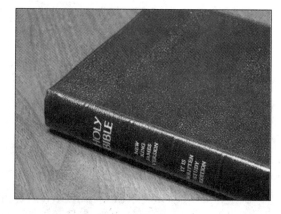

- It **provides** the audience with the **biblical content** of the meetings.
- It **answers** their **questions** and stimulates them to dig deeper into the truths presented.

The well-chosen **treasured gift book or Bible** with **study helps** will **keep the audience coming back.** When their interest in the meetings wanes a little and distractions tend to keep them from attending on a given night, a **unique incentive** may encourage them to return.

Be sure you choose a gift book of value or Bible for anyone who comes fourteen to sixteen nights.

You can use small, less expensive books for special weekends like the weekend you preach on the Sabbath, baptism, or the true church. You will **stabilize attendance** with a **top-quality attendance award.** You may use such books as *What the Bible Says About* or *The World's Next Super Power* as attendance awards.

PRACTICAL TIPS

- Provide a **copy of the lecture** of the evening for each person attending.
- Provide **attendance awards** as incentives on select nights.
- Direct the audience to the **resource table** where they can purchase more literature.
- Direct attendees to **the Bible school** where they can receive **free** Bible study guides.

> "The **discourses** presenting the reasons of our faith should be **published in little leaflets,** and circulated as widely as possible. . . .
>
> ". . . Thus the **falsehoods** and **misrepresentations** which the **enemy** of truth constantly **tries** to keep in circulation would be revealed in their true character, and the **people** would **have** an **opportunity** of **knowing just what the minister said**" (EVANGELISM, P. 160).

11 | Encouraging People to Invite Their Friends

There is **nothing more effective** in building your evangelistic audience than **friends inviting friends.** When Andrew came to Jesus, he then went and found his brother Peter and brought him to Jesus.

> "He **first found his own brother** Simon, and said to him, 'We have found the Messiah' (which is translated, the Christ)" (JOHN 1:41).

The Samaritan woman left her water pot by the well and ran to tell others about Jesus.

> "The woman then **left her waterpot,** went her way into the city, and said to the men, '**Come, see** a Man who told me all things that I ever did. Could this be the Christ?' " (JOHN 4:28, 29).

The result of her invitation was multitudes coming to hear Jesus. John adds this thrilling extra bit of information.

> "And many of the **Samaritans** of that city **believed** in Him **because of the word of the woman** who testified, 'He told me all that I ever did' " (JOHN 4:39).

Multitudes came to hear Jesus preach because of one changed woman. **People are the best advertising!**

Encourage people attending your meetings to **invite their friends** and **offer** an **incentive** for those who bring people to the evangelistic meeting.

We have often used 4x6 **quality prints** from Nathan Greene such as ***The Family of God, The Invitation,*** and ***Jesus and the Lamb. Wait*** until your **second or third weekend** before you launch your incentive program for friends. We give the **picture to both** the **friend** and their **invitee.** Provide schedules each evening for people to give to their friends.

People like to share something good they have found. **Encourage them to invite their family, friends, and working associates.**

12 | Weekly Mailings

Weekly mailings serve as constant reminders of the upcoming topics. They also provide an opportunity to promote any special features such as a health, musical programs, or the question-and-answer periods.

At times we include a **special coupon** in the weekly mailing for a gift book. We have included a copy of four separate attendance building letters in the appendix on pages 194–197.

Remember, if you are out of touch, few people will come. Keep the evangelistic meetings before your audience. With the **competing interests** to keep people away, **weekly mailings place them in the forefront of their thinking.**

Our weekly mailings are normally **mailed on Wednesday** to build up the weekend attendance.

Usually we advertise our Friday, Saturday, and Sunday nights in one letter. **Letters** are **mailed** to all attendees—**Adventists** and **visitors** alike.

13 | Special Features

Special features add spice to your meetings like salt to a meal. You may feature
- Special **musical** groups
- A **video** on the life of Christ
- An exciting **mission story**
- A **health presentation**

We schedule a variety of special features throughout the series. On Saturday night, we will typically start early with an outstanding musical feature. During the week, we will focus on health features. These health features make a big difference in people wanting to attend the meetings. People are interested in their health and enjoy a health feature in the evening program.

Often a person may be considering whether to come to the meeting.

They may be tired, extremely busy, or distracted by another competing interest. **A special feature** that they particularly want to see or hear may be the **catalyst that brings them back** that evening for a message leading to a decision for Jesus.

14 | Giving the Attendees Practical Help With Life's Problems and Challenges

When people's needs are met, they continue to come to the meetings. When they feel that the meetings are giving them practical help for their daily needs, they will not want to stay away.

PRACTICAL TIPS

- **Offer** a **class** to help people **overcome undesirable habits** such as smoking, alcohol, and drugs.
- **Offer** people **help** with the problems in their families, their marriages, and their health and they will continue to come.
- **Offer** a **counseling** service at select periods during the day.
- **Offer to pray** specifically for those facing life's problems.

15 | Establishing a "Resource Center" to Build the Attendees' Spiritual Library

When people come to spiritual meetings based on prophecy, questions will surface. They will seek reading materials on the topics presented.

If you do not provide it, someone else will. Carefully select new reading material to place at the sales table which correlates with the topic you are presenting. Our **bestsellers at the resource table are the CDs and DVDs of the meetings.** People like to share the message they have just heard with their family and friends. They also want to review the message they have just heard.

Develop a **systemic approach** to sales, which follows the outline of the topics you present in your meetings. For example, **don't put books** on the **sales table** about the Sabbath, the state of the dead, or the mark of the beast **until you have presented those topics.**

Some people will keep coming because their questions are being answered through the literature they are reading, the DVDs they are watching, and the CDs they are listening to. They will look forward to visiting the resource table each evening to see what new items have been placed on it. Many who do not make immediate decisions will eventually decide for Christ and His church based on the material that they have purchased at the resource table.

16 | Providing CDs/DVDs of the Actual Meeting

Audio and video **recordings** of the **meetings** give people an opportunity to **review the messages** over again. We have regularly baptized people whose schedule has allowed them to come to only some of the meetings but who have **listened to the CDs.** If a person misses a meeting, our visitors **drop off a CD** from the **lending library** for them to catch up on what they missed. Husbands and wives regularly bring home CDs or DVDs for their families. Sometimes whole families have been converted through the CD/DVD ministry. **Here is how to get started:**

- **Duplicate audio tapes, CDs,** or both of the sermons being preached each evening.
- **Sell them at your resource center** and give the people an opportunity to hear the message again.
- Many new people will come to the meeting and **buy** the CDs or DVDs.

  It may not be financially possible for every church that conducts an evangelistic meeting to tape DVDs, but try to have some lecture material available.

- The **CDs of the messages enable** people to **hear any message they might have**

missed so they do not have gaps in their thinking process.

- **Establish a CD/DVD lending library** for people to check out up to two CDs/DVDs. When they return the CDs/DVDs they have taken, they can choose two more.

17 | Through Conducting a Question-and-Answer Period One to Two Nights a Week During the Evangelistic Meetings

Dissonance occurs when new truth challenges preconceived opinions and cherished ideas. The more **questions dominate the thinking,** the more likely a person is to drop out of the meeting. By providing an outlet for our guests to ask their questions, we are reducing their mental conflict and preparing them to receive Bible truth.

- Many people will keep coming to the meetings if they know this is a **place where they can ask questions** and **receive biblical answers.**
- You can **deal with objections** during the **question-and-answer period** that you might not be able to deal with in the sermon.

Some final thoughts on building attendance

It is the **preached Word** ignited by the Holy Spirit that **impresses truth on the heart.** When your audience senses they are hearing an urgent present-truth message, which is out of the common order of things, they will return night after night.

When hearts are stirred by the truths of God's Word, they will return.
When lives are changed, they will return.
When hearts are touched by divine grace, they will return.
When Jesus is uplifted by the Holy Spirit, they will return.
When Revelation's message is unfolded, they will return.
When the Lord's coming is prominent in every message, they will return.
They will not want to miss a single meeting.

May your **meetings** be so **filled with the Spirit** and so **rooted in the Word** that the **audience** will make **sacrifices to come** every evening.

CHAPTER 10

RECORD KEEPING

Nothing will substitute for biblical, Spirit-filled preaching in **building your audience.** People will return each evening to hear the Word of God preached if a Spirit-filled evangelist preaches a Spirit-filled message from the Bible. But there are some things that keep your audience coming back to the meetings and actually increase your attendance.

One of the best ways to motivate people to continue attending the meetings is **to give literature each evening on the topic presented. You can also give attendees** books and Bibles as an incentive for attending the meetings regularly. Accurate records are kept through a ticket book or a scanner card tracking system. The ticket book or scanning card system are not only great assets in keeping accurate records but are very **valuable to the person** attending the meetings.

The **ticket book/scanner card system** is **used** not only as a means of **providing** the **guests with more information** on the topics that are presented each evening, but also as a way of **keeping accurate visitation records.** Accurate records ensure that each name is followed up. **Each name is a sacred trust.** The purpose of record keeping is to provide the evangelist, pastor, and lay Bible workers with an accurate visitation list so they can visit interests shortly after they attend the meetings.

REGISTRATION PROCEDURE

TICKET BOOK/SCANNER CARD EXPLANATION

To **register** guests attending the **Revelation of Hope** evangelistic meetings, follow the instructions below.

Night #1

When individuals come on opening night, or for the first time, the following things happen to register all attendees for the Revelation of Hope evangelistic meetings:

1. Hosts and hostesses **distribute a ticket book or envelope with scanner card to all attendees coming** to the Revelation of Hope meetings as they enter the auditorium the first night.
2. **The pastor explains the registration system clearly in the announcement period on opening night.** Be sure to take adequate time to describe the registration process clearly to the entire audience. **He will explain the entire registration form** including how they

learned about the lectures.

3. The pastor encourages attendees to **fill out the registration form** in the ticket book/envelope right then. After filling out their names, addresses, phone numbers, and how they learned of the meetings, attendees are informed that the ticket book/scanner card is to be **kept** throughout the series and brought back each evening.

4. **The pastor explains that every attendee will exchange the envelope or ticket book registration form for a copy of the lecture magazine** as they go out at the end of the meeting. **Each ticket book has a number.** The number on each ticket corresponds to the evening meeting and has the individual's personal registration number on it. On the way out of the meeting, the individual gives the ticket to the host or hostess at the door. He/she in turn gives them a copy of the **lecture magazine** for the evening. The ticket book is valuable because the attendees desire the lecture magazine for the evening.

NOTE: If you use the **scanner card system:**
- The person **fills out the registration form on the envelope.**
- The **person keeps their scanner card and brings it back** each evening.
- **The person scans their card each evening when they come to the meeting.**

5. The ticket book or scanner card not only gives attendees a free copy of the lecture, but also **qualifies** them for **gift books, Bibles,** and **pictures.**

6. After the **registration form** on page 1 in the ticket book or scanner card envelope is filled out and returned to the record-keeping personnel, the information is placed on the **computerized master list.**

7. **Ticket books**—Exchange ticket for a magazine each evening.
   - **Each ticket book has a number.** That number on each ticket corresponds to the evening meeting and has the individual's personal registration number on it. On the way out of the meeting, the individual gives the ticket to the host or hostess at the door. He/she in turn gives them a copy of the **lecture magazine** for the evening. The ticket book is valuable because the attendees desire the lecture magazine for the evening.

Scanner cards—Scan the person's card when they come in.
Note: People attending the Revelation of Hope meetings register only once for the entire series.

- Once they have registered, they are **entitled to various incentives to build their spiritual library.**
- Every person attending who **scans their ticket receives a free copy of the lecture summary on the way out.**
- After they have **recorded their attendance by scanning the designated number of meetings,** they will **receive various incentives.**

NEW REGISTRATIONS AFTER THE FIRST NIGHT—NIGHTS 2–24

People who attend the evangelistic series for the first time from night two until the end of the series register **at the registration table** to receive their ticket book or scanner card.
- **Have the hostesses at the door greeting people** as they enter **ask** if they have their scanner card.

- **If attendees don't seem to understand, the host/hostess will** know they are attending for the first time.
- Host/hostess **will send them to the registration table.**
- Each evening the host/hostess **should be alert for people who are not scanning their cards and invite them to register.**

At the registration table:

- Have each new person **fill out the registration form (ticket book) or envelope (scanner card) including how they learned about the lectures.**
- **Inform them** that **they need to scan their card each evening** as they come in before the meeting begins.
- Have **sign-up sheets each evening** for people who have **forgotten their ticket book or scanner card.**
- Registration personnel are **responsible for distributing all gift incentives** at the registration table.
- **The list** of people **eligible for the incentive** for that evening will be **given to them by the head of registration.**
- **All gifts and incentives** will be **brought to the meeting** by the **head of the registration table.**

Keeping accurate records is vital for a strong **visitation program.**

THE TICKET BOOK/SCANNER CARD SYSTEM

There are two systems we have used in tracking evangelistic names.

Ticket book system

- The ticket books can be used in countries where the scanner cards may not be available or where you need a simple cost-efficient system. Although we used the ticket books for years, we have found that **the scanner system is much faster and more complete.** It gives us more data so we can be more effective in our visitation.

- The tickets are printed and a personal identification number is printed on each ticket book above the number of the night of the evangelistic meeting.
- The larger number in the picture represents the night of the evangelistic meeting. The smaller number, 23,209, is the person's number who is attending the meeting. The smaller number is the one that identifies the attendee coming to the Revelation of Hope evangelistic meeting.

Scanner card system

The scanner card is a small plastic card with a hole that can be placed on a key chain. It is similar to a grocery scanner card. The number on the scanner card is matched to the number on the registration envelope and placed inside. This number identifies the person coming to the evangelistic meetings. The scanner card is kept by the attendee who scans in each evening at the meetings. The envelope is returned to the record-keeping personnel.

RECORD-KEEPING PERSONNEL RESPONSIBILITIES

1. **Give ticket book registration form or scanner card envelope to the hosts and hostesses** to be distributed **at the door** as people enter the auditorium on the **FIRST NIGHT ONLY.** Every person that attends should receive a registration form whether they are a church member or a guest.

2. **Register all "new" people after the first night at the registration table.** A table is set up with ticket books or plastic scanner cards in envelopes. Anyone who attends for the first time after the opening meeting registers at the registration table with the record-keeping personnel.
   - Arrange to have tables eight feet in length where people can come and register quickly and efficiently.

3. **Collect all tickets** each evening after the meeting from the hosts and hostesses. If you are not using the computer networking system, the tickets must be placed in numerical order and recorded on a numbering sheet.
   - If you are using the **scanning system,** you will scan the person's card as they come in each evening.

4. After the **registration form** in the ticket book or scanner card envelope is filled out, it is returned to the record-keeping personnel. All the information is entered on the **computerized master list. The "tracking system"** provides all the information including: All the attendee's information.
   - Person's ticket number (from ticket book or scanner envelope)
   - Name, address, and phone numbers
   - The nightly attendance
   - How the attendee learned about the meetings
   - Religion of person attending

5. **Record-keeping personnel prints out an alphabetical list from the master list.** If someone forgets to bring their ticket book, you can find their name quickly by the use of the alphabetical list.
   - **Ticket book system**—If someone accidentally forgets their ticket book, simply write their ticket number on a blank ticket and give them a ticket corresponding to that evening's lecture and place their number on the ticket.
   - **Scanner system**—You simply look up their number and enter it into the computer or you can locate their number on the alphabetical list.

6. **Registration personnel enter all decisions** from the decision cards on the computerized master list.

7. **Registration personnel runs address labels** for the weekly mailing and assist in sending the mailing out.

8. **Print visitation cards** from the computerized "evangelistic tracking system."
   - Give the visitation cards to the evangelist to distribute to every participating pastor, Bible instructor, and those on the visitation team.

NOTE: All names of non–Seventh-day Adventist members are entered on a visitation card and each worker receives these names. Every non-Adventist is assigned to a worker.

VISITATION CARD

1. The evangelist, pastors, and all workers receive a sheet titled **"Visitation Card" for every non–Seventh-day Adventist member.**
- This visitation card is the **only pass** into the home.
2. This **visitation card** contains the following information:
- The person's ticket number
- Name, address, city, state, zip code
- Phone
- E-mail
- Referred—(how they learned about the Revelation of Hope meetings
- Notes—Any known information about this person including:
  - age
  - church affiliation
  - any requests for more material/information/visit, etc.
- Nights attended
- A check in the box stating the person believes the following:
  - Salvation
  - Second coming of Christ
  - Sabbath
  - Lifestyle
  - Death
  - Baptism
  - True church
- A check in the box titled **"personal visit"** means the interest has requested a personal visit from the pastor or Bible instructor.
- *Search for Certainty* (SFC) Bible lessons completed. These checked boxes indicate how many SFC Bible lessons your interest has completed.
- Visitation Notes: This is for you to write any important information about your interest.
- In the right-hand corner is the **visitor's name.**
- This line is for the pastor, Bible worker, or lay person who visits this name.

WORKERS' REPORTS

- At every worker's meeting, the worker will receive a **master sheet** of his/her interests. **No name assigned to a worker is exchanged with another worker.** If you **exchange a name (visitation card)** with another worker for any reason, you must follow the procedures below. This is very important so that several pastors do not visit the same names of non–Seventh-day Adventist guests in their home.
  - Make a **duplicate copy.**
  - **Cross out your name** and **write the name of the person you exchange with on both copies.**
  - **Return** one copy to record keeping.
  - Please note: **Any attendee name** that is **traded with another worker** should

put all information on the visitation card only. Cross out the visitor's name as many times as the visitation card is traded.

- Leave the final name of the pastor/Bible instructor/lay worker at the bottom of the list.
- Place the visitation card in the "To Be Entered" box, which will be returned to the record-keeping personnel.
- The record-keeping personnel want only one final copy. Thank you!

The pastor/Bible instructor/lay worker who ends up with the name should be the only one to have the visitation card. Don't make a copy and give it to another worker. **Give them the original.**

- It is your responsibility to **transfer the nightly attendance** from your master attendance record to your visitation card.
- You will **receive a new copy** of all newly exchanged visitation cards.
- All new **unassigned visitation cards** will be given throughout the series. Record keeping will keep duplicate copies.
- All **decisions** will be recorded on the visitation card.
- You will also receive the original decision card for visitation purposes.
- All **baptisms** will be recorded. A separate sheet of all decisions for baptism will be given to each visitor with a list of all your interests who have checked for baptism. You will have the joy of seeing many of your interests baptized.

May God richly bless you as you conduct your evangelistic meetings and visit the interests on your list!

CHAPTER 11

EVANGELISTIC VISITATION

Although the **preached Word** is of utmost importance, **visitation** is **equally important.** After Bible **truth** has been **presented** in a public evangelistic meeting, the audience will have questions. Preaching alone without visitation in the home will be minimally effective. **Answering questions** overcomes a person's prejudices. Understanding each individual's feelings, concerns, and challenges, can only be accomplished in person-to-person contacts.

Think for a moment of the times that Jesus spent speaking eternal truth to individuals.

- He met privately with **Nicodemus** at night and
- then the **Samaritan woman** at Jacob's well.
- He appealed individually to **Peter, James, John, Matthew, Phillip, and Andrew.**
- He spoke personally to the **demoniacs, the Roman centurion, Zacchaeus,**
- the **thief** on the cross, and a host of others.

Jesus recognized the value of listening to the questions, understanding the needs, and appealing to one person at a time. Jesus knew that through one converted person whose life was changed by the gospel, scores of people would be influenced for the kingdom of God. The Savior preached to the multitudes but wisely ministered to individuals.

Commenting on Christ's evangelistic strategy, Ellen White makes this **enlightening statement: "To a great degree this [successful soul winning] must be accomplished by personal labor. This was Christ's method.** His work was largely made up of personal interviews. He had a faithful regard for the **one-soul audience.** Through that one soul the message was often extended to thousands.

"**We are not to wait for souls to come to us;** we must seek them out where they are. When the word has been preached in the pulpit, the work has but just begun. There are multitudes who will never be reached by the gospel unless it is carried to them" **(CHRIST'S OBJECT LESSONS, P. 229).**

Ellen White stresses the critical importance of personal visitation in these unmistakable words:

"If **half the time** now spent in **preaching,** were given to **house-to-house** labor, **favorable results** would be seen" **(EVANGELISM, P. 463).**

Systematic Visitation and Goals for Each Visit

Visitation is **essential** in **public evangelism.** We plan to **visit the guests** attending our meetings **at least once a week** during the evangelistic series. In addition to in-home visits, we schedule regular visits before and after meetings at the auditorium or church. This enables us to save a great deal of time traveling to the individual's home, avoids unnecessary distractions which may arise during our in-home visits, and maximizes the interested person's time since they will be at the auditorium for the meeting.

This section will help you to understand:

- **Who to Visit?**
- **How to Visit?**
- **When to Visit?**

We will first cover **who to visit** in a reaping series of public evangelism.
- **WHO TO VISIT?**

FOUR BIBLICAL PRINCIPLES

An **understanding** of these principles **will increase** your **success** as an evangelistic worker. To **neglect** these **principles** is to **minimize** your **effectiveness.**

They are the unchangeable laws of the harvest. They apply both in the natural and physical world. In *Christian Education,* page 116, we read this fascinating statement: **"There are great laws that govern the world of nature, and spiritual things are controlled by principles equally certain; the means for an end must be employed, if the desired results are to be attained."** Here are four soul-winning principles deeply etched into the fabric of the New Testament. Let's learn vital lessons from these laws of the harvest.

PRINCIPLE #1

SPIRITUAL FRUIT RIPENS AT DIFFERENT STAGES

- **Look for the ripest fruit and pick it first.**

> "And He said, 'The kingdom of God is as if a man should **scatter seed** on the ground, and should **sleep by night** and **rise by day,** and the **seed should sprout** and **grow,** he himself **does not know how.** For the earth yields crops by itself: first the blade, then the head, after that the full grain in the head. But when the **grain ripens,** immediately he puts in the sickle, because the **harvest has come'** " (MARK 4:26–29).

Successful evangelistic workers *know how* to carefully **evaluate interests** coming to the evangelistic series. They zero in on the best interests. As one church growth guru said, **"We must win the winnable while they are winnable or soon they will not be winnable."** In other words,
- Follow the **law** of the **harvest.**
- Look for the **ripe fruit** and pick it. We often enter into the faithful labors of others. They have sown the gospel seed and we reap the harvest.

1 Corinthians 3:6–9

"I **planted,** Apollos **watered,** but *God gave* the **increase.** So then neither he who plants is anything, nor he who waters, but God who gives the increase. Now he who plants and he who waters are one, and each one will receive his own reward according to his own labor. **For we are God's fellow workers;** you are God's field, you are God's building."

The Holy Spirit is preparing a harvest in your city. There are people who are open and receptive to gospel truth now. Jesus' own disciples made the mistake of thinking that the harvest was at some future time. The Master corrected their misunderstanding by declaring, "Do you not say, 'There are still four months and then comes the harvest'? Behold, I say to you, **lift up your eyes and look at the fields, for they are already white for harvest!**" (JOHN 4:35). The disciples were looking forward to a future harvest in some other more favorable place, but Jesus saw opportunities to reap an immediate harvest right in the place they were.

As you keep your eyes open for souls, **God will lead you to those all around you** that He has prepared for reaping now.

PEOPLE WHO ARE RIPE FOR HARVEST

Possible candidates for baptism:
- **Seventh-day Adventist** *young people*
- Spouses **of Seventh-day Adventists**
- Relatives **and** friends **of Seventh-day Adventists**
- Visitors **attending Adventist churches**
- People with **previous contacts** through our seminars, Bible studies, literature, or television and radio programs

PRINCIPLE #2

RIPE FRUIT NOT PICKED ROTS ON THE VINE

When people are **convicted of truth** and **do not act** upon it, it is **possible they may walk away** from it. Evangelistic visitation compels convicted seekers to action. In the context of visitation, their questions are answered and decisions made for eternity.

The apostle Paul emphasizes this vital law of the harvest in 2 CORINTHIANS 6:2.

"For He says: 'In an acceptable time I have heard you, and in the day of salvation I have helped you.' Behold, **now** is the accepted **time;** behold, **now** is the day of **salvation.**"

When Paul appealed to the Roman ruler Felix and urged him to make a decision for Christ, Felix came under deep conviction but allowed his fears to keep him from making a decision.

> "Now as he reasoned about righteousness, self-control, and the judgment to come, Felix was afraid and answered, '**Go away** for **now;** when I have a **convenient time** I **will call** for you' " (ACTS 24:25).

Felix delayed his decision and never made a commitment for Christ.

In the context of the **evangelistic meetings,** your **best interests** will tend to be
1. People who **regularly attend** the evangelistic **meetings.**
2. People who **request literature** via the decision card.
3. People who **make significant decisions** on the card.
4. People who are **taking personal Bible studies through the Bible school.**

Spend most of your time nurturing your best interests. Meet with them personally, **develop** relationships, **answer** their questions, **study** God's Word, **invite** them **to make eternal decisions,** and you will have an abundant harvest.

The question every evangelist or pastor must ask is:

"Who are my best interests?" "Which prospects are ripe for harvest?"

It is **better to develop positive relationships with a few top interests** than **surface relationships with casual interests** who have little interest in the life-changing truths of the Bible and may simply be curiosity seekers who desire to take up your time.

Learn to distinguish between an interest and a prospect.

- **An Interest**—A person who is eager not only to **learn** but to **accept.**
- **A Prospect**—Someone who will **ask** all kinds of **questions,** keep you busy, but is not really interested.

One way of telling the difference between an interest and a prospect is this:
- **Interests make changes** in their lives when they hear the truth. It may take time but they are moving forward.
- **Prospects** tend to **debate truth.** They are filled with questions but there is little evidence of any spiritual fruitage in their life.

Here are some questions we ask about each person we work with:
- "What is this person's **attitude toward truth**? Do they seem to have a heart hunger to do what God says?"
- "Have there been **any changes in this individual's life** as they have heard truth?"
- "Is **there** any indication of **spiritual progress**?" If the answers are Yes, the person is a good interest.

To maintain the interest, keep visiting so the spiritual fruit does not rot on the vine. **Cultivate** the interest. **Give them literature, books, or sermon CDs or DVDs.** You will be amazed as how you sow the seed, God will grow the seed.

PRINCIPLE #3

Under the right condition, some *fruit ripens very quickly* and it surprises you.

Spiritual fruit tends to ripen very quickly in public evangelism. In a few meetings, people can make dramatic changes in their lives. **Seed sown through the years rapidly comes to harvest under the ministry of the Holy Spirit.** Think of what happened in the book of Acts. The seed Jesus sowed during the three years of His earthly ministry yielded an incredible harvest.

"Then those who **gladly received his word were baptized;** and that day about three thousand souls were added to them" **(ACTS 2:41).**

"However, many of those who heard the word believed; and the number of the men came to be about five thousand" **(ACTS 4:4).**

Expect God to work miracles in the lives of people coming to your meetings.

- Often a **person regularly attending** your meetings may experience more dramatic changes in their life in a week than a person receiving Bible studies for six months.
- **Evangelism** produces a greenhouse effect where **fruit ripens quickly.** Don't be misled into thinking that a person who has been an apparent interest for months or years is a better interest than someone who has **walked into your meetings due to a handbill** or some other form of evangelistic advertising. God may surprise you.

Time does not grow spiritual fruit. The **Spirit** does. Watch for the **Spirit's working and reap** the harvest.

PRINCIPLE #4

SOME FRUIT RIPENS MORE SLOWLY, BUT DON'T LOSE HEART

One of the **fundamental laws of the harvest** is that fruit ripens at different times. Some fruit ripens today but a great deal will ripen in the future. In public evangelism, we will reap what others have sown and others will reap what we have sown.

> "And let us not grow weary while doing good, for in due season we shall reap if we do not lose heart" **(GALATIANS 6:9).**

We have regularly baptized people who attended an evangelistic meeting or took Bible studies years ago. **Evangelism is a constant process of sowing and reaping.**

We <u>sow</u> while we <u>reap</u> and <u>reap</u> while we <u>sow</u>.

The Irreducible Laws of the Harvest

1. **Spiritual fruit ripens at different stages.** Concentrate on the ripe fruit.
2. **Spiritual ripe fruit not picked rots on the vine.** Prayerfully watch for an individual's growing interest and make appeals.
3. **Some spiritual fruit ripens more quickly under the right conditions.** Watch what God is doing in the lives of people attending your meetings.
4. **Some spiritual fruit ripens more slowly, but don't lose heart.** Remember, although God will give you an immediate harvest, there will be a much greater future harvest.

In our evangelistic ministry, we would do well to remember this statement:

> "Today in His great harvest-field **God has need of sowers and of reapers.** Let those who go forth into the work, some to sow and some to reap, remember that **they are never to take to themselves the glory for the success of their work.** God's appointed agencies have been before them, preparing the way for the sowing of the seed and the reaping of the harvest" **(GOSPEL WORKERS, P. 409).**

WHEN AND HOW TO VISIT

Week #1

We have placed priority on visiting three groups of people the first week of the meetings.

- **The goal of our visitation the first week is to build as large of an attendance as possible at our evangelistic meetings, to give as many people as possible an opportunity to make eternal decisions.**

1. **When an individual has attended one meeting and then misses two consecutive meetings,** we visit them at the end of the first week.
   - **Visit** briefly at the door with the **goal** of encouraging the person to **attend another meeting** and to **separate** prospects from curiosity seekers.
2. **Visit** your **"good"** interests on the interest list who have **not yet attended** the meetings.
   - **The goal** is to encourage the person to begin attending the meetings.
   - **Visitation literature:** Revelation of Hope handbill
3. **Visit** those who have checked the "Peace of Mind" response card distributed at the meetings.
   - **The goal** of the visit is to lead seekers to Christ and Christians to a deeper relationship with Christ.

Visitation literature: *Steps to Christ*

Week #2

The goal of our visitation for week two is to continue to build attendance while at the same time developing relationships and answering questions.

1. **Visit everyone coming** to the meetings.
   - **The goal** of this visit is to follow up on the presentation of the gospel in the public meeting and **clarify questions** surrounding the second coming of Christ.
   - **The visit reviews the essential elements of salvation** and **leads** the individual **to a commitment** or re-commitment to Christ in the light of Jesus' soon return.
2. **Visit** those who have **checked** "Revelation's Final Judgment" **response card.**

Visitation literature: Choose something on the second coming of Christ.

Week #3

During this third week of visitation, we **focus on clarifying questions regarding the law and the Sabbath** and attempt **to lead as many people** as possible **to begin keeping the Bible Sabbath.**

1. **Visit** all those who have **checked** "The Great Religious Cover Up" **response card.**
2. **Visit** each person who has attended "The **Sabbath**" **and/or "The Change of the Sabbath"** presentation.
   - The **goals** of this visit are:
     - To **determine** the **conviction** of each person who has heard the Sabbath presentation.

- To **answer questions** regarding the Sabbath.
- To **lead to decision** those who are convicted regarding the Sabbath.
- To **keep** those **coming** to the meetings who are not yet ready to make a commitment.
- To **ascertain** the attendee's **commitment** to the **truths** presented thus far.
- To **answer questions and meet objections.**
- To **encourage** the attendee to **follow** all the truth that God graciously reveals.
- **Emphasize** the **joy** and **peace** that accompany daily obedience to God's will.
- **Clarify** the **Sabbath truth.** Do this in the context of a warm, loving relationship with such questions as:
    - "**Have you ever heard** a message on the Bible Sabbath before?" "Is the Sabbath new to you?"
    - "Is the Bible's **teaching** regarding the **Sabbath clear**?" "Do you have any questions on the Bible Sabbath?"
    - "Have you ever **thought about keeping** the Bible Sabbath?"
    - "What would it **mean personally** for you if you decide to keep the Sabbath?"

If the response to the visit is positive, **encourage** the person to **visit your church** the very next Sabbath. **Leave** some pertinent piece of **literature** on the Sabbath. Conclude your visit with an earnest prayer, allowing Jesus to guide us in all of our decision making.

Visitation literature: *When God Said Remember*

Week #4

By the fourth week of your meetings, you will see the powerful working of the Holy Spirit. By now you have presented the major doctrinal truths of Scripture and people are making significant life changes. Many of them will decide for baptism during this week.

- **Visit** each person who has responded to the appeal to be **baptized.**
- **Confirm** their **decision** to be baptized.
- **Set baptismal dates** with key prospects.
- **Encourage** each person who has decided for baptism and those who are thinking about it to **join** the **baptismal class.**
- **Clarify questions.**

Appeal for decisions on the true church and baptism for those who seem ready.

Focus on the **fruit** that is **ripe.** It is better to visit a few top prospects, spending more time with each one, than to frantically attempt to answer the questions of all casual interests.

Focus your attention on the individuals who have begun **to keep the Sabbath** or who have indicated a **desire for baptism.**

Visitation literature: Baptismal booklet, *In His Steps*

Week #5

The last week of your evangelistic series **is decision week. Evaluate** all of your best interests. Prayerfully ask, **"Who might be ready to make a decision now?" Focus also on those who are good interests but who may not be ready for an immediate decision.**

- **Visit** those who have **checked** the "Why So Many Denominations?" **response card.**
- **Visit** each person a **second time** who has responded to the appeal to be baptized and to **those** who are on the verge of making the **decision to be baptized.**
- **Lead** top interests to a **full surrender** to Jesus Christ and baptism.
- **Set baptismal days** with your key interests.
- **Review** the **baptismal certificate** with the person.

Visitation literature: "The World's Next Super Power," for top interests.

SAMPLE VISITS

Sample Visit #1—Getting Acquainted Call

For those who have **attended** the Revelation of Hope **one time** and have not returned.

Purpose of the Visit

1. **To become acquainted** with individuals who have attended the evangelistic meetings once and have not returned.
2. **To encourage them to come back.** The vast majority of people who come to one meeting early in the series and don't return are not offended. Often, they simply **need a little more motivation to return.** Many are planning to return. They desire to return to the meetings, yet a variety of circumstances may have hindered them. They may have **planned other activities before** the lecture series started. **Unexpected visitors** may have kept them away. **Sickness** may have hindered them. It may be that the **business** of their lives have so worn them down that they're just too tired to attend.

Often a **visit** at the right time during the **first week** will get people to come back at this very fragile time in their experience of learning to know God. Your visit can make a significant difference in their lives.

The Visit at the Door:

- This is what we call a **"pop call."**
- Do not enter the home, visit **at the door only.**
- Do not take more than **five minutes.**

The following is an **outline of the visit** that will take place at the door. Only under rare circumstances will visitors enter the home. Visits usually will **take no more than five minutes.** During this first visit, the discussion goes something like this:

Visitor says:

- "Good afternoon, my **name** is _____ **from** the Revelation of Hope **lecture series.** We're so happy that you were able to **come** to the meeting last evening.
- "It's exciting to see the large number of people who are **interested** in **Bible prophecy**

today. Thousands are **interested** in what the **Word** of God has to say about the future.

- "They're **looking** for meaning and **purpose** and **security** in their own lives. And they're finding it as they study Bible prophecy.
- "We just wanted to **drop by** and **give** you this little **pamphlet,** which is a brief summary of the things Pastor _____ said on the last two evenings. We know you'll enjoy reading it."

At this point, pause, and then say:

- "Did you get a **complete schedule** of our meetings? Here is one.
- "In the next two meetings, Pastor _____ will be **discussing** two very interesting and **fascinating topics.**"
- Look at the schedule and tell them what the next two topics are.
- "I know you will **enjoy** these powerful Bible-centered messages."
- "I sure hope that you'll be **able to attend.**
- "Do you think it's **possible** for you **to come** out to the meeting on Friday and Saturday night?"
- "Great, we'll **see you at** the **meeting.**"

Visitation Literature: Evangelistic handbill

Sample Visit #2—Accepting/Growing in Jesus Visit

Purpose of the Visit

For those who have **checked** the **response card** on **"Salvation"**

Sample Visit in the Home:

- "Good afternoon, _____. I'm _____ from the **Revelation of Hope** series and I'm so delighted to see you again.
- "I'm happy to see that you've been able to **come** on a **regular basis.**
- "To help you to grow in Christ and to deepen your relationship with Him, I've **brought** you a copy of the book *Steps to Christ.*
- *"Steps to Christ* has been **translated** into hundreds of languages with millions of copies in print. Some consider it to be the most outstanding book ever written on the practical aspects of the Christian life.
- "I know this book will be a real **blessing** to you. (Pause.)
- "_____, as you have been attending the meetings, is this a **new experience** for you or have you ever attended meetings like this before?
- "Were you brought up in a **Christian home**? Have you ever made a decision to commit your life fully to Christ?"

Listen and respond accordingly.

"We look forward to **seeing you** at the **meeting.** When we accept Christ, He unfolds His plan for our lives."

Goals of the Visit:

- To **give** them the **book** *Steps to Christ* to deepen your relationship with the interest.
- To **listen** carefully to what people are saying regarding their own spiritual experience.
- To **spend** a **few moments** deepening their commitment to and their relationship with Christ.
- To have some basic **assurance** that this **person has made** an intelligent **commitment to Christ** and that he/she desires to follow Him in his/her life.

Sample Visit #3—Clear and Set Visit

Purpose of the Visit

To evaluate the prospect's openness for truth and prepare them to follow further truth.

Visit in the Home:

Visitor: "John and Mary, we are **delighted you have been coming** to the meetings. Are you **enjoying** the presentations each evening? Are you **learning** a great deal? **What is the most important thing you have learned** at the meetings so far?"
Listen carefully.
Visitor: "Do you have any questions on anything we have gone over at the meetings?"
Listen carefully once again and respond with a Bible text.
Visitor: "Jesus gave us a wonderful statement of truth when He said, 'I am the way, the truth, and the life' **(JOHN 14:6).** Jesus is the only way to salvation. When we accept Him as our way of salvation, He promises to lead us to His truth so we can live His life.

"Before I leave, **would you like me to pray** for both of us to be always sensitive to follow God's truth wherever it leads?"

This visit prepares your prospect to have an open heart for the Sabbath truth, which is coming.

Sample Visit #4—The Sabbath Truth Visit

Purpose of the Visit

To ascertain the depth of **conviction** regarding the **Sabbath** and **encourage** people to **attend** the very **next Sabbath.**

(It is presumed that I have been in the home at least twice and preferably three times before this visit takes place.)

Visit in the Home:

"John and Mary, **I'm so glad to see each of you again today. I appreciated the opportunity of getting acquainted with you** since you have been coming to the meetings. **I've enjoyed the visits I've had in your home so much.**

"**How is your week going? Is there anything significant going on in your lives this week?**"

At this point, we might talk about: their **work,** their **children,** something brief but to the point that indicates my desire to be in touch with what's going on in their personal lives.

After a brief discussion of John and Mary's lives, we move into three specific questions:

SABBATH QUESTION #1

"**John and Mary, have you ever heard a message on the Bible Sabbath before or is this the first time that you have ever heard anything like this?**"

After their response to the question, usually you will know something about what they are thinking regarding the Bible Sabbath. Their response might be:

"**Yes**, I've always wondered about the Bible Sabbath. I learned it from a Sunday School teacher sometime ago."

"**Yes,** as I read the Ten Commandments I was confused about the one that said, 'Remember the Sabbath day to keep it holy,' and I never understood why we went to church on Sunday."

"**Yes,** I have taken the Discover Bible Lessons and I studied about the Sabbath."

"**No,** this is new to me. I have never heard a message on the Bible Sabbath before."

Many who have never heard the message on the true Bible Sabbath will usually appreciate spending a little time reviewing the message on the Sabbath. To review the subject deepens the conviction.

Here are five Bible texts we use to briefly review the Sabbath truth:
- **Genesis 2:1–3**
- **Exodus 20:8–11**
- **Ezekiel 20:12**
- **Luke 4:16**
- **Acts 13:42–44**

After we have read those texts, we will then ask other questions.

SABBATH QUESTION #2

"**Do you have any questions on the Bible Sabbath?**"
"**Is the Bible Sabbath clear to you?**"
"**Are there any Bible passages you wonder about?**"
- Usually, this brings out **specific questions or objections,** which are then answered.
- The individual may have **questions that are not answered** at this point. These questions can loom large in the mind and generate doubts.
- The **questions may even lead to doubt** and a loss of confidence in the truthfulness of our presentations.
- All intelligent **decisions are based on adequate information.**
- An individual might raise questions regarding Colossians 2:14–17; Romans 14:1–3,

or issues on law and grace.

- *Studying Together,* by Mark Finley, provides concise answers to these questions. It is a handbook for personal workers. If you do not have a copy, you will want to be sure to get one.

After we have answered questions that have arisen, we then ask the third question on the Bible Sabbath.

SABBATH QUESTION #3

"Now, John and Mary, have you ever <u>thought</u> about keeping the Bible Sabbath?
"Is there anything that may keep you from beginning to <u>observe</u> the Sabbath?"
We carefully observe as John and Mary respond. If the response is favorable, we'll then add:
"Well, we hope you will be able to be with us in the special service this coming Sabbath morning."
The most important Sabbath for John and Mary to keep is the next one.
Once they have heard the message on the Sabbath and the change, we'll do everything to encourage them to attend church the very next Sabbath morning.
NEGATIVE RESPONSE—If the response they have is hesitant or somewhat negative, we will urge them to earnestly pray about it, be honest with God, and continue studying the Sabbath. Encourage them not to miss one meeting because future presentations will answer their questions and clarify the Sabbath. We might say:
"I know this is new to you, and we will be praying that God will help you in this situation. I am confident that the Lord will make truth plain to you. Be sure not to miss one meeting because each upcoming meeting will be a vital link in a chain of connected truth. Let's pray together now and ask God to provide the answers you seek. I know you have an honest heart and only desire to do His will."
This visit is specifically designed to help John and Mary:

- **Clarify** the information regarding the Sabbath.
- **Answer** any questions they might have.
- **Keep the Sabbath** if the information is clear and they are convicted of the truth.
- **Encourage** them to attend church the very next Sabbath.

If they have not yet made the decision, the purpose of the visit is:

- **To discover** what hinders them.
- **Attempt to** answer any questions.
- **To urge** them to continue to follow Jesus.

Note: Give each interest who attends the Sabbath presentation a copy of the book, ***When God Says Remember***. *When God Says Remember* gives the **Bible basis for the Sabbath.**

- It also covers the history and background of the Sabbath, as well as the change of the Sabbath to Sunday.
- It shares some Sabbath-keeping principles and makes a strong case for the historicity of the Sabbath down through the centuries.
- It will help solidify their decision to keep the Sabbath and reinforce the Sabbath truth in their minds.

SAMPLE VISIT #5—Baptismal Decision Visit

Purpose of the Visit

The **purpose** of this **visit** is to solidify the decisions people have made regarding baptism. During this week of our meetings, we will **concentrate** on those people who have already made a **decision for baptism or who are seriously thinking about it.** They have raised their hands, stood, come forward in a public appeal, filled out a decision card for baptism, or made a decision in their home.

At this point, we are attempting to **crystallize** the **conviction** regarding baptism and **answer questions.** It is also to **deepen the knowledge base** of those who have made the decision to be baptized.

The Visit in the Home:

"Good evening, John and Mary. It's so good to see you again. I'm glad that we can **spend** a little **time together** in our weekly appointment.

"I was so **glad** to see **you attending church** the last few Sabbaths. I'm just delighted with the **friendship** we've developed and I've enjoyed coming to your home.

"I **noted** that **you came forward** in our response the other evening looking forward to **baptism** (or that you checked a card to be baptized).

"Jesus says in Matthew 28:19, 20, '**Go** therefore and **make** disciples of all the nations, **baptizing** them in the name of the Father and of the Son and of the Holy Spirit, teaching them to **observe** all things that I have commanded you; and lo, I am with you always, even to the end of the age.'

"Did you notice the steps? Jesus said,
- **Go** therefore and
- **Teach** all nations,
- **Baptizing** them in the name of the Father, Son, and Holy Spirit."

Baptism is a double symbol.

- It is a symbol that we have **committed our lives to Christ** and we desire to follow Him.
- It is also a symbol that we believe that we have **found God's truth** and long to walk in it and **become part of His body** of believers.

Engage your interests in a positive discussion about their baptism by asking questions such as:

"Have you been **thinking about being baptized** for a while now?"

"Have you ever been **baptized** the Bible way, by immersion, before?"

Once you have engaged in a friendly discussion, share this thought: "We have prepared a brief review of the **key doctrines** of Scripture to help you prepare for Bible baptism. It briefly reviews such topics as:
- The Bible and the authority of Scripture
- Salvation by grace

- The second coming of Jesus
- The law
- The Sabbath
- The truth about death
- The body as the temple of God"

"Let's **review** these **essential teachings** of the **Bible** to answer any questions preliminary to your baptism. Here is a copy of a **baptismal booklet.** If you have any questions at all, please feel free to ask them. I will leave this booklet with you today and plan to return later in the week to review it." We usually spend two or three times reviewing the material contained in the baptismal booklet. If it is more convenient, we meet our interests before or after the evangelistic meeting at the meeting venue. *In His Steps* is an excellent product, but use the baptismal material relevant to your needs.

Affirm your joy at their commitment to be baptized and share with them that all of heaven is rejoicing at this important decision.

Visitation Literature: Use baptismal material relevant to your needs.

SAMPLE VISIT #6—True Church Visit

The Purpose of the Visit

The **purpose** of this last visit is to **help people** who have **not yet decided to make their full decision** to follow truth all the way. The visit may proceed something like this:

The Visit in the Home:

"John and Mary, what a **delight** it is to see how you have been **growing in Christ** as you have been coming to the meetings.

"There are many people who wonder, **Does God have a church today?**

"**Is it possible to discover God's true church?**

"Today during our Bible study, I thought we would **review** some of the things that we have gone over in the past few nights in the meetings.

"Would turn in your Bibles to **Revelation 12:17?**

"You will recall that Revelation 12:17 is a **key text** in the book of Revelation that **outlines the characteristics of God's true church.**

"It says, 'And the **dragon** [that is Satan] was **enraged** [angry] with the **woman** [the church] and he went to **make war** with the rest of her offspring, who **keep the commandments of God** and have the **testimony of Jesus Christ.**'

"Here, God's remnant, His **final church, is identified** as that church that keeps His commandments. In **Revelation 14:6,** God's church is identified as **preaching** His **last-day message** to every nation, kindred, tongue, and people.

"This message includes:
- the **everlasting gospel**
- the fact of **Christ's soon return**
- a call in the light of a judgment hour to **worship** the Creator on His **Sabbath**
- a message of **mental, physical, and spiritual restoration.**

"John and Mary, as you study this message in Revelation 14, it becomes **clear** that **God does have a church today** that is **teaching** the **truths of His Word.** Let's **review** some of those basic truths to make sure they are clear in your mind.

"**Is it clear to you that the Bible is the Word of God?**

"Do you **understand** that **Christ is coming again** and that the only way to be saved is to accept Christ?

"That we are not saved by our works, but **saved by grace**? [EPHESIANS 2:8].

"Jesus said, Do you love Me? 'If you **love Me, keep My commandments'** [JOHN 14:15]. Does that sound clear to you?

"Do you have any **questions** about the **Bible Sabbath**?

"Do you have any **questions** about **why there are so many denominations**?

"You remember, the **reason** there are **so many denominations** is that the **followers of these church leaders often stopped where they stopped.** They went no further.

"But just as it took over **four hundred years,** from A.D. 100 to A.D. 500, for the **church to go into the Dark Ages,** it would take **four or five hundred years to come out of the Dark Ages.** This is why God raised up the Advent movement.

"The **Seventh-day Adventist Church is not another church; it is not another denomination.**

"It is a **divine movement of destiny** raised up by God **to restore the truths of Scripture** that have been long lost sight of down through the ages.

"So the **Adventist Church** is **to restore the truth of God's Word.** It is to stand on the shoulders of these great giants of the past. It is to accept the truths that the Reformers accepted.

"You remember the **evangelist saying,** 'That's why in a sense, I'm a **Waldensian** because I believe the **Bible** is the only source of faith and practice. I'm a **Hussite** because I believe **obedience to God** should be our only motto. I'm a **Lutheran** evangelical Christian because I believe, as Luther taught, that **salvation is** only **by grace.** In a sense, I'm a **Methodist** because I believe that **obedience to God** is the response of gratitude for what Christ has done for me. I'm a **Baptist** in a sense because I believe in **baptism by immersion.** I'm an **Adventist** because I believe in the **literal second coming of Christ.** And, of course, I'm a **Seventh-day Adventist** because I believe in the **Sabbath**. . . . I believe the **Seventh-day Adventist Church** has gathered all the **teachings of truth** together.'

"John and Mary, **is it clear** to you that God does have a people on earth today and that **God is calling** men and women to be a **part of His truth church**?

"Would you like, through your **baptism, to become part of God's commandment-keeping church** on earth? To become a part of a body of people that are teaching like Jesus taught when He was here on earth?

"**Is there anything that would keep you from being baptized this coming week?"** If they have questions, kindly answer them. If there is resistance, try to find out why, answer their objections, and attempt to lead them to a decision. If you sense the obstacles are too great for the individual to make a decision now, invite them to submit it to God in prayer and join them in praying about it right there. Often after prayer, people will make their decision.

If there are no major obstacles, you may do two things:

    1. Place a baptismal manual in their hands at this point and set up an appointment to go over the manual.

2. **Set a specific baptismal date.**

Literature: *In His Steps* baptismal manual and the book

Your visitation will pay rich dividends for the kingdom of God. One visit can make an eternal difference. As you develop relationships in the home, answer your interests' questions and make Christ-centered appeals. Many will make decisions for Christ.

The heart of **evangelistic success lies with visitation** in the homes.

With a prayer in your heart, **visit!**
With a Bible in your hand, **visit!**
With truth-filled literature under your arm, **visit!**
With a smile on your face and joy in your heart, **visit!**

Watch what God does!

CHAPTER 12

CONDUCTING A BIBLE SCHOOL

One of the major purposes of any evangelistic meeting is to lead people to a deeper knowledge of God's Word. God's Word is life changing. It is one thing for people to hear an evangelist preach, but it is quite another for them to study the Word of God themselves. The scriptural admonition is, "**Study** to shew thyself approved unto God, a workman that needeth not be ashamed, rightly dividing the word of truth" (2 TIMOTHY 2:15, KJV).

Ellen White adds,

> "**None but those who have fortified the mind with the truths of the Bible will stand through the last great conflict.** To every soul will come the searching test: Shall I obey God rather than men? The decisive hour is even now at hand. Are our feet planted on the rock of God's immutable word? Are we prepared to stand firm in defense of the commandments of God and the faith of Jesus?" (THE GREAT CONTROVERSY, PP. 593, 594).

Often Bible workers have studied the Bible with people for several months or even a year and they have never made a decision to change their lifestyle; but when they attend public evangelistic meetings, they grow spiritually very quickly. If they enroll in the Bible school and do the lessons in the privacy of their home while attending the meetings, they make giant steps forward.

Our goal in evangelistic meetings is not only to preach to people but also **to anchor them in the Word of God.** We are convinced that the only way to accomplish this is to get people **studying the Bible** for themselves. This is precisely **why we launch a Bible school in every one of our evangelistic meetings.** When people study God's Word for themselves, their conviction of truth deepens as their informational base expands.

When challenges and difficulties come and questions about the new truths they are learning are raised, they will not be moved. The Word is fixed in their minds. One of the most effective ways of reinforcing the truths the evangelist preaches is to **enroll people in the Bible school** during your evangelistic meetings.

Six Advantages of Establishing a Bible School in Evangelistic Meetings

01 | ### To acquaint people with the teachings of the Bible

Scores of people who attend your evangelistic meetings **will have little or no knowledge of the**

Bible. They will have difficulty finding the books of the Bible and may not understand the basic teachings and stories of the Bible. Taking a systematic series of Bible lessons through **the Bible school will deepen their knowledge of Scripture and acquaint them** with the fundamental teachings of the Word of God.

02 | To help people understand God's end-time message in His Word

Seventh-day Adventists have been given a unique message to preach to the world. The **three angels' messages of Revelation 14:6–12** are totally new for many people attending the evangelistic meetings. Even most Christians do not grasp God's end-time message. It is difficult for them after hearing only a few sermons to understand its implication. Studying the Bible school lessons will greatly help them grasp God's last-day truths.

03 | To establish relationships with the Bible school staff

Each evening our **guests enrolled in the Bible school pick up their lessons, complete them at home,** and **return them** at the next evangelistic meeting. This necessitates coming to the Bible school on a regular basis and **they will naturally develop relationships with the lay Bible instructor** who corrects their lessons. It is in the context of these relationships that their faith will grow, their knowledge of the Bible increase, and their decisions solidify.

04 | To provide an opportunity for people to study God's Word in the privacy of their own home

As people come to evangelistic meetings and new truths are presented, **they will have questions.** These questions will lead them on a journey of discovery and they will seek answers. If we do not provide them an opportunity to deepen their faith through intensive Bible study, they will seek answers elsewhere. The Bible lessons provide people who are seeking with answers to their deepest questions without anyone pressuring them to accept them. In the privacy of their own home, at their own pace, on their own time schedule, they can discover truth for themselves.

05 | To maximize the evangelistic attendees' use of time

In a world jam-packed with activities, many busy people struggle to find time to do everything they want to do. It is our experience through the years that **people will come early to the meetings to do their Bible lessons.** In Moscow's Olympic Stadium in 1992, over ten thousand people participated in our Bible school. It was an amazing sight to witness hundreds of people scattered throughout the vastness of that huge auditorium studying the Word of God. Although the numbers of people studying the Bible lessons were not as large as in Moscow, we have **conducted successful Bible schools in conjunction with our evangelistic meetings in North America** as well. One of our greatest joys is to see people with their Bibles opened, lessons on their laps, searching God's Word before the evening evangelistic meetings begin.

06 | ## To encourage the attendees to continue studying the Bible after the evangelistic meetings end

Although some people will complete the Bible lessons during the series, many will not. **The lay Bible instructors who have developed relationships with the Bible students during the evangelistic meetings will have an open door to continue their studies.** The impact of the evangelistic meetings will be extended through the Bible school. The New Testament church followed up with Peter's evangelistic sermon on Pentecost with home visitation. The record states,

> "And they **continued steadfastly in the apostles' doctrine and fellowship,** in the breaking of bread, and in prayers" (ACTS 2:42).
>
> "How I kept back nothing that was helpful, but proclaimed it to you, and **taught you publicly** and from house to house" (ACTS 20:20).

The Bible school is one means of effectively combining the proclamation of God's Word with personal visitation. In public evangelism, this is a winning combination.

How to Set Up and Operate the Bible School

Giving priority to the Bible school atmosphere will stimulate more people to enroll. We have observed that if we **put the Bible school in a prominent place with a clearly visible sign, more people will participate** than if it is hidden in a corner. In our Bible schools, we set up an eight-foot table with a black tablecloth with the words "Revelation of Hope."

A Revelation of Hope **Bible school banner** is placed on the wall above the table. **We want to be certain that no one misses the Bible school sign.**

At least **two file boxes** are placed upon the table. One with the new lessons and the other for completed lessons to be corrected. Once the completed lessons are corrected, they are returned to the Bible student.

Each prospective Bible student fills out and completes and returns a **registration form** before receiving their first lesson. You will find a copy of this registration form in the appendix on page 205.

We also provide a Bible for those who register for the lessons and don't have one.

Although there are a variety of Bible study guides that can be used, we use *Search for Certainty* Bible lessons. They are a **set of thirty Christ-centered, prophetic lessons.** Each lesson **presents Bible truths as a link in a connected chain.** The lessons are systematically arranged. One lesson flows logically into the next. The lesson titles and topics are in the appendix on pages 203, 204.

Often our lay Bible instructors study with people who lose interest and drop out of the Bible studies, but when they are invited to the evangelistic meetings, their interest is renewed. To motivate them to attend the evangelistic series, you may say something like this:

"You know, we are so happy for the relationship we have developed with you over the last few weeks and months. We are just so thankful for the opportunity we have had of studying the Bible together. A really good friend of mine will be conducting a series of lectures on Bible prophecy. This series of meetings will be very exciting.

- He will be using graphics and talking about topics like the times we are living in today.
- About what the future holds.
- The signs of Jesus' return.
- The second coming of Jesus.
- The prophecies of Daniel and Revelation, and much more.

"I was thinking about you and wanted to invite you as my special guest. Do you think you might be able to attend this weekend? The first meeting begins Friday night. Here is a four-color brochure about the meetings.

"I know you would be really delighted to hear these presentations. **I have a reserved seat for the first night.** I can reserve one seat if you would like to come. Do you think it might be possible for you to attend with me?"

If they say, **"Sure, I can come Friday night,"** then you can say, **"Great, I'll be happy to pick you up." Or you can say, "I'll see you there."**

Many of these people will attend the evangelistic meetings. The prophetic preaching will rekindle their interest in the Bible. When they hear the announcements made about the Bible school, they will renew their Bible study once again. When they enroll in the Bible school and begin studying systematically, the truths they have previously studied will flood into their minds.

After studying the Bible, listening to the lectures, and reading the many magazines and books they receive at the meetings, they often **make a decision to be baptized.**

STAFF:

- Choose a leader and coleader.
- Choose four to six people who will correct the lessons depending on how many sign up.
- Choose two to three people giving out lessons at the Bible table.
- Choose one person who is on hand to answer questions the guests might have as they come to the meetings.

MATERIALS:

- Sign—which says, "BIBLE SCHOOL"
- File boxes—For blank lessons
- File boxes—For completed lessons
- Bible lessons (*Search for Certainty*)

The Bible school staff has direct contact with your best interests coming to the meetings. People who are seeking want to learn more. They will naturally gravitate to the Bible school.

- It is for this reason that you want to select some of your best lay leaders as Bible school staff.

- If it is possible, choose your Bible school staff from church members who have had previous training and experience as lay Bible instructors.
- Be sure to choose people who are friendly and know how to build relationships. The Bible school is a place of biblical instruction and relationship building.

The Bible school deepens the interest of those who have never studied the Bible before, but it also leads those who have to commitment and a decision for baptism.

When the Bible school is organized well and run efficiently by a friendly, knowledgeable staff, it will produce lasting results for the kingdom of God.

CHAPTER 13

HOW TO HANDLE OBJECTIONS

Often after an evangelistic meeting or during my visitation of interests in their homes, I am confronted with a barrage of questions. There are times some people strongly object to a statement I have made or some biblical truth I have shared. Actually, questions reveal what people are thinking and objections demonstrate their deep interest in the topic.

How Do You View Questions?

If you find questions threatening, you may try to ignore them. You might even be tempted to answer them curtly. But questions need not be feared, they are doorways into hearts and minds. Objections are God's way of revealing what is in the heart of the one who objects. Questions are God's way of clearing up misunderstandings. At times, what one person vocalizes is in the minds of others.

In this chapter, I will share a few dynamic principles for answering people's questions and we will discover an effective strategy for handling objections. Of course, we want to go a step beyond to understanding why people have objections and what hinders them from making positive decisions. Lastly, we want to discuss how to turn the objection into an opportunity to appeal for decision.

The Five *R*s of Meeting Objections

When questions or objections are vocalized, the five *R*s of meeting objections will help you to turn the objection into a doorway for decision. The way in which you answer the questioner will either prepare the mind for decision or prejudice the mind against it.

RESPECT THE PERSON

The first *R* stands for **RESPECT.** If you treat the questioner with dignity, attempting to understand where they are coming from and why they ask the question, their minds will be more open than if you appear shocked or become curt in your answer.

Although the scribes and Pharisees placed Him under tremendous pressure, Jesus showed them respect. **When one of them asked Him a leading question, Jesus responded by declaring, "You are not far from the kingdom of God" (MARK 12:34).**

Look for something in the question with which you can **agree.** If you can, **compliment** the person who has raised the question. Ellen G. White says: **"The manner in which the truth is presented often has much to do with determining whether it will be accepted or rejected" (TESTIMONIES, VOL. 4, PP. 404, 405).**

And, "agree with the people on every point where you can consistently do so" (EVANGELISM, P. 141).

Often, I'll make comments like: "Thank you for that question. I'm sure that others are asking the same thing." Or, "I can understand why you might feel that way. This question has come up before."

For example, suppose that after a presentation on the Sabbath someone asks, "I thought we were under grace and not under the law. It's not really necessary to keep the Sabbath, is it?" My response might begin, "Thank you for being wise enough to ask such a good question."

Once, after a presentation on the mark of the beast, a staunch Roman Catholic stood up and said, "I'm confused, perplexed, and troubled over what I've heard tonight, and I think that the majority of the people here are too. How can what I've heard be true?"

I could have either become defensive or attempted to understand why she responded the way she did. I smiled and said, "Thank you so much for your honesty. May I ask you a question? Have you been coming to our meetings each night or is this your first or second night here?"

Most of the people in that audience had been attending regularly and I did not recall seeing this particular woman before.

She responded, "Sir, this is my first night here."

Immediately, I said, "If this meeting were the first of this series I had attended, I probably would ask some of the same questions. You've started in the middle of the stream. I sure hope we haven't drowned you—I can see by your questions that you're an honest person. Could I sit down with you sometime and give you the background of the subject we presented tonight?"

Showing respect for individuals disarms them and prepares their minds for the reception of truth. Incidentally, this woman allowed me to explain to her the issues surrounding the mark of the beast and she attended church the very next Sabbath. This does not always happen, but you'll win a lot more people if you show respect for them than if you don't.

REPEAT THE QUESTION

The second *R* is **REPEAT** the question by paraphrasing it. This process demonstrates that you have understood the question. For example, a person might say, "I always thought that my mother was up in heaven, but you teach that she's in the earth. It's cold and dark and I don't like the thought of her being down there."

I might respond like this, "Mary, thank you for your question. It's a very good question. Many people have said similar things before. Let me be sure I understand you. Your basic concern is that you don't like to think of your mother underneath the earth. You're afraid that if you accept what we've studied tonight on the state of man in death, you'll have to picture her in a cold, dark place. Is this your question?"

Repeating a question someone asks you has immense value. First, it shows respect to the person who has asked it. It breaks down prejudice in their mind and lets them know you are listening to them and what they said is important to you. Second, it gives the person the opportunity to clarify what they meant by their question. Often, we answer questions we think people asked when in reality they asked something else. Thirdly, repeating the question gives you a split-second opportunity for the Holy Spirit to impress you with the answer to the question. There have been many times when someone has asked me a question and when I have repeated their question, the Holy Spirit impresses me with an answer.

REFER TO A BIBLE TEXT OR FUTURE TOPIC

This leads to my third *R,* which is **REFER.** If the question is on the topic of the evening, refer the individual to a particular text. Give a short answer and then move on. In his book *The Art of Personal Evangelism,* Alonzo Wearner says, "It is not our arguments which God has promised to bless but His word." In answering questions, it is far better to read one or two clear texts, make assertions, and then continue with the presentation. The third volume of the *Testimonies* gives us this principle: **"There are occasions where their glaring misrepresentations will have to be met. When this is the case, it should be done** *promptly* and *briefly*, **and we should then pass on to our work" (TESTIMONIES, VOL. 3, P. 37).**

Lengthy answers often confuse the mind and create unnecessary friction. Often we attempt to prove too much. A succinct answer is much better. Suppose a person says, "How can it possibly be true that when you die, you rest and don't immediately go to heaven? Jesus told the thief on the cross that he was going to be in heaven with Him that day."

Using the principles we've learned thus far, you might answer like this, "Thank you so much for your question. That is a very good question. *[Respect.]* Do I understand correctly that your major concern is over the subject of the thief on the cross? You wonder, If Jesus assured the thief that they would be in Paradise on Friday, how could it be true that the dead sleep?" *[Repeat and paraphrase.]*

When they respond positively, continue, "The Bible refers some sixteen hundred times to the soul, but not once does it speak of an immortal soul. In fifty-three places, the Bible says death is but a sleep. Let's turn to the book of John, chapter 20, verse 19 and onward, and study a little bit about Christ's resurrection and what He *really* said to the thief that day."

Along the same lines, many times an individual will raise a question in a group that is on the particular topic after an evangelistic meeting, but I realize that I cannot answer it fully due to time and the circumstances. In this case, I generally attempt to give a short answer that will satisfy the majority of the group and use the question as an opportunity to make an appointment with the questioner for one-to-one Bible study.

For example, Bill raises a question regarding the use of alcohol. *Respecting* Bill as an individual, *repeating* his question, *referring* him to a Bible text, I attempt to answer it. The rest of the group appears convinced, but I can tell by the look on his face that my answer has not fully satisfied Bill. What shall I do? Labor with Bill for twenty minutes and risk losing the rest of the group? An added difficulty is that when a person has made a strong statement publicly, they usually will not change their position publicly due to the embarrassment they would suffer. At all costs, I want to protect that person's image.

If it appears that Bill does not find my brief answer convincing, I might respond something like this: "Bill, that's such a good question that it's going to take me more time than I have in class tonight to answer it well. Can we get together sometime in the next couple of days? Maybe we can set up an appointment as to when I can answer your question more fully." The question that he has asked has become a launching pad for personal Bible study. My response shows both respect for Bill—I haven't entered into direct conflict with him—and also concern on my part that his question be fully answered.

REVEAL THAT THE ANSWER WILL COME

If the question concerns a topic you will be covering some evening later in your meetings, use the fourth *R,* which is simply to **REVEAL** that you will be discussing the topic later.

Be specific. Let's suppose an individual raises a question about the rapture and the second coming of Christ. You might say, for example, "Thank you for asking the question. I greatly appreciate your openness. That subject is so important that three weeks from tonight we will devote an entire presentation to it. That session is entitled 'Revelation's Hope for Tomorrow,' or the 'Second Coming of Christ.' I know you won't want to miss that particular class."

One pastor was teaching a Revelation seminar and referred questions to a future class five or six times in the first three classes. In about the fifth or sixth class session, someone again asked a question that was the subject of a future class. Before the pastor could respond, a class member spoke up and said, "Don't worry, Harry, that's coming up in class number 15." Of course, the whole class broke into laughter!

Truth must be revealed progressively. The mind is so constructed that it will not tolerate many ideas at once—no matter how true they are. Surprisingly enough, you will find referring people to future classes will actually build your attendance.

Jesus once told His disciples, "I still have many things to say to you, but you cannot bear them now" (JOHN 16:12).

Solomon states it clearly, "But the path of the just is like the shining sun, that shines ever brighter unto the perfect day" (PROVERBS 4:18). In other words, the darkness gradually fades as the sun continually rises. God does not throw a cosmic switch to turn the lights on after a night of darkness. Light is good but if there is too much too quick, we can easily be blinded. When a question is raised regarding a future topic, refer the person to the meeting in which their specific question will be answered.

REMEMBER, YOU DO NOT HAVE THE ANSWER TO EVERY QUESTION

The last *R* stands for REMEMBER. Remember that you don't know everything, and be willing to admit it. Questions will be raised that will be extremely difficult to answer. There'll be some questions that you've never heard before. If you pose as a walking Bible encyclopedia, you are merely setting yourself up for embarrassment. If people ask you questions for which you don't know the answers and you attempt to fake it by making up an answer, your audience will generally see through you.

You won't lose any credibility by saying, "You know, that's an outstanding question. I'm still learning too—I don't know the answer to that one. Maybe somebody else would like to give an answer. If not, let's go home and look this one up. Try a Bible concordance. I've got a good Bible dictionary and some commentaries and I'll certainly do a lot of searching.

"It's important to **remember Deuteronomy 29:29, 'The secret things belong to the LORD our God, but those things which are revealed belong to us and to our children forever.'** There are some questions that God has not fully answered. The Bible is plain on those subjects that relate to our eternal salvation, but there are some questions for which we won't have answers until we can ask Jesus about them in heaven."

Remember that you don't have to have all the answers. Admitting that you don't will certainly enhance your stature before your interests. Remember one other thing: God is Sovereign; He is in control.

Understanding Objections

To effectively answer objections necessitates understanding something about what's going on in the questioner's mind. Why do people have objections? What can we do to turn these objections into doors of opportunity?

In his outstanding book, *Getting Through to People*, Dr. Jesse S. Nirenberg points out that five basic human characteristics form the basis for people's objections:

1. People are resistant to change. Change tends to knock them off balance. They fear the unknown. Their habits may have become deeply entrenched. Some people find it extremely discomforting to accept a new idea or to try something new.

All new ideas cause friction. If the new idea can't be harmonized with what the person already thinks or feels comfortable with, or if too many ideas come all at once, the individual is likely to object.

2. Most people have a tendency to filter everything through their past. Their frame of reference is the way they have looked at things all their lives. Our prejudices, background, and ways of viewing things influence what we perceive.

3. People tend to see what they are looking for. Many people, recognizing that new truth calls for moral change, reinterpret it, and hear what they want to hear. Others see what they suppose they are seeing.

What do you see in the boxes below?

Snake in the grass	Busy as a bee	Paris in the the springtime

"Oh," you say, "I see 'snake in the grass, busy as a bee, and Paris in the springtime.' "

Do you really? Look at them again and again. Did you notice that the word "the" appears twice in one of the boxes: "Paris in the the springtime." Most people don't. Why? They see what they are accustomed to or familiar with. They see what they think they ought to. Many people raise objections because they think they hear something that we're not actually saying. I have preached scores of times on the Sabbath and its change and appealed for people to keep the Sabbath and, more often than not, someone will say, "Are you saying that if I do not keep the Sabbath I will be lost? What about my loved ones who never kept the Sabbath and were sincere Christians? I just cannot believe they are lost." Of course, I never suggested they were. The person heard me say something I never came close to saying. People's questions provide you with an opportunity to clear up their misunderstandings regarding what you were really saying.

4. People may have unwarranted assumptions. They may assume the dead go to heaven or that Jesus is coming in a secret rapture, or that Sunday is kept in honor of the Resurrection. They regard these assumptions as facts. They may, in fact, use these assumptions as the criteria by which they evaluate truth. They are likely to raise objections when their assumptions are challenged.

5. Some people object because of what Nirenberg calls habitual secretiveness. Expressing doubts makes them feel insecure. They want to keep everything inside—they feel much more secure that way. They have objections but they will not express them. In this instance, you will have to ask a lot of questions to discover what they are really thinking. Questions like these:

Is the Sabbath new to you?

Is the Sabbath plain?

If all you had was your Bible, would the Sabbath be clear to you?

Do you have any questions regarding the Bible Sabbath?

Are there any particular texts that trouble you?

Is there any good reason you could not begin keeping the Bible Sabbath fairly soon?

It is extremely important, then, to understand how to present truth in such a way that it will raise as little resistance as possible and when objections do rise, handle them respectfully, satisfactorily, and as soon as possible.

Cognitive Consistency

In his book *Soul Winning Made Easier,* Kembleton Wiggins discusses in some detail an amazing psychological principle called *cognitive consistency.* **This principle suggests that before a person integrates a new concept into his life, he wants to see that it is in some way consistent with what he already believes.**

When new ideas are presented, a person looks for a reference point in their thinking, some anchor point. If they cannot find that anchor point, they will object to and resist the new idea. If the prospect sees that the new idea is anchored to some reference point he has already accepted, then it is far more likely that he will accept the new idea.

Cognitive consistency leads us to a powerful technique. **Jesus said, "If I am lifted up from the earth, [I] will draw all peoples to Myself"** (JOHN 12:32), **and on another occasion, "I am the way, the truth, and the life"** (JOHN 14:6).

To present the truth as it is in Jesus means that before we present doctrinal truth, either in a Bible study, a Daniel seminar, a Revelation seminar, or a regular evangelistic meeting, men and women must first be led to Christ.

When we have led men and women to Jesus Christ, He becomes the reference point for everything else.

He becomes the North Star by which men and women set their courses.

He becomes the Foundation upon which the house is built.

He becomes the Truth by which all other truth is evaluated.

In the book *Evangelism,* Ellen G. White makes this perceptive observation: **"Great wisdom is required in dealing with human minds, even in giving a reason of the hope that is within us. . . . You dwell too much upon special ideas and doctrines, and the heart of the unbeliever is not softened. To try to impress him is like striking upon cold iron. . . .**

". . . And when the heart is all melted and subdued by the love of Jesus, the inquiry will be, 'Lord, what must I do to be saved?' " (PP. 247, 248).

As men and women are led to Jesus Christ, as they see the majesty of His love, the magnificence of His grace, they develop a desire to follow Him. Then, as each doctrine is tied to Jesus, presented logically and systematically as it is in Him, the friction that new ideas naturally develop is minimized. Thus the Second Coming is presented not merely as an event in which Jesus destroys the world, but as the Supreme Lover coming for His church. The state of the dead is presented as Jesus' triumph over the grave when He reunites His people with Himself. The Sabbath becomes a sign of love between Christ and the believer, a tangible witness to our belief in Creation, a witness to our acceptance of His sacrifice on the cross and our rest in Him for eternal life **(SEE HEBREWS 4)**.

If men and women are led to love Jesus and surrender their lives to Him, and if each new truth is presented as something that Jesus loves immensely, it will be the rejecting of any of these truths that will create friction or tension in the mind. To reject the truth then becomes not merely the rejection of a doctrine but the rejection of something that Jesus loves, a rejection of Jesus Himself. As men and women raise questions and present objections, we must show them the relationship of the doctrine that they are questioning to Jesus. Continue to lead them back to the reference point—Jesus Christ.

> *The Desire of Ages* affirms, "The wonderful love of Christ will melt and subdue hearts, when the mere reiteration of doctrine would accomplish nothing"
> (P. 826).

Each objection is an opportunity to reveal what Jesus teaches about a given subject. It provides the open door to reveal Jesus' desire for the individual to enter into full happiness as he accepts that subject. Each objection allows the perceptive teacher to show how a given subject relates to Jesus' way of life.

Present to your audience the overwhelming magnificence of Christ's love for them. Lead them to know Him personally. Then present one testing truth at a time. Make that particular truth clear in the minds of your students. Reveal to them how Christ loves this particular truth and desires their ultimate happiness. Show them that if they do not follow Jesus' will all the way, it displeases Him because it ultimately hurts them. Watch how the walls of prejudice disintegrate.

Resistance will fade away and scores of people who you didn't think would accept truth will accept it readily.

CHAPTER 14

EVANGELISTIC PRINCIPLES OF DECISIONS

The evangelistic principles that I'm going to share with you here on how to get more decisions are principles that I have put into practice for over forty years in my evangelistic preaching. They are not abstract theories that I think might possibly work. **They are biblical, Christ-centered principles that I know change lives.** They have transformed my ministry. I believe that they'll transform yours. They are solidly based on the Bible, the Spirit of Prophecy, and the teachings of modern science. As you put them into practice, you'll notice that they make a significant difference.

A Quartet of Decision Inhibitors

It seems to me that there are **four major challenges to people making decisions in evangelistic preaching.** I call these challenges decision *inhibitors*. They hold a person back from acting on truth that is clearly understood. If you are aware of these inhibitors, you can avoid them, or at least understand how to minimize their negative effects.

1. Information Overload. The first inhibitor is the problem of information overload. In an evangelistic series, individuals regularly attend three to five nights a week. During this period, they receive a lot of information, learning new doctrines quickly. **People can get too much, too fast, without the time to assimilate it.** As a result, they may feel off balance or generally ill at ease. Often this spiritual confusion leads them to avoid making a decision regarding what they have learned.

The "Clear and Set" Principle

You can use the **"clear and set" principle to avoid information overload.** If unanswered questions accumulate, an individual will, in all probability, either decide to continue to attend your evangelistic meetings but not respond, or will drop out of the series altogether. It is absolutely vital to deal with each new issue as it is presented. This principle teaches that only as the listeners understand and act upon truths presented can they be ready to receive and accept more truths. **At every new step, the evangelist must ascertain whether the hearer accepts or rejects the message.** The lay person or pastor who conducts an evangelistic series, believing that those attending will accept truth en masse at the conclusion of the meetings, is tragically mistaken. Any doctrines that appear hazy or inconsistent hinder further progress. Clearly understood truths become stepping-stones for a progressive understanding of God's Word. Ellen White emphasizes this "clearing and setting" process:

> **"Inquire how the subjects presented appear to the hearers, and whether the matter is clear to their minds"** (EVANGELISM, P. 429).

"The sacred responsibility rests upon the minister to watch for souls as one that must give an account. He must interest himself in the souls for whom he labors, finding out all that perplexes and troubles them and hinders them from walking in the light of the truth" (THE REVIEW AND HERALD, AUG. 30, 1892).

Seven Major Decisions

Throughout the series there are seven major decisions to clear your prospect on.

First is the decision regarding Jesus Christ—The decision to accept Jesus as both Savior and Lord.

Second is the decision to be ready for Christ's coming—To surrender any habits, attitudes, or practices that would keep the individual from being prepared for His coming.

Third is a decision to obey Christ, to follow His explicit instruction—"If you love Me keep My commandments" (JOHN 14:15).

The fourth decision involves keeping the Bible Sabbath—Following Christ in observing the seventh day of the week, Saturday, as the Sabbath outlined in Scripture. To wait until the end of the meetings before inviting people to church is a colossal mistake. Once the Sabbath is presented, it is important to answer questions about it and to invite people to church the very next Sabbath. All of them will not come but many will. The very fact that you have given your attendees an opportunity to come will work upon the minds of those who don't come, encouraging them to consider it.

The fifth major decision has to do with the state of man in death. Very often if an individual is not led to decision on the truth about death, they are vulnerable to Satan's deceptions.

The sixth concerns healthful living. As people progress through the seminar, they need to understand the importance of the fact that their bodies are the temples of the Holy Spirit. As the truth about healthful living is preached, the Spirit will convict them to give up alcohol, tobacco, undesirable habits, and unclean foods.

Seventh, there is baptism. Once this topic is presented, it is helpful to set a date for the first baptism. The Holy Spirit will be working upon the minds of the people, leading them to decide to be baptized. As you present each of these subjects, you must determine whether the interested individuals have merely heard what has been presented or whether they have made an intelligent commitment to accept it. At this juncture, visitation is of paramount importance.

Whenever we follow the "clear and set" principle, we are following Jesus' model of presenting truth. He said, "I am the way, the truth, and the life" (JOHN 14:6). Leading our prospects to understand Jesus as the way of salvation opens them to following the truth that He has revealed in His Word, so that they can live the life that He desires them to live. Proverbs 4:18 says, "The path of the just is like the shining sun, that shines ever brighter unto the perfect day." Just as the sun rises gradually upon the earth, dispelling the darkness, so likewise Jesus, the Son of Righteousness, arises in the heart, dispelling our spiritual darkness. The unfolding of truth is progressive. At each step in this unfolding process, the truth of God's Word must be made plain. If any of the foundational blocks in the temple of truth appear flawed or poorly placed, the individual will resist entering because he fears that the temple will come crashing down upon him. Be sure to secure each building block as you place it in the foundation.

2. The Programmed Non-Response Syndrome. The second great danger or inhibitor in the decision-making process is what some students of human behavior have termed the "programmed non-response syndrome." When we have adequate information to make a decision and our emotions are stimulated prompting us to make it, and we refuse because of real or apparent obstacles, we are likely to steel our minds against the decision. This syndrome occurs when an individual repeatedly fails to respond to information or emotional stimuli. **Repeatedly repressing one's response may easily result in the loss of the capacity to respond.**

For example, **Americans spend an average of four hours per person per day watching television.** That's 1,460 hours per person per year! Some researchers in the field of human emotions believe excessive television watching may result in the failure to respond to human need. For example, every time a television drama arouses an individual's emotions and they feel motivated to act, they likely go through a process of rationalization. They may say to themselves, "This isn't really happening, this is only make-believe." Consequently, that puts their conscience to sleep again and again. They are stimulated and then relax. They are moved but repress their response.

You may wonder how this applies to evangelism. **If people sit through an entire series of meetings without responding, they will lose their capacity to respond. That is why you must give people opportunities to respond.**

Counseling a minister who failed to make earnest appeals, Ellen G. White asserted that people "**leave the meeting feeling less inclined to accept the service of Christ than when they came**" (TESTIMONIES, VOL. 4, P. 447). And she commented to another pastor/evangelist,

"If there is not a decided application of the truth to their hearts, if words are not spoken at the right moment, calling for decision from the weight of evidence already presented, the convicted ones pass on without identifying themselves with Christ, the golden opportunity passes, and they have not yielded, and they go farther and farther away from the truth, farther away from Jesus and never take their stand on the Lord's side" (EVANGELISM, P. 283).

In practical terms, what has happened?

- They have listened carefully.
- Their minds have been enlightened.
- Their emotions have been aroused.
- They have been convicted of the truth.
- They have been stimulated to action. But there has been no opportunity for response. Since they cannot respond, they repress their desire to respond. The mind becomes less inclined to respond and the heart hardened.

Avoiding the Non-Response Syndrome

How can we avoid the programmed non-response syndrome? What practical steps can we take to give people opportunities to respond?

First, strongly appeal to people to make decisions at the end of each major point of doctrinal truth. Checking the card is a response to the Holy Spirit's call regarding the information presented. Experience reveals that pastors who overlook the decision cards or neglect utilizing them get far fewer decisions.

Second, make calls during your closing prayer, on a regular basis.

Ask questions like these:

- "As we pray, is there someone who has a habit that would keep you from being ready for the coming of Jesus? Tonight you'd like to ask Jesus to forgive you. You wish to surrender that habit to Him. Just raise your hand and I'll pray for you."

After a presentation on the Sabbath, simply ask, "Tonight as we pray, if the Sabbath truth is clear to you, please raise your hand. I'll pray that the Lord will help you to begin to put the Sabbath into practice in your life." And after a presentation on baptism, "If you're thinking about baptism, would you just raise your hand and I'll pray that God will give you the courage and strength to follow Jesus." Since expression deepens impression, acting upon knowledge received deepens the desire to perform the act for which audience members have raised their hands.

Third, when people begin to respond, visit them in their homes. Reinforce the decision they have made in the evangelistic meeting. This reconfirmation process helps to solidify the decision. Dr. William James, formerly a professor of psychology at Harvard University, once stated that when you are deeply moved by a concert or a play, you should not fail to act on the good emotions that have been aroused. He advised that if you can do nothing else, speak kindly to the taxi driver and tip him generously, kiss your wife and help her with a household chore. You must act in some constructive way unless you want to inhibit to a degree your future ability to act and repress the noble emotions you feel.
This is precisely the point. The action need not be large, but it is extremely important that we help people to act.

3. The Upper-Layer Approach. The third great inhibitor of decisions is what I call the "upper-layer approach." The upper-layer approach appeals to the head and not the heart. As someone has said, a message from the head reaches the head. A message from the heart reaches the heart. Many people who come to evangelistic meetings are not intending to change their lives. Many of them come out of intellectual curiosity. They want to learn something new and different.

The answer to helping people make lasting changes in their lives is understanding the importance of the will and how people make positive choices. According to Ellen White, "Everything depends on the right action of the will" **(STEPS TO CHRIST, P. 47).**

Elements That Lead to Decision

What is it that prompts the will? What essential elements make up the process that leads to a decision?

First, all intelligent decisions are based on

1. <u>INFORMATION</u>. Seventh-day Adventist evangelists are usually very strong on this point. People coming to our meetings may have some questions but typically they will have a solid information base. **But most people do not make a decision because of information alone. They must experience**
2. <u>CONVICTION</u>, the *second* essential element, as well. Information asks, What are the facts? Conviction asks, What is right? Conviction has to do with conscience.

Throughout the series, it is important to show the attendees the relationship of the topic presented to the will of God. It's important to show the interest that a failure to respond in a certain way is displeasing to Jesus. **Conviction has to do with a sense of rightness and wrongness in relationship to God's will.** Therefore, as we present a topic like the Sabbath, we ask,

- "Is the Sabbath **clear** to you?
- Do you have any **questions** about the Bible Sabbath?
- Can you see that it is God's will for you to **keep** the seventh-day Sabbath?"

Such questions take interested people a step beyond information. We are not merely interested that they *believe* that Saturday is the seventh-day Sabbath. We want them to understand that it is God's will for them to keep it.

We might ask further, "Can you see that Jesus kept the Sabbath? Is it clear to you that those who violate Jesus' will displease Him?" These questions will create a certain tension within a person. They convey that following Christ means acting a certain way. Living in harmony with God's will usually involves changes in our lifestyle.

In asking questions that bring conviction, we must be careful not to judge others prematurely. To avoid this, we constantly ask,

- "Can you see that this is God's will?"
- "Can you see that this is the direction that God wants you to go?"
- "Is it clear to you that if you follow this you'll be pleasing Jesus?"

We try continually to relate the information that they're learning to the will of God. The successful evangelist must be more than merely a conveyer of information.

He/she must become an agent God's Spirit can use to initiate conviction that leads to changes in the individual's course of action.

But in addition to information and conviction, there is a *third* element essential to decision-making. This element, of the utmost importance, is

3. <u>**DESIRE**</u>. An individual may have enough information to act, be convicted that they ought to act and still not act. How many people have you known that had all the facts about the negative effects of smoking, were convinced they should give up smoking, thought about giving it up, but still smoked. Why? There is one fundamental reason: they desired to smoke more than they desired to quit. No one forced them to smoke. For them, the benefits of smoking were greater than the benefits of quitting.

The Minimax Principle

The word *minimax* is derived from two words—minimum and maximum. There's a psychological principle that says that people will tend to act if the liabilities of their actions are low (minimum) and the benefits of their actions are high (maximum). In his book *The Mind Changers*, Emory Griffin points out that students of human behavior have concluded that minimax is the main factor in motivation.

When someone noticed that one crew of longshoremen in San Francisco unloaded twice as much cargo in half the time and with less breakage than any other crew, researchers were eager to find out why. As they probed, they discovered that while each group had dollies available, only the most efficient group used them.

Apparently, the rough, burly longshoremen were trying to live up to a macho image. Even the word *dolly* was repulsive to them. Most foremen were attempting to motivate their crews with lines like "The rules say you have to use the dolly," and "Use it or you may get fired."

The foreman who motivated his crew most successfully presented the benefits. He yelled things like, "Save your back, stupid; use the cart." In effect, his message was, "Smart guys have healthy backs. They're not going to doctors or chiropractors all the time, because they are wise enough to use the dolly."

This same principle of emphasizing benefits applies to spiritual things as well. Maximizing the eternal benefits of right action will produce dramatically greater results than focusing on the negative consequences of wrong action.

Notice how Jesus motivated men and women to act in harmony with His will. Jesus said, "Assuredly, I say to you, there is no one who has left house or brothers or sisters or father or mother or wife or children or lands, for My sake and the gospel's, who *shall not receive a hundredfold now in this time—* houses and brothers and sisters and mothers and children and lands, with persecutions—*and in the age to come, eternal life*" (MARK 10:29, 30).

Jesus acknowledged the reality that accepting His way of life often produced conflict. But He emphasized the benefits, which far outweighed the liabilities.

What benefits did Jesus offer?

- **Peace of mind** (JOHN 14:27)
- **Forgiveness of sin** (1 JOHN 1:9)
- **Freedom from guilt** (ROMANS 8:1)
- **Spiritual power** (JOHN 1:12)
- **The abiding presence of the Spirit of God** (JOHN 14:8)
- **The hope of heaven and of living eternally with Him** (MATTHEW 16:27)

If you want people to act, share with them the benefits that they'll get from acting. If you emphasize the negative consequences of acting, they are likely not to act.

For example, suppose that people have indicated that they have come to believe in the seventh-day Sabbath and that it is God's will for them to keep the Sabbath. How successful would I be if I proceeded with my appeal like this: "If you keep the Sabbath you may lose your job, you may lose your wife, your friends may forsake you, you may lose your home and car, but God will be pleased. How many of you will do it?"

Such an appeal is so negative that individuals would be frightened from making a decision.

On the other hand, I can say, "You may find it necessary to make some sacrifices to follow Jesus and keep the Sabbath, but if you do, God will give you a new peace. You'll have the joy of knowing that Christ is by your side. You'll have the certainty that you are doing His will. Most of all, you will have the absolute assurance that your hand is in His. You will sense you are on a path that will lead you to heaven." I would rather have that assurance than anything else in life, wouldn't you?

"Do you desire to please Jesus? By raising your hand you declare, 'Lord, I trust You and I know that You will guide me as I follow You.' If you desire to say, 'Yes, Jesus, I will follow Your Word,' raise your hand right now! I'll pray for you."

Notice the difference in the two appeals. One is positive and the other extremely negative.

In regard to every lesson that you teach, ask yourself, "Am I pointing out adequately in this lesson the benefits of right-doing? Am I emphasizing sufficiently the joy, the peace, and the happiness that comes with following this aspect of Jesus' teachings? Am I constantly pointing the students beyond the doctrine to the joy that fills heaven when men and women follow truth?"

4. Lack of 20/20 Vision. The last factor hindering decision is what I call the "lack of 20/20 vision." Paul indicated that he had this 20/20 vision when he said, "How I kept back nothing that was helpful, but proclaimed it to you, and taught you publicly and from house to house" (ACTS 20:20).

A lack of 20/20 vision is a lack of perception. It means that the seminar teacher does not see things clearly. Some individuals who lack skills in personal visitation try to hide behind the seminar approach, whether it is a Daniel seminar, a Revelation seminar, or one of the many health-related seminars. Seminars can give one the appearance of being a soul winner. But Acts 20:20 makes it clear that seminars cannot stand alone. You cannot do soul winning by proxy.

Jesus was an outstanding Personal Worker. He met privately with Nicodemus and appealed to his heart. He led the woman at the well to the conviction that He was the Messiah. He visited in the house of Simon the Pharisee, showing concern for his soul. Jesus appealed to Mary Magdalene after the crowd was dismissed. He worked with her individually. He said to Zacchaeus, "Come down, I'm going to your house today."

Without one-to-one work with those attending, the public seminar will not be as successful as it might have been. Ellen White clearly points this out:

> "If one half of the sermonizing were done, and **double the amount of personal labor** given to souls in their homes and in congregations, a result would be seen that would be surprising" **(EVANGELISM, P. 430).**

> And, "For years I have been shown that house-to-house labor is the work that will make the preaching of the Word a success" **(EVANGELISM, P. 433).**

I have seen these words confirmed. In one of our conferences, I trained the pastors to conduct Revelation seminars, and then we launched a conference-wide Revelation seminar program. As the results came in, I noticed a trend. Although generally the results were good, and we praised God for what happened, those pastors who did not actively follow the outlined visitation program had significantly fewer results than those pastors who did.

If you desire to have outstanding results in your work, you must have 20/20 vision, the vision of Acts. That book relates that the disciples preached the Word of God in public and in private. While it tells of Peter, James, and John preaching to the crowds, it also often shows them dealing directly with individuals. Even the apostle Paul, that great missionary, says in the book of Galatians that he preached to some privately, lest his preaching be in vain.

CHAPTER 15

MAKING EFFECTIVE APPEALS

Robert Boothby was an extremely **effective evangelist** throughout the Midwestern and Eastern United States a generation ago. Pastor Boothby gave particularly **powerful appeals. Thousands responded** to his calls through the years. On one occasion, he was **conducting an evangelistic series** in Washington, D.C., while he conducted an evangelistic field school for ministerial students.

A young pastor asked Pastor Boothby about the secret of effective appeals. The veteran evangelist answered with a question.

> "Young man, you **do not expect to get decisions every time** you preach, do you?" The young preacher answered, "No, pastor, **not every time,** but I wish I got more than I do." As quick as a flash, Pastor Boothby responded, "Young man, *unless* you preach like you expect to get decisions every time you preach, you will get very few. You must preach like you expect people to respond."

Preaching With Expectation

The apostle Paul preached with expectation. The book of Acts ends with the apostle's statement of ringing confidence that **God would change lives through his preaching.** His words assure us that **God will also use our preaching for the advancement of His kingdom.** Here are Paul's words of encouragement for all evangelistic preachers:

Making Appeals

" 'Therefore **let it be known** to you that the **salvation of God has been sent to the Gentiles, and they will hear it!'**... Then Paul dwelt two whole years in his own rented house, and received all who came to him, preaching the kingdom of God and teaching the things which concern the Lord Jesus Christ with all confidence, no one forbidding him" (**ACTS 28:28–31**).

The apostle Paul knew he was a **God called man** with a **God-inspired message** on a **God-ordained mission.** There was no question in his mind about the success of the mission. For him, the proclamation of the gospel and the preaching of the Word carried with them life-changing power.

Paul declares,

> "For I am not ashamed of the **gospel** of Christ, for it **is the power of God to salvation** for everyone who **believes,** for the Jew first and also for the Greek" (**ROMANS 1:16**).

The gospel is the power of God for salvation. Preached powerfully, it transforms lives.

Paul preached with "all confidence," knowing he would have results for his labors. He echoed the same thought to the church at Galatia when he wrote, "We shall reap if we do not lose heart" (GALATIANS 6:9).

God's Word will not return void. It will accomplish the thing God desires (ISAIAH 55:11).

Every evening as you preach:

- **Believe** God is going to use you to touch somebody for the kingdom.
- **Believe** the Holy Spirit is going to use your words and some boy, some girl, some man, some woman is going to be saved in God's kingdom.
- **Believe** that God is going to use you powerfully.
- **Preach** with expectation.
- **Preach** with anticipation.
- **Preach with confidence.**

"**If** you have the divinely inspired **confidence** that **God is going to use you** to lead scores of people to Christ and His truth, you will have far greater **success** than if you merely hope someone will respond."

The great purpose of Seventh-day Adventist evangelistic preaching is threefold:

1. **To lead** people to make a decision for Jesus Christ.
2. **To lead** people to make decisions to follow Jesus' end-time truth.
3. **To lead** people to become part of Jesus' end-time church.

Adventist evangelistic preaching that does not include these three aspects of appeals falls far short of God's ideal and will have minimal results.

- It is the **work** of the **evangelist** to preach and make appeals.
- It is the **work** of the **Holy Spirit** to convince and convict people of their need of Christ and plant within their minds the desire to follow truth.

Appeals provide divine opportunities for your audience to respond to your preaching. They are channels for the Holy Spirit's working. A **failure to make appeals** is a failure to give God the opportunity to transform lives.

Appeals provide your audience with the opportunity to commit to do what they have heard.

The apostle James makes it clear that **"faith by itself, if it does not have works, is dead"** (JAMES 2:17). "Even the **demons believe—and tremble!**" (JAMES 2:19).

Paul adds, "(For not the hearers of the law are just in the sight of God, but **the doers of the law will be justified**)" (ROMANS 2:13).

Jesus weighs in on the conversation this way. "Not everyone who says to Me, 'Lord, Lord,' shall enter the kingdom of heaven, but he who does the will of My Father in heaven" (MATTHEW 7:21).

The **function** of **all preaching** is to **motivate people to action**. It is to lead them not only to know but to do the will of God. Without appeals, hearts are hardened. If a person is convicted of what they ought to do, have sufficient information to act and do not, it is likely the conviction will gradually wear away.

"**If there is not a decided application of the truth** to their hearts, if words are not spoken at the right moment, **calling for decision** from the weight of evidence already presented, the convicted ones pass on without identifying themselves with Christ, the golden opportunity passes, and they have not yielded, and **they go farther and farther away from the truth, farther away from Jesus and never take their stand on the Lord's side**" (EVANGELISM, P. 283).

According to this statement, when an evangelist fails to make appeals, four things happen:

1. "**The convicted ones pass on without identifying themselves with Christ.**"
Psychologists call this "**programmed non-response.**" When the heart is convicted of truth, and the mind understands truth, a failure to act hardens the heart. When the intellect is informed and the Spirit moved, a failure to act makes people less capable of acting and they lose the ability to respond if they do not act on what they know to be right.

2. "**The golden opportunity passes.**"
There are divine moments when the Spirit prompts action. Jesus says,
"**Walk while you have the light,** lest darkness overtake you" (JOHN 12:35).
The apostle Paul adds, "**Now** is the day of salvation" (2 CORINTHIANS 6:2).
It is a dangerous thing to carelessly shrug off the Spirit's promptings.

Appeals take advantage of the divine moments when people are open for decision.

---

3. The "**convicted ones**" drift further from Jesus and His truth.
A failure to act on the truth does not leave our hearers in the same place they were before they heard truth. If they do not respond, they are worse than if they never heard (JOHN 9:39-41).

4. The "**convicted ones**" never take their stand on the Lord's side.
Repeated rejection of the truth leads to a hardness of heart and a callousness of mind. Speaking to us as well as to Israel, the apostle Paul declares, "Today, if you will hear His voice, do not harden your hearts as in the rebellion" (HEBREWS 3:7, 8).

Throughout the Bible, strong appeals played a major role in God's plan of saving people. The biblical prophets, the New Testament evangelists, and Jesus Himself made strong appeals.

Questions are sometimes asked:
- **Why make appeals** if God already knows the heart? **Doesn't God know** the hearts of the people in the audience?
- **Why is it necessary** to make any kind of visible response?

First—Making Appeals Is Biblical

God Made the First Appeal

When Adam and Eve sinned, God would not let them go without making an earnest appeal.

Heaven's first appeal is given in Genesis just after Adam and Eve sinned and were hiding from God. The record states, "Then the LORD God **called** to Adam and said to him, **'Where are you?'** " (GENESIS 3:9).

We make calls because God made the Bible's first call.

Moses Made Appeals

EXODUS 32:26: "Then Moses stood in the entrance of the camp, and said, 'Whoever is on the LORD's side—come to me!' And all the sons of Levi gathered themselves together to him."

Moses would not let Israel be lost in idolatry without an earnest appeal.

Elijah Made Appeals

1 KINGS 18:21: "And Elijah came to all the people, and said, 'How long will you falter between two opinions? If the LORD is God, follow Him; but if Baal, follow him.' "

Elijah powerfully made appeals.

Jesus Made Appeals

Jesus repeatedly called His disciples publically.

MATTHEW 9:9: "As Jesus passed on from there, He saw a man named Matthew sitting at the tax office. And He said to him, 'Follow Me.' So he arose and followed Him."

Revelation Ends With a Biblical Appeal

The entire Bible ends with God's final appeal.

REVELATION 22:17: "And the Spirit and the bride say, **'Come!'** And let him who hears say, **'Come!'** And let him who thirsts **come.** Whoever desires, let him take the water of life freely."

Making appeals is biblical. It is at the very heart of Scripture. To neglect to make appeals is to neglect to follow the scriptural model and the clear example of Jesus.

As you preach, **it is vital that you invite people to make decisions** for Christ and His truth.

Second—Making Appeals Changes Lives

Every time you preach, **the Holy Spirit impresses the minds** of the **hearers** with the truth you proclaim. New light dawns on darkened minds. New truths burst upon the consciousness. As you make appeals, your audience has the opportunity to respond to the working of the Holy Spirit and make life-changing decisions. **When the impressions of truth are the strongest, the opportunity for decision is the greatest.**

Third—Without Appeals, People Often Hear But Do Not Act

Conviction must **lead** to **action.** Conviction not acted upon leads to complacent inaction. Someone well said that impression without expression leads to depression. When God impresses truth upon the heart and people are not led to act upon it, the conviction to act gradually leaves them and they drift further from Jesus, hardening their minds to truth.

"When persons who are under conviction are not brought to make a decision at the earliest period possible, there is danger that the conviction will gradually wear away" **(EVANGELISM, P. 298).**

Fourth—Actions Intensify Inner Belief

Action is faith strengthening. When an individual acts on a certain belief, then that belief strengthens.

- It is not only true that **thoughts lead to actions.**
- It is also true that **actions intensify and deepen thought** patterns.
- If you want to lead a person to think a certain way, **help them to act on their present convictions.** Our actions influence our thoughts. The wise man puts it this way, **"Commit your works to the LORD, and your thoughts will be established"** (PROVERBS 16:3).

In your evangelistic meeting, **if you lead people to take action on the truth presented, their belief in the truth they act upon will intensify.**

Truth acted upon is truth believed. Individuals never really believe truth until they put it into practice in their lives. By this we mean that **truth lived is truth believed.** Appeals provide people an opportunity to respond to the truth the Holy Spirit has been placing in their hearts.

> "The **convicted sinner** has something to do besides repent; he must **act** his part in order to be accepted by God. He must **believe** that God accepts his repentance, according to His promise. "Without faith it is impossible to please Him: for He that cometh to God must believe that He is, and that He is a rewarder of them that diligently seek Him" **(EVANGELISM, P. 287).**

UNDERSTANDING THE HUMAN MIND

Jesus was a master at understanding the human mind. He observed the people He appealed to and tailored His appeals to reach the inner recesses of their hearts but always followed the basic laws of the mind. Just as there are laws of physiology that govern our bodies, there are laws equally certain that govern our minds. Ellen White gives this wise counsel to all soul winners:

"Mechanics, lawyers, merchants, men of all trades and professions, educate themselves that they may become masters of their business. Should the followers of Christ be less intelligent, and while professedly engaged in His service be ignorant of the ways and means to be employed? The enterprise of gaining everlasting life is above every earthly consideration. **In order to lead souls to Jesus there must be a** knowledge of human nature and a study of the human mind. Much careful **thought and fervent prayer are required** to know how to approach men and women upon the great subject of truth" **(TESTIMONIES, VOL. 4, P. 67).**

Remember what we studied in the chapter on Decisions. **Individuals will choose to act if the information is clear, their conviction to act is strong, and their desire to act is high.** The choice to decide to act on a given issue depends on the answer to **three basic questions:**

1. **Is the information clear** or are there questions inhibiting the person's decision? Do they understand what the Bible clearly teaches on the subject?
2. **Is the person's conviction to act strong?** Do they sense that if they do not act they are not in harmony with God's will?
3. **Is the person's desire to act high?** Do they see the benefits of taking the step and do they desire to act?

> **Throughout your sermon, present a strong informational base, weave in elements of conviction and desire, and watch what God does.**

KEY POINTS IN MAKING APPEALS

1. **Pray about your appeal.** Ask the Holy Spirit to give you the right words. I often arrive at the auditorium early to pray for the power of the Holy Spirit in my sermon and especially upon my appeal. Invite your intercessory prayer group to pray earnestly during your appeals.
2. **Appeal from a sincere heart.** Let **your concern** regarding the eternal salvation of your audience flow from your heart. Avoid pleading, coaxing, urging. **Let the Spirit work.** Don't worry about a few moments of silence while the piano plays softly. **It may seem like an eternity to you, but the Spirit is gently pleading.**
3. **Make your appeal specific** so that the audience will know exactly what they are asked to respond to. General appeals do not change lives and poorly worded confusing appeals leave an audience bewildered.

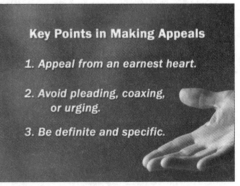

Key Points in Making Appeals

1. *Appeal from an earnest heart.*
2. *Avoid pleading, coaxing, or urging.*
3. *Be definite and specific.*

Prepare your evangelistic sermons with the deliberate purpose of giving opportunity of **expression** of some kind that will lead **to acceptance** of the truth presented. Intelligent decisions are based on **adequate information** impressed upon the mind by the Holy Spirit. In evangelistic visitation, **tell key interests** that you are going to make a call and invite them to lead the way.

THE ALTAR CALL

1. **Leave** plenty of **time for the altar call. Shorten preliminaries** if necessary on the nights of an altar call.
2. Have **altar calls on scheduled nights** whether you feel like it or not, if there are non-members present.

3. Hold major **calls** for **ten or at most twenty minutes.**
4. Invite the **pianist to play** appeal songs such as "Just as I Am," "All to Jesus I Surrender," "Softly and Tenderly Jesus Is Calling," and so on. At times, it is extremely effective to place the words of the song on the screen and have the entire congregation sing together during the appeal.
5. **Invite everyone to stand to sing together.** This will make it easier for some to make their way to the aisles to come forward.
6. **Close with prayer.** Ask those who came forward to remain for a short time as the audience is dismissed.
7. Place a **card** and pencil in the hands of each one who came forward. Ask them to **fill out the card.**

NINE CALLS OR APPEALS

There are **AT LEAST nine** different types of calls you can make in your evangelistic preaching. Each one has its place. Someone said, **"Any method used exclusively is a poor method." In other words, vary your calls.** Some people will respond to one type of call and other people will respond to another type of appeal.

01 | Hand-raising call

The hand-raising call is a rather gentle **appeal that elicits a significant response.** It is helpful to use at the beginning of the series. It helps the audience to take small steps and prepares them for larger steps later. There are two types of hand-raising calls.

- General hand-raising calls obviously invite people to make a general decision. Most of your audience will raise their hands for this type of appeal. Here are a few examples of general hand-raising calls.

General

- "**How many** of you want to be ready when Jesus comes?"
- "**How many** of you want to tell Jesus you love Him enough to obey Him?"
- "**How many** of you want to say, 'Jesus, I will follow wherever You lead'?"

Specific

Here are some examples of specific hand-raising calls.
- **"Is there anything in your life that would keep you from surrendering to Jesus?"** "Tonight, if you want to surrender that specific thing to Him, just raise your hand."
- **"Do you sense the Holy Spirit calling you to be baptized?"** Would you like to raise your hand right now and say, 'Yes, Lord, I will follow You all the way into the baptismal waters'?"

02 | Kneeling call

A kneeling call moves an audience to surrender their lives more deeply to Jesus. It is often more effective in a church setting than in a public hall. After a sermon on the Cross or the divinity of Christ, the appeal may go something like this: "Is there some burden you struggle with, health problems, financial problems, family problems, **that you would like to kneel** and talk to God about?"

"If the Spirit is leading you and you would like to kneel, I'm inviting you to drop to your knees right now." The value of the kneeling call is that it allows the Holy Spirit to speak to people's hearts as they kneel, committing their lives to Jesus. I remember one kneeling call I made in a church in one of Chicago's suburbs. The Holy Spirit was markedly present. As people knelt and prayed, there was crying throughout the church. Hearts were deeply moved by the Holy Spirit.

03 | Standing call

This is sometimes the hardest call to make. As an individual stands, they sometimes feel everyone is staring at them. I rarely use standing calls for testing truths and use them only when I desire a general response. **Standing calls for prayer at the close of the meeting can be extremely powerful** if they are combined with an altar call during a song at the end of the sermon.

04 | Card call

We use response/decision cards once a week on the key topics of the week. The response cards provide an individual the opportunity to make a decision in their seats without having to come forward. **For many people, it is much easier to check a card than it is to respond to an altar call.** The cards are counted out ahead of time and distributed row by row by the ushers in that particular section. Here is the general outline of the response cards.

- First line—**General** spiritual commitment
- Second line—**Is specific** regarding the topic you presented that evening
- Third line—Generally a **baptism** appeal
- Fourth line—Provides further **reading material** on the topic

As the cards are distributed, I explain to my audience that they can write a prayer request or question on the back blank side of the card. We invite the ushers to collect the cards and bring them forward for me to pray over. Response cards are also effective on Sabbath mornings.

Note: There are eight different decision cards in the appendix on pages 213–216.

05 | Prayer call

The **prayer call is a special invitation** for people to come forward who desire prayer for some problem, difficulty, challenge, or need in their life. Usually I announce the night of the prayer call ahead of time and share with the audience a few promises on prayer and my belief that God will work mightily in their lives.

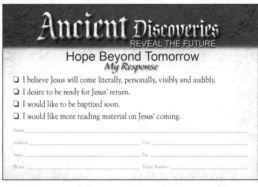

- **Invite pastors and lay leaders to join those coming forward** and pray with the people who have specific needs.
- I encourage the **evangelist to offer prayer** for those who have come forward first, then invite those who want spiritual counseling or further prayer to remain to pray with one of our pastors.

06 | Altar call

During the **altar call, people are invited forward to make a complete surrender to Jesus.** There are times when some who have not responded to any other type of appeal will be **moved by the Holy Spirit to come forward in the altar call.** I recall the father of one of our members who we were praying and laboring for. Nothing seemed to move him. He did not respond to any of my calls. He never filled out a response card, never raised his hand or stood, and appeared unmoved by all of my appeals. The night I made an altar call for baptism, his daughter responded
and he could hold back no more. He bolted forward. What a sight to see this man standing at the altar with his non-Adventist daughter and Adventist son, weeping with their arms around one another.

HOW TO GIVE AN ALTAR CALL FOR BAPTISM—WHAT TO SAY

"**Do you sense God is calling you to follow Jesus in Bible baptism?** When Jesus was baptized, the Father spoke from heaven and said, 'This is My beloved Son, in whom I am well pleased' **(MATTHEW 3:17). As you walk into the waters of baptism, you are pleasing Jesus.** There is no greater joy in life than knowing that you are making the One who loves you with an immense love, happy. **My appeal focuses on three specific groups this evening. God may be speaking to your heart.** This may be the night for you to make the most important decision of your life."

FIRST—"Those of you who have **never been baptized by immersion,** I want to give you an opportunity to make that decision tonight. You have never made a personal decision to be baptized, and I'm inviting you to come forward."

SECOND—"Those who have been baptized, but since that time the Lord has given you added light, and **now you would like to take the step of uniting with His last-day movement that keeps all of God's commandments** and honors the simple faith of Jesus.

- You may be a church member.
- You may have accepted Christ long ago and walked with Him through the years, but now
- He is calling you to take another step in your walk with Him. I want to invite you to take that step tonight."

FINALLY—"I have another invitation tonight. **Those of you who used to walk with God's people, but for a time have fallen away.** Tonight **I want to invite you to come back.**

"**If you are in one of these three groups, will you come forward just now as the pianist plays softly?**

"Many of you are having great battles in your heart right now. God will give those of you in the valley of decision the strength you need to make a decision.

"**Yes, God bless you.** Are there others who will come? **Don't put it off,** my friend. Jesus is appealing to you tonight. **The longer you wait, the harder it is to take that step.** There will never be a more convenient time. **Make that step for Jesus tonight.**"

07 | Combination call

The combination call blends more than one call into a single appeal. Sometimes after the ushers have collected the response/decision cards, I invite the audience to stand and sing the appeal song. While they are standing, **I invite those who have checked the decision card for baptism to come forward** for a special prayer to receive God's power to sustain their decision.

08 | Meditation call

The **meditation call is a simple, effective call** that although it does not produce a visible response, it touches people's hearts and prompts them to make major decisions. In this call, I invite people to **remain in their seats during the closing appeal song and meditate upon the music, allowing the Holy Spirit to impress them** with the decision God is leading them to make.

09 | After-meeting call

The after-meeting call always takes place in **combination with either one of our card calls, altar calls, or standing calls.** Once people have responded to a specific call, we invite them to remain after the meeting to get specific instruction on how to live a victorious Christian life. This is especially effective on the sermon on **healthful living.** Immediately after the sermon, we invite people who want **help quitting smoking** or overcoming some undesirable habit to join us for the after-meeting.

Appeals Based on the Ten Things Jesus Offers

People tend to act if the benefits of their acts are high and the consequences of their acts are low. A careful study of Jesus' appeals reveals that He offered to meet the deepest needs of the human heart for those who followed Him.

Weave the benefits listed below into your appeals and watch your results increase.

1. **Peace**—John 14:27
2. **Happiness**—John 10:10; John 13:17
3. **Holy Spirit**—John 14:15, 16
4. **Influence**—John 1:40, 41; Romans 14:7
5. **Pleasing God**—John 8:29; Matthew 3:16,17
6. **Light/Truth**—John 12:35
7. **Fellowship**—John 15:13–15
8. **Power**—John 1:12
9. **Eternal life**—John 3:16
10. **Place in the Father's house**—John 14:1–3

The Holy Spirit works through the consecrated evangelist as he/she opens the Word of God and makes heartfelt appeals. The story is told of Billy Graham preaching in London's Wembley Stadium.

Evidently, the **British press was quite critical** of Billy's appeals. They particularly took him to task for using the hymn, **"Just as I Am."** They claimed that it was pure emotionalism, manipulating the audience. Billy decided to make a **straight-forward appeal with no music at all.** When he began the appeal, very few came forward. The veteran evangelist stood with his arms folded, praying in silence. As he continued to pray, **hundreds began to move toward the front.** He continued this practice for **thirty straight nights with no music during his appeals at all.** Hundreds continued to pour forward to make decisions for Christ. The journalists were amazed. They wrote in the British press, **"Give Us Back 'Just as I Am.' The Silence Is Killing Us."**

As you, too, make appeals, the Holy Spirit will work mightily on the hearts of your audience and you will see miracles of divine grace.

CHAPTER 16

BAPTISM

Baptism is one of the most important subjects in the New Testament. It is **mentioned more than eighty times.** Before His ascension to heaven, Jesus commissioned His disciples to "Go therefore and make disciples of all the nations, baptizing them in the name of the Father and of the Son and of the Holy Spirit" **(MATTHEW 28:19, 20).** The book of Acts records that the disciples followed their Lord's instructions and tens of thousands of people were baptized.

The New Testament church baptized adult believers who committed their lives to Christ, repented of their sins, and obeyed His Word. Christ commissioned His disciples to instruct people in the principles of the Christian life. When they accepted the claims of His love and became His disciples, the sign of their allegiance to a new life was baptism.

Final words are extremely important. Parting words are usually significant. Picture a family gathered around a hospital bed eagerly trying to catch every word of a dying loved one. **Last words make a difference. Christ's last words were some of the most significant** He ever uttered. His final command to His disciples was, **"Go into all the world and preach the gospel to every creature" (MARK 16:15).**

As an evangelist, as you preach God's Word, make powerful, Spirit-filled appeals, and invite people to follow Jesus in baptism, you are obeying Christ's two-thousand-year-old command. Christ commissioned His disciples in every age to instruct people in the principles of the Christian life. When they accepted the claims of His love and became disciples, the sign of their allegiance to a new life was baptism.

The subject of baptism does raise many questions in the minds of evangelists, pastors, and church members.

- **How** important is biblical baptism?
- **What** are the essential steps an individual must take before baptism?
- **Why** were there so many apparent rapid baptisms in the New Testament?
- **How** can a pastor or evangelist determine if a person is ready for baptism?
- **How** can an individual's baptismal service be the most meaningful? In this chapter, we will seek answers to these questions.

THE IMPORTANCE OF BIBLICAL BAPTISM

Jesus declared: **"He who believes and is baptized will be saved;** but he who does not believe will be condemned" **(MARK 16:16).** It should not escape our attention that in these words the Master is specifying not just one but two important things—*believing* and *being baptized.*

Those who try to **minimize the importance of baptism often overlook the implications of Jesus' words.** Theoretically, there may be some circumstances beyond one's control that prevent someone from being baptized—like the **thief on the cross**—but from a practical standpoint, such cases are few and far between. We have baptized prisoners behind penitentiary walls in **makeshift prison baptistries** and a young man dying of cancer in a **bathtub.** I have discovered that it often **depends more on the person's *will* than on circumstances.**

The people asked the apostles,

> " 'Men and brethren, what shall we do?' Then Peter said to them, '*Repent,* and let every one of you *be baptized* in the name of Jesus Christ for the remission of sins; and you shall receive the gift of the Holy Spirit.' . . . Then **those who gladly received his word were baptized;** and that day about three thousand souls were added to them" (ACTS 2:37, 38, 41).

Once again, the Word of God tells "every one of us" to do two important things—*repent* and *be baptized.* Baptism is much more than a lifeless ritual. It is a deeply **spiritual symbol of complete, total commitment to Christ, the burial of the old life and resurrection to a new life in Christ.**

FIVE CHARACTERISTICS OF RAPID BAPTISMS IN THE NEW TESTAMENT

01 | Previous instruction

In most instances, there was evidence of previous instruction.
- The *three* **thousand baptized on the Day of Pentecost** were Jews who were familiar with the basic teachings of the Old Testament and influenced by the three-and-a-half-year ministry of Jesus.
- The **Ethiopian Jew** was returning from worshiping at Jerusalem, studying the book of Isaiah.
- **Cornelius** was a God-fearing man, seeking truth and studying the Scriptures.

The Bible focuses on the moment of decision not the months of preparation.

02 | Evidence of the presence of the supernatural

In the **rapid baptisms** in the New Testament, there is the evidence of the supernatural.
- The gift of tongues or real languages was poured out at Pentecost.
- The Philippian jailer witnessed a strange earthquake.
- The miraculous protection of the apostle Peter. Both Cornelius and Peter were guided by dreams.
- Philip miraculously appeared to the Ethiopian on the Gaza road.

03 | Acceptance of a present-truth prophetic message

In each rapid baptism in the New Testament, there was the **acceptance of a present-truth prophetic message.** The disciples revealed from the Old Testament Scriptures that Christ was the Messiah of prophecy. Seeing the fulfillment of prophecy in Jesus' life and accepting Jesus as the Messiah, multitudes were baptized.

04 | The willingness to stand alone

In New Testament time and culture, Christianity was not popular. **For an individual to become a Christian meant they were willing to step out of their cultural background and stand alone for Jesus.** At times it meant losing their jobs, friends, family, and even their lives. Accepting Jesus meant giving their all to Him.

05 | Personal initiative

When the Holy Spirit moves in someone's life, the initiative for baptism is theirs. **They do not need to be coaxed, coerced, or pressured.** In every instance of a rapid baptism in the New Testament, the individual being baptized requested the baptism.

How do these principles we have discovered in the book of Acts apply to our evangelistic meetings today? **Here are some questions I raise in my mind regarding candidates for baptism:**

- Are they committed to Jesus?
- Are they willing to stand alone for Jesus if necessary?
- Do they have a basic grasp of God's end-time prophetic message for this final generation?
- Is there evidence of the supernatural in their lives?
- What changes have they made?
- Is the initiative for baptism theirs?

READINESS FOR BAPTISM

The Four Biblical Characteristics That Determine Readiness for Baptism

Readiness for baptism is not determined by how many evangelistic meetings a person has attended or even how long they have been attending church. **It is determined by the following factors:**

1. **REPENTANCE:** "Then Peter said to them, '*Repent*, and let every one of you be baptized in the name of Jesus Christ for the remission of sins; and you shall receive the gift of the Holy Spirit' "(ACTS 2:38). **Repentance is a deep sorrow for sin. It means a conscious desire to turn from those things that violate God's will and sadden His heart.**
   - Does this individual **demonstrate a genuine sorrow for sin** and the desire to turn from the things that break Jesus' heart?

- What **specific changes** have they made in their lives?

2. **BELIEF:** "Now as they went down the road, they came to some water. And the [Ethiopian] eunuch said, 'See, here is water. What hinders me from being baptized?' Then Philip said, 'If you *believe* with all your heart, you may.' And he answered and said, 'I *believe* that Jesus Christ is the Son of God' " (ACTS 8:36, 37).

New Testament belief is not merely intellectual assent.

- **It is a living faith in Jesus** that is transformational.
- **It is the acceptance of Jesus** as both my Savior and Lord—my dying Lamb and living Priest—the One who came and will come again.
- It includes **accepting the free gift of salvation** and the **life-changing teachings of Jesus.** This belief is more than simply an acceptance of a particular creed.
- It is a **heart commitment** to Jesus and His Word.
- It is **a turning to Him** with all the heart, a belief that He is the Savior, who alone can forgive sin and give victory in my life.

Baptism is more than just adding numbers to the church. It is a visible symbol of a heart that loves Jesus so much that he/she longs to be with Him throughout all eternity.

3. **INSTRUCTION:** The words of Jesus regarding baptism are too plain to be misunderstood. His disciples were to continue "*teaching* them to observe all things that I have commanded you; and lo, I am with you always, even to the end of the age" (MATTHEW 28:20).

Although **learning is a lifelong process** and **one should never wait until they feel they have grasped all truth before baptism,** it is **necessary to understand basic scriptural truths** before making such a significant decision.

Before each person is baptized, they should be instructed in the essential truths of Scripture as understood by Seventh-day Adventists. In the New Testament, baptism signifies union with Christ and union with His church. Consequently, each individual we baptize should be clear on both their commitment to Jesus and His church.

Ellen White cautions church evangelists and pastors from baptizing people prematurely.

"**The preparation for baptism is a matter that needs to be carefully considered. The new converts to the truth should be faithfully instructed in the plain 'Thus saith the Lord.'** The Word of the Lord is to be read and explained to them point by point" (EVANGELISM, P. 308).

During our evangelistic meetings, **we provide an opportunity for people to review the message a minimum of at least three times before baptism.**

- They **hear** God's **Word preached.**
- They **participate** in the **Bible school** by studying the *Search for Certainty* lessons and either
- **Attend** our **baptismal class** or **review the *In His Steps* baptismal manual** in their homes.

Adequate preparation of each baptismal candidate significantly reduces apostasies. It anchors baptismal candidates in the truth and helps to prevent them from being swept away by the winds of heresy.

Baptism comes after all the essentials of the Seventh-day Adventist Church have been presented in the evangelistic meetings, **pastors' Bible class,** and **baptismal class,** and often after the person **has completed all thirty of the** *Search for Certainty* **Bible lessons.**

4. **PRACTICE: Jesus' instruction** to His disciples regarding baptism adds this fascinating expression: **"teaching them to observe all things that I have commanded"** (MATTHEW 28:19). **The disciples were not only to teach new converts, they were to lead them to act on what they were taught.**

This fourth requirement is also described in ROMANS 6:4 in a little different way but with the same significance: "Therefore we were buried with Him through baptism into death, that just as Christ was raised from the dead by the glory of the Father, even so **we** also **should walk in newness of life.**"

If a person understands truth but is not practicing it and has not integrated it into their lifestyle, they are certainly not ready for baptism.

- It is possible to understand the Sabbath but not keep it.
- A person may have the knowledge that tobacco is harmful but keep smoking.
- An individual may accept Jesus intellectually but still live like they were before because although they believe, they have not really been converted. The apostle James states it clearly, "You believe that there is one God. You do well. Even the demons believe—and tremble!" (JAMES 2:19).

All who enter upon the new life should understand, **prior** to their **baptism,** that the Lord requires their undivided affections. "The **practicing** of the **truth** is **essential.** The bearing of fruit testifies to the character of the tree" (EVANGELISM, P. 308).

"But when a person presents himself as a **candidate** for **church membership,** we are to **examine** the **fruit of his life,** and leave the responsibility of his motive with himself" (THE REVIEW AND HERALD, JAN. 10, 1893).

Teaching New Converts a New Lifestyle

"There is need of a more **thorough preparation** on the part of **candidates** for **baptism.** They are in need of more **faithful instruction** than has usually been given them. The **principles** of the **Christian life** should be **made plain** to those who have newly come to the truth. None can depend upon their profession of faith as proof that they have a saving connection with Christ. We are not only to say, 'I believe,' but to **practice** the **truth**" (TESTIMONIES, VOL. 6, PP. 91, 92).

A great responsibility rests upon the pastor to do his work with thoroughness. The **baptismal candidate** should be led along step by step until every essential point has been brought before them.

1. It is the person preparing the candidates responsibility to be sure the person being baptized is fully **grounded in the truth** and has made a full surrender.
2. It is the person preparing the candidates responsibility to see that a person is **practicing the truth** before baptism is administered.
3. It is the person preparing the candidates responsibility to be sure the **person being baptized has given up tobacco, alcohol,** and **unclean foods.**
4. It is the person preparing the candidates responsibility to assign the newly baptized person a **"spiritual guardian."** Having a spiritual guardian will help the newly baptized member to integrate into the church more rapidly.

Ways of Maximizing the Baptismal Potential

1. **Make appeals Sabbath morning in the participating churches.**
2. **Make appeals in the evangelistic meeting.**
   - Use the various appeals from the chapter on appeals.
3. **Make appeals in the home.**
4. **Consolidate your baptismal prospects into a baptismal class.**
   - See pages 207, 208 for baptismal statement of faith—Class #1
   - See pages 209, 210 for baptismal statement of faith—Class #2
5. **Plan baptismal dates**
   - Planning baptismal dates is very important—it gives the person a certain time to look forward to for his/her baptism.
6. **Conduct some baptisms in the evening evangelistic meetings.** Seeing people baptized is a strong motivation to be baptized.
7. **Make every baptism special.** In a sense, a baptism is like a wedding. It is a union with Christ and His church. We like to provide flowers for each person baptized and share their testimony. After the baptismal service, we supply them with a packet of gift books to solidify their newfound faith.

REBAPTISM

The question is sometimes asked about rebaptism

Remember that Paul met a group of believers in the upper coasts of Philippi and rebaptized them. They had been baptized by John the Baptist but did not understand a doctrine as significant as the Holy Spirit. When they understood the fullness of truth, they were rebaptized. In almost every evangelistic meeting that we hold, there will be **committed Christians** who attend our meetings, **were baptized by immersion once, and desire to be baptized again** because they **want to unite with God's remnant church.** An **understanding of God's prophetic message** for today compels their consciences to be **rebaptized.** Others who once walked with Jesus but who have **drifted away** in open apostasy may also desire to **recommit their lives to Christ in rebaptism.** Notice these two clear statements from the pen of inspiration.

"The Lord calls for a decided reformation. **And when a soul is truly reconverted, let him be**

rebaptized. Let him renew his covenant with God, and God will renew His covenant with him. . . . Reconversion must take place among the members, that as God's witnesses they may testify to the authoritative power of the truth that sanctifies the soul" (EVANGELISM, P. 375).

"The **honest seeker after truth will not plead ignorance of the law** as an excuse for transgression. Light was within his reach. God's Word is plain, and Christ has bidden him search the Scriptures. He reveres God's law as holy, just, and good, and he repents of his transgression. By faith he pleads the atoning blood of Christ, and grasps the promise of pardon. **His former baptism does not satisfy him now.** He has seen himself a sinner, condemned by the law of God. He has experienced anew a death to sin, and he desires again to be buried with Christ by baptism, that he may rise to walk in newness of life. Such a course is in harmony with the example of Paul in baptizing the Jewish converts. **That incident was recorded by the Holy Spirit as an instructive lesson for the church**" (EVANGELISM, P. 372).

> **Rebaptism is not a necessity** for committed, converted Christians **but it is a choice that** many of them make **when they hear God's last-day message. If they do not choose rebaptism, they certainly can become members of the Seventh-day Adventist Church by profession of faith.**

There are few events in the life of the church that **encourage church members** more than a baptismal service. **A carefully planned baptismal service inspires every person present.** When new believers give their testimonies and share their stories of how they came to Jesus and learned about His true church, the entire church is inspired .

- **Regular baptisms** give the church a sense of God's presence and power.
- **Plan regular baptisms** throughout your evangelistic meetings rather than a single large baptism at the end of the series, and God will be honored and the church will rejoice. Once church members have a taste of seeing people baptized,
- They will **long for more souls won** for Christ and
- **Be inspired** to become actively involved in evangelism.

Evangelism rightly done is the culture for more evangelism. Baptisms spawn more baptisms.

CHAPTER 17

CONSERVING THE GAINS

Baptism is not a panacea to solve all spiritual problems. Often, immediately after baptism, new believers are faced with difficult challenges. There is the challenge of relating to non-Adventist relatives; the challenge of developing new friends; and the challenge of consistently living in harmony with the high standards of the Bible. **The challenge of integrating new doctrinal beliefs into their lifestyle and living as a Seventh-day Adventist is a significant one that each newly baptized believer faces.**

This critical problem must be addressed by the church. It is very likely that many will become discouraged shortly after baptism. If there is little tolerance for their mistakes, no sympathetic understanding for the trials they experience, and if criticism destroys the blessing of their newfound faith, apostasies will be high. **New members cannot be expected to survive if they are left alone. They are spiritual babes.** Any baby that does not receive adequate attention will die. Baptism is a symbol of new birth. It is not an indication that the new convert is fully mature. Therefore, it is the **responsibility of the church** to take careful steps to help each new member grow and develop a deeper relationship with Christ.

Let's suppose you have a new baby son. You may regularly rise two or three times a night to meet his needs. Changing his diapers will occupy a significant portion of your time. In infancy, babies are incapable of doing anything for themselves. But will you feel that the baby is a failure because he/she needs so much attention? Certainly not! This is exactly what we expect babies to be like. Likewise, **we should not think that new members are failures if, even after baptism, they need lots of care and attention.** Babes in the faith are expected to be like that. At times they will stumble and fall. Lifestyle transitions are difficult. It is possible that many of their friends and relatives have withdrawn from them. They desperately need the warm hand of friendship. It's only kindness, care, concern, and continued instruction that will provide the environment to enable them to keep growing.

Some time ago, the *Reader's Digest* featured an article called "The Awesome Power of Human Love." It was the **study of two orphanages. In one orphanage:**

- The children did not develop adequate motor skills.
- They failed to crawl or walk at the right time.
- Their vocabulary was limited and their learning ability delayed. As the researchers studied the situation, they found that the attendants at this particular orphanage treated the children crudely. They disliked their jobs. They did only what were the bare necessities. They performed only those tasks they were obligated to do. The children were often left alone and allowed to cry for hours on end.

At another orphanage not too far away, the children developed beautifully.

- In this orphanage, researchers found a dedicated, committed staff. Nurses deeply cared for the children.
- The children developed adequate motor skills. They walked and crawled at the right

times. But most of all,

- They developed lovely, cheerful dispositions. Love does make a difference. In the context of a loving, nurturing environment, the children developed normally even in an orphanage.

People thrive in an atmosphere of love. Surely, an atmosphere of a loving church encourages growth. Ellen White puts it this way:

> "**Those who have newly come to the faith should be patiently and tenderly dealt with,** and it is the duty of the older members of the church to devise ways and means to provide help and sympathy and instruction for those who have conscientiously withdrawn from other churches for the truth's sake, and thus cut themselves off from the pastoral labor to which they have been accustomed" (EVANGELISM, P. 351).

She then continues with this practical instruction:

> "After individuals have been converted to the truth, they need to be looked after. . . . These newly converted ones need nursing,—watchful attention, help, and encouragement. **These should not be left alone, a prey to Satan's most powerful temptations;** they need to be educated in regard to their duties, to be kindly dealt with, to be led along, and to be visited and prayed with. These souls need the meat apportioned to every man in due season" (IBID.).

After carefully evaluating the experience of new converts to the Seventh-day Adventist Church, we have discovered that there are **often four major crises** in the lives of new believers. Just as the early stages of a baby's life are critical, so are the first two years of a convert's life. These years set a pattern of spiritual growth and development for the rest of his or her life.

FOUR MAJOR CRISES IN THE LIVES OF NEW BELIEVERS

01 | The Crisis of Discouragement

This crisis occurs when individuals fail to live up to the high standards that they have espoused immediately previous to their baptism. In baptism, they make a public commitment to accept certain biblical truths and live by certain biblical standards. But shortly after baptism, they often discover tendencies from their old life still present. They may be impatient or unkind with a colleague at work, struggle with keeping the Sabbath holy, lapse into old lifestyle habits, or fail to be Christlike in their homes. When these old habit patterns, whatever they are, grip them again, they may enter into a period of discouragement. Discouraged, with feelings of inadequacy, they may feel they are living a hypocritical life. **Their natural reaction is to abandon their relationship with the church.** The church represents the commitments to standards and a lifestyle they feel incapable of maintaining. Guilt led Adam and Eve to be uncomfortable in God's presence and flee. It's doing the same in the lives of many people today.

Symptoms:

The main symptoms of the crisis of discouragement are absenteeism at church or any significant change in attendance patterns at social events or prayer meetings. It is also identified by a recognizable loss of cheerfulness in the Christian life. It may manifest itself in the obvious lack of desire to linger at church. A hurried handshake, a discouraged countenance, or a somber disposition may be indications of the crisis of discouragement.

Solutions:

The individual going through the crisis of discouragement can often be helped if the crisis is detected quickly.

- A phone call, a reassuring word, a prayer, a brief note, a pastoral visit—all can be like rays of hope in the darkness. These individuals certainly do not need condemnation. To sense their discouragement, to listen to their problems and offer genuine, sincere encouragement is often all they need. When an individual is already carrying a heavy load of guilt, the last thing they need is somebody condemning them further.
- What they need is someone graciously speaking words of hope and encouragement. The apostle Paul gave the church at Galatia this wise counsel, "Bear one another's burdens, and so fulfill the law of Christ" **(GALATIANS 6:2)**. It was wise counsel two thousand years ago, and it is still wise counsel today.

02 | The Crisis of Integration

This crisis takes place when a new convert fails to replace the old friends in their life with new ones. It occurs when a person accepts the doctrines of the church, but is not integrated into its social structure. Since human beings are social as well as physical, mental, and spiritual creatures, a failure to connect with people in the church makes them feel like they do not really belong. The crisis of integration happens when an individual does not become a part of the social network of the church. They feel alone. They may feel awkward in their own families because of their new commitment. **They crave friendship and social support. The New Testament church provided a warm, loving environment for new converts** (ACTS 2:42–47).

Symptoms:

The new member begins arriving late at church or leaving immediately after the closing hymn. They may sit by themselves and rarely attend the social functions of the church. If they do, they keep to themselves. Their church experience is reduced to simply attending on Sabbath mornings. They believe the doctrines but feel like a stranger in the church. This type of individual will generally not attend Sabbath School. They associate very little with church members and have no close friends in the church. They may go on like this for weeks and months, **but sooner or later, unless they develop a network of friends within the church, they will leave.**

Solutions:

These individuals need immediate personal attention.

- Make active attempts to help them develop some new friendships within the church.
- Special efforts must be made to invite them to church social functions.

- Phone calls for social events will be more effective than a letter or public announcement.
- Warm, loving fellowship and deep, personal relationships are a significant factor in preventing apostasy.
- An invitation to Sabbath dinner, or a social outing to an Adventist institution such as one of our hospitals, schools, or the Adventist Book Center, provide some of the best preventive medicine.

During the first six months, more individuals leave the church because of the crisis of discouragement or the crisis of integration than for any other single reason. Yet the tide of apostasy can be stemmed here. Warm, loving fellowship and deep, personal relationships are a significant factor in preventing apostasy. Some church growth studies indicate that unless a new convert can identify at least seven people in the church by name that they've developed friendships with, the likelihood of their leaving the church is rather high. The fewer the friends they have in the church, the higher the apostasy. The more friends they have in the church, the lower the apostasy.

03 | Crisis of Lifestyle

The crisis generally takes place from a year to a year and a half after baptism. It occurs when an individual fails to integrate the value system of Scripture and the Seventh-day Adventist Church into their lifestyle. Typically, they have not incorporated family worship into their schedule. Grace at meals is spasmodic. The Sabbath is kept carelessly. They continue to attend the old places of amusement. Although they are present in church on Sabbath morning, the pull of the old life is extremely strong. Their personal experience is still superficial. The seeds of the gospel have taken root, but there is little depth. They do not have a personal devotional life and spend little time in prayer and Bible study. In brief, they do not really know Jesus.

Symptoms:

This new member often will not attend Sabbath School; they will almost certainly miss prayer meeting. There is a general superficiality about their Christian experience. They have not developed any outreach ministry in their lives. There is a failure to read denominational journals and a lack of attendance at the special meetings of the church, such as camp meeting. They speak in generalities regarding the church, but there is little involvement in it or apparent spiritual growth.

Solutions:

The great need for one experiencing this crisis is a meaningful devotional life.
- Be sure they have Adventist literature at home suited to their needs and interests.
- An outstanding stimulus to foster spiritual growth for this already Laodicean Adventist is to involve him or her in a small group Bible study with meaningful prayer bands, study, and witness. In the setting of a small group of six to eight individuals, spiritual growth will more likely occur.

04 | Crisis of Leadership

This crisis usually occurs after an individual has demonstrated faithfulness to Christ and His church. Let's assume the church is relatively small. They begin to be integrated into the leadership structure. Perhaps they are placed on the nominating committee. They begin to see the inner workings of the church. Its "halo of holiness" is tarnished. They recognize that all the church members are not "saints." During the nominating committee meetings, there's a frank evaluation of church members elected to office. The imperfect decisions and functions of committees and boards perplexes him or her. The shock of belonging to a church composed of real, erring humans discourages him or her.

Symptoms:

This crisis may express itself in criticism, gossip, breaking of confidences after a committee meeting, or a general feeling of discouragement. At times a person going through the crisis of leadership may, after sitting on the nominating committee, refuse to take a church office. There may be criticism on one hand and deep feelings of anxiety on the other.

Solutions:

Usually, one or two counseling sessions focusing on the divine origin of the church and the weakness and inadequacy of any human leadership is enough to help this person. The crisis of leadership generally occurs because an individual does not have the spiritual maturity to recognize the "humanness" of individual church members.

- It is helpful if pastors explain to each new Adventist elected to a leadership position the frailty of all human beings and the urgent necessity of cooperating together.
- In areas where truth is not at stake, church committees must remember that for the sake of new members, if for no other reason, unity is more important than individual opinions.

In each of **the crises** which we have discussed—
- The crisis of **discouragement,**
- The crisis of **integration,**
- The crisis of **lifestyle,** and
- The crisis of **leadership,**

one major ingredient is needed to avert apostasy: caring love. A love which continually says, "I am interested in you, I am concerned, I care." Love manifested in a phone call, a brief note, a smile, a warm handshake, an invitation to dinner, may be more effective than a sermon. We would do well to remember the words of a little boy from Harlem who, when he passed by a street preacher preaching about God's love, stopped, planted his feet firmly, and shouted, "Mister, I want to see love with skin on it."

Soul winning is the most wonderful work in the world. In soul winning, God and the soul winner work side by side. The greatest, deepest joy in life is to work along with God. To blend quiet meditation and moments alone with God in prayer with active labor is the life that God designs for each of His followers. It is this life of successful soul-winning adventure that I invite you to enter into today.

Nurturing New Converts

The devil zeroes in on new believers. His goal is to sever their relationship with the body of Christ, for it's in the context of the church that new believers are nurtured and grow up to become mature Christians.

It is very likely that some will become discouraged shortly after their baptism. If there is **little tolerance** for their mistakes, no conscious effort to **integrate them** into the social network of the church, and no carefully planned **process of after-care** to reinforce their new doctrinal understanding, apostasies will be needlessly high.

Baptism is a symbol of the new birth. It is certainly not an indication that the new convert is fully mature. It is the responsibility of the church to take careful steps to help each church member develop a deep abiding relationship with Christ and a secure relationship with His church. **Here are two additional principles for establishing and holding new converts.**

01 | Repeat the Message a Second Time

Do not assume that because a new convert heard the message once, he/she fully understands it. To repeat the message a second time solidifies it in the mind of the new believer. It anchors their faith. Since new believers are often eager to share their newfound faith, a repetition of the great truths of the Bible provides them with an excellent opportunity to invite their friends.

Ellen White reaffirms the principle of repetition in these words:

> "When the arguments for present truth are presented for the first time, it is difficult to fasten the points upon the mind. And although some may see sufficiently to decide, yet for all this, there is need of going all over the very same ground again, and giving another course of lectures.
>
> ". . . After the first efforts have been made in a place by giving a course of lectures, **there is really greater necessity for a second course than for the first.** The truth is new and startling, and the people need to have the same [truth] presented the second time, to get the points distinct and the ideas fixed in the mind" **(EVANGELISM, P. 334).**

To "fasten the truth" upon the mind, we recommend one of two approaches. *What the Bible Says About* is a **Bible study resource covering multiple topics with hundreds of Bible texts.** Topics include both Bible doctrines, the prophecies of Daniel and Revelation, and practical lifestyle subjects. We suggest:

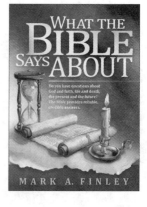

- Choosing a variety of the major themes from *What the Bible Says About,* providing each attendee the book, and reviewing the theme twice a week for thirteen weeks covering twenty-six topics. Each chapter will have far more Bible texts than you can cover in a single session. Typical chapters have fifty to one hundred texts.

- As the teacher, read through the chapter in advance and choose ten to fifteen texts for class members to mark in their Bibles. This study approach will fasten God's Word in their minds, anchor them in His truth, and prepare them to share it with others.
- You could alternatively use the book *Studying Together,* by Mark Finley. It is much less exhaustive in the treatment of each subject, but it does cover essentially the same material and has the benefit of choosing the ten to fifteen texts to review and mark.

The other possibility to follow up your evangelistic meetings is to conduct an **Unsealing Daniel's Mysteries** seminar. **Unsealing Daniel's Mysteries** covers the **entire book of Daniel, chapter by chapter.** It especially focuses on three aspects of Daniel:

1. The character of God
2. Prophetic outlines
3. Practical living at the end time.

This seminar has been attended by thousands of people around the world. **Each session centers on these essential questions:**

- What does this chapter say about God? How does it portray His action in human history and in our personal lives?
- What does this chapter say about end-time events?
- How does it describe the past, the present, and the future?
- What does this chapter say about life today?
- How does it provide help for daily living? The core of these chapter-by-chapter studies in Daniel is God's triumph over the powers of evil and His ultimate victory in the universe. We have listed the main theme of each chapter below.

  Chapter 1—The God who turns defeat into victory

  Chapter 2—The God who guides the future

  Chapter 3—The God who delivers His people

  Chapter 4—The God who is the King over all

  Chapter 5—The God of justice and judgment

  Chapter 6—The God who is steadfast forever

  Chapter 7—The God whose kingdom triumphs

  Chapter 8—The God whose truth triumphs

  Chapter 9—The God who keeps His appointments

  Chapter 10—The God who hears our prayers

  Chapter 11—The God whose people triumph

  Chapter 12—The God whose plans and purposes triumph

The *Unsealing Daniel's Mysteries* lessons are designed to be done at home, but reviewed in class. We prefer pre-enrolling people for the class the last weekend of the evangelistic series and giving out the first lesson the last night of the series. In this way, we **pre-enroll the largest number of people for the Unsealing Daniel's Mysteries series.** The Daniel series is conducted twice a week. We normally conduct the class on Tuesday or Wednesday evenings and Sabbath mornings as a pastor's Bible class. This has multiple advantages.

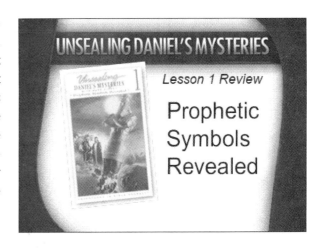

Advantages of Unsealing Daniel's Mysteries Seminar

1. After an intensive evangelistic series, it only asks people to **attend one night per week.**
2. It solidifies **Sabbath morning attendance.**
3. It provides an opportunity for new converts to **study the book of Daniel** for a period of time after the evangelistic meetings, outside of the regular Sabbath School lessons.

Some churches prefer an alternative plan. Previous to the evangelistic meetings, they have established a small group network with house groups geographically situated throughout their city. **New converts** may be **invited** to **attend the house group** closest to their home. **On Sabbath mornings, all groups meet together to study Daniel in the pastor's Bible class.** There are still two Unsealing Daniel's Mysteries classes meetings per week—**one in homes** and the other **at the church on Sabbath mornings**.

02	**Visitation**

Visitation is extremely critical if new members are to grow in Christ and feel at home in the church. **It is possible for a new convert to be doctrinally convinced, but not socially integrated into the church.** The individual has been baptized but still feels like an outsider. They feel uncomfortable with this new group of people whom they have never known before. Caring love, practically demonstrated in a brief visit, a note, a casual phone call, a warm handshake, or an invitation to dinner makes an incredible difference in the lives of new converts. Here's how inspiration puts it:

> "**Church Patiently to Help New Converts.**—Those who have newly come to the faith should be patiently and tenderly dealt with, and it is the duty of the older members of the church to devise ways and means to provide help and sympathy and instruction for those who have conscientiously withdrawn from other churches for the truth's sake, and thus cut themselves off from the pastoral labor to which they have been accustomed. The church has a special responsibility laid upon her to attend to these souls who have followed the first rays of light they have received; and if the members of the church neglect this duty, they will be unfaithful to the trust that God has given them" (EVANGELISM, P. 351).

Immediately following the evangelistic meetings, we suggest that **each pastor organize visitation teams to visit the new converts.** We generally visit our new converts every other week for the first twelve weeks. This provides an opportunity for them to bond with different church members. During the twelve-week process, we rotate the new converts' names so different people are visiting them.

The visitation schedule is organized as follows:

WEEK 1:

Each new convert is visited by a member of the visitation team and given a copy of *The Desire of Ages,* plus invited to a fellowship dinner the next Sabbath at church.
- The theme of the visit is:
- Knowing Christ through personal devotions

WEEK 3:

Each new convert receives a visit by a member of the visitation team and is given a copy of the *Adventist Review*, *Signs of the Times,* and the Union paper. The theme of the visit is the international, worldwide nature of the Seventh-day Adventist Church **(MATTHEW 24:14; REVELATION 14:6, 7).**

WEEK 5:

Each new convert is visited by a member of the visitation team and given a personal invitation to dinner. The theme of the visit based on Genesis 2:1–3 is the joy of Sabbath keeping.

WEEK 7:

Each new convert is visited by a member of the visitation team and given a copy of *Studying Together*. The theme of the visit is lovingly sharing your faith with others.

WEEK 9:

Each new convert is visited by a member of the visitation team and given a copy of *The Great Controversy*. The theme of the visit is God's deliverance at the end time. Read together the last four pages in *The Great Controversy.*

WEEK 11:

Each new convert is visited by a member of the visitation team and given the **Sabbath School lesson quarterly** for the coming quarter, as well as an invitation to the fellowship dinner at the church the next Sabbath.

This follow-up strategy blends continuing doctrinal Bible studies, personal devotions, and warm fellowship. It provides opportunities for the new convert to share challenges he/she is facing as well as prayer requests.

As you implement these principles, the Holy Spirit will help you to grow strong disciples for Christ. New converts will mature into solid Christians. Some will become leaders in your church. **Many will actively share their faith with their relatives and friends.**

As a rock thrown into a pond that sends its ripples across the water, the influence of this after-care program will have a ripple effect on scores of lives. **Only eternity will reveal its lasting influence.**

It is possible to spend enormous efforts to lead people into the church and few efforts to retain them. Our philosophy is not that we dip them and drop them but that we immerse them and instruct them.

Our love for people compels us to continue nurturing new believers. The gospel demands it, and Jesus would have us do no less.

CHAPTER 18

The Message Triumphant

The promises of God are sure. His work will triumph gloriously. His message of truth will be speedily proclaimed to the ends of the earth. In His end-time sermon in Matthew, chapter 24, after describing the signs of the times, Jesus declared, "And this gospel of the kingdom shall be preached in all the world as a witness to all the nations, and then the end will come" **(MATTHEW 24:14).**

The aged apostle John, exiled on the Isle of Patmos, was taken off into prophetic vision and saw three angels flying in the midst of heaven "having the everlasting gospel to preach to . . . every nation, tribe, tongue, and people" **(REVELATION 14:6, 7).**

God's message is soon to triumph gloriously. He gives us the awesome privilege of participating with Him in the most exciting work in the world. His last-day message will speedily span the globe and tens of thousands will accept His urgent appeal to be ready for His soon return.

No matter how difficult evangelism is, no matter how few may be involved, it will increase until the world is enlightened with the glory of the righteousness of Christ.

"After these things I saw another angel coming down from heaven, having great authority, and the **earth was illuminated with his glory**" **(REVELATION 18:1).**

> ". . . When the storm of **persecution** really **breaks upon us,** the true sheep will hear the true Shepherd's voice. **Self-denying efforts** will be put forth **to save the lost,** and many who have strayed from the fold will come back to follow the great Shepherd. The **people of God will draw together** and present to the enemy a united front. . . .
>
> ". . . Then will the message of the third angel swell to a loud cry, and the whole earth will be lightened with the glory of the Lord" **(TESTIMONIES, VOL. 6, P. 401).**

We believe that **these prophecies are being fulfilled today.** Twenty-first-century technology provides the church with unprecedented opportunities to reach the entire planet with the gospel quickly. **Through radio, television, Internet, and publishing, God is doing some amazing things.**

- Recently, **one hundred and fifty million copies of** *The Great Controversy* were distributed **worldwide. Thirty million copies of the book** *When God Says Remember* **on the Bible Sabbath** were given away in less than a year.
- Millions more truth-filled pieces of literature have been and are being distributed.
- Adventist **television networks** continue to broadcast Bible truths in multiple languages and prepare programs in fifty-four media centers internationally.
- **Satellites** set in orbit for secular, commercial purposes now carry Christ-centered Adventist programming circling the globe.

Since 1995, we have witnessed a resurgence of evangelism around the world. The **NET '95 evangelism** initiative represented a new major thrust in soul winning for the Seventh-day Adventist Church in North America. It utilized satellite technology to extend the reach of public evangelism.

The NET '95 Discoveries in Prophecy evangelistic campaign was the **first full series of satellite evangelistic meetings** held in the history of the Seventh-day Adventist Church. NET '95 was the beginning of a **new era in evangelism.** From February 18 to March 25, 1995, the signal was beamed to the North American churches. I still remember the overwhelming feeling of God's providential work that swept over me as I walked onto the platform in the Chattanooga Convention Center and knew that **the TV signal beaming God's message was traveling twenty-three thousand miles into space and returning to churches all over America in less than a second.** All across the Division, churches conducted their own simultaneous evangelistic programs with the nightly messages projected live on their own large life-size screens. Programming was tape-delayed in various time zones so that each local church could have the series in prime time.

In Net '95, 676 churches participated with an opening night attendance of 66,165 of which 22,601 were not members of the Adventist Church. The non-member attendance grew to more than twenty-three thousand. This was greater than opening night attendance. Approximately three thousand attended the local meetings in the Chattanooga Convention Center.

The results of the NET '95 satellite evangelistic meetings were outstanding.

- By June 1, 1995, a total of **4,518 had joined the Adventist Church.**
- After the series was over, there were **4,597** people actively involved in **Bible studies** who had not been baptized yet.
- A careful analysis of the Net '95 event revealed that the number of those who were baptized or joined the Seventh-day Adventist Church by profession of faith swelled to **more than eight thousand.**

This was the **largest evangelistic campaign** by an individual evangelist in the history of the Seventh-day Adventist Church. It was the dawning of a new day of opportunity.

The Discoveries in Prophecy NET evangelistic meetings put a new spark of life into public evangelism. Satellite evangelism definitely and positively impacted the Seventh-day Adventist Church. Pastors and church members caught a new vision of the possibility of evangelism in their local congregations. **Net '95 demonstrated that public evangelism is still possible today.**

NET '95 was followed by **NET '96** with over **eighteen thousand baptisms** in North America alone. NET '96 was the first satellite event to include **forty countries** in **twelve languages.** Numerous other satellite evangelistic meetings followed until satellite evangelism became a way of life for the Seventh-day Adventist Church. To date, there have been well **over 250 satellite evangelistic series with over 1.5 million people baptized.**

Could satellite evangelism be a fulfillment of prophecy? Ellen White says:

> **"I saw jets of light** shining from cities and villages, and from the high places and the low places of the earth. God's Word was obeyed, and as a result there were memorials for Him in every city and village. His truth was proclaimed throughout the world" (TESTIMONIES, VOL. 9, PP. 28, 29).

The Bible does reveal that the everlasting gospel of the three angels' messages will triumph in a blaze of evangelism.

- Evangelism will increase more and more until the whole world is lightened with the glory of God. There has been a renewed interest in evangelistic proclamation in recent years in the Seventh-day Adventist Church.
- Over 179,000 Adventist young people conducted nearly 50,000 evangelistic meetings from 2006–2008. Tens of thousands of Adventist lay people have proclaimed the

evangelistic message for these last days using the New Beginnings or Truth for the End-Time Graphics.

- Thousands of pastors have conducted their own evangelistic meetings using the Revelation of Hope materials. Currently, the Seventh-day Adventist Church is focusing on **"Mission to the Cities."** This massive comprehensive evangelistic outreach includes all aspects of evangelism and is targeting 650 cities. There will be four hundred evangelistic meetings conducted in New York City alone, with over six hundred churches involved. Cities like Sao Paulo, Brazil; Buenos Aires, Argentina; Mexico City; Tokyo, Japan; London, England; Seoul, Korea; Manila, Philippines; Moscow, Russia; Johannesburg, South Africa; Lagos, Nigeria; and scores of other cities worldwide are in the midst of a major evangelistic thrust.

But the **greatest evangelistic thrust is yet to come.** It will precede the close of probation and the coming of the Lord. Revelation says, **"The earth was illuminated with his glory"** (REVELATION 18:1). Every person on planet earth will have the opportunity to hear the everlasting gospel. Every individual will be faced with the choice to accept or reject God's eternal end-time message.

Every believer will be involved in the work of evangelism. Thousands will be seen going from home to home opening the Word of God to everyone who is willing to listen. Others will be distributing literature and still more will be preaching God's Word wherever they can get an audience.

> "In **visions** of the night, **representations passed before me** of a great **reformatory movement among God's people.** Many were **praising God.** The **sick were healed,** and other **miracles were wrought.** A spirit of intercession was seen, even as was manifested before the great Day of Pentecost. Hundreds and **thousands** were **seen visiting families** and opening before them the word of God. Hearts were convicted by the power of the Holy Spirit, and a spirit of genuine conversion was manifest. On every side **doors were thrown open to the proclamation of the truth.** The world seemed to be lightened with the heavenly influence" (TESTIMONIES, VOL. 9, P. 126).

What will pastors and church members be doing at this time? Not hovering over a group of inactive church members. Every minister who is called of God, every committed lay person will focus on one thing—**proclaiming the third angel's message with power.**

Believers will use their varied gifts of the Spirit to share God's truth everywhere. Every Christian will be involved in witnessing for Jesus. We all will not do the same thing, but we all will do something.

Jesus said that the main objective of receiving the Holy Spirit is power for effective witnessing to lead souls to Him. He said, "But **you shall receive power** when the Holy Spirit has come upon you; and you shall be witnesses to Me in Jerusalem, and in all Judea and Samaria, and to the end of the earth" (ACTS 1:8).

The signs of the times are **everywhere.**

Natural disasters, America's skyrocketing national debt, the world's struggling economies, international terrorism, rising crime, nuclear threats, political instability, and school violence clearly reveal we are on the threshold of great and solemn events. In these critical hours of earth's history, **our loving Lord gives to each one of us the privilege of cooperating with Him in His mission of redeeming this lost world.** The Holy Spirit will be poured out abundantly in the fullness of heaven's power to **fulfill the gospel commission.**

"For He will finish the work and cut it short in righteousness, because the LORD will make a short work upon the earth" (ROMANS 9:28).

God could have used the angels to finish His work on earth, and angels certainly play a role in guiding people to hear truth, but God has chosen us to proclaim it.

- **Angels do not give Bible studies, God's people do.**
- **Angels do not preach evangelistic sermons, God's people do.**
- **Angels do not make evangelistic appeals, God's people do.**
- **God has chosen each one of us to joyously join Him in His mission of reaching the world. His promises will be fulfilled.**

"Servants of God, with their faces lighted up and shining with holy consecration, will hasten from place to place to proclaim the message from heaven. **By thousands of voices, all over the earth,** the warning will be given. Miracles will be wrought, the sick will be healed, and signs and wonders will follow the believers. . . . Thus the inhabitants of the earth will be brought to take their stand" **(THE GREAT CONTROVERSY, P. 612).**

This is heaven's **picture of evangelism in the last days.**

The work is soon to close and there will be thousands of voices proclaiming God's truth. Will one of them be yours? God will use His people in a mighty way. Will you unite with tens of thousands of others in this last final proclamation of the gospel?

"Our watchword is to be, Onward, ever onward! Angels of heaven will go before us to prepare the way. **Our burden for the regions beyond can never be laid down till the whole earth is lightened with the glory of the Lord**" **(GOSPEL WORKERS, P. 470).**

Angels will open doors, the Holy Spirit will impress hearts, but God uses people to proclaim His message—people upon whom He pours out His Holy Spirit. His promise is that "the people who know their God shall be strong, and carry out great exploits" **(DANIEL 11:32).**

- **You were born** into this world at this time **to share Jesus' love** with a dying world.
- **He longs to use you** in ways you have never thought of. You are to do "exploits" for Him.
- **You may never have held a public evangelist meeting before and have read this manual** and desire to become involved in public evangelism. You may be a little fearful and have some concerns. Remember, **God does not call the qualified. He qualifies those He calls.** Under the unction of His Spirit, you can powerfully proclaim His end-time truth. Do not allow your fears to hold you back. **Step out in faith and watch what God does with your life.** You may be a veteran evangelist with years of experience and are impressed God desires to give you even greater results.
- **Apply the principles found in this evangelistic manual** and allow God to expand your horizons. You may be a church administrator, pastor, or lay person, and God is calling you. Whether you are young or old, male or female, educated or uneducated, rich or poor, God's call to evangelism is for you. If He impresses you to be involved in

conducting a public evangelistic meeting, He promises to give you success. God does not sponsor failures. We can step out in faith and leave the ultimate results to Him.

May our wonderful Lord powerfully bless your ministry and empower you with His Holy Spirit, so you can become one of tens of thousands of evangelists preaching His message of divine truth, for the most outstanding evangelistic sermons are yet to be preached and the most successful evangelistic meetings are yet to be held.

Praise His name you have been called for a purpose and can be used of God to make an eternal difference for His kingdom.

Form Letters

Dear _____,

It is a pleasure for me to write to you on behalf of the Seventh-day Adventist Church. Recently, (first/last name), has begun attending our church and is currently preparing for baptism and church membership. (First name) has run into one difficulty. Currently, he/she is required to work on Saturday. In harmony with the teachings throughout the Bible and specifically the clear mandate in the Ten Commandments to "Remember the Sabbath," Seventh-day Adventists observe the Sabbath from sundown Friday evening to sundown Saturday evening.

(First name) enjoys his/her job and certainly does not want to lose it. This places him/her in a dilemma. Based on his/her religious convictions, he/she is unable to work on the Bible Sabbath. In harmony with his/her first amendment rights, the Seventh-day Adventist Church would like to officially request that you grant (first/last name) his/her Sabbaths off. He/she is willing to work any other time, including Sundays or extra hours during the week. (Employer's name), I am confident you will be richly repaid for this important decision by (name's) faithfulness and hard work to his/her job. I am also confident God will honor you for your willingness to allow an employee to worship in harmony with the dictates of his/her conscience.

Historically, the United States has honored the diverse religious beliefs of its citizens. Its rich heritage in religious liberty is admired by countries all over the world. One million Seventh-day Adventists throughout the United States salute you in preserving this vital aspect of American life. Thank you in advance for granting this request.

Sincerely in Christ,

(Pastor's name)

Dear Friend:

What an exciting time to be alive! We have entered the twenty-first century. Ours is a generation that blends optimism regarding the future with serious concern. We are optimistic about society's technological advances with new breakthroughs in health care and disease control. But we are also concerned about waning moral values, the rapid deterioration of the family unit, and rampant sex and violence on television. Electrical energy shortages, an uncertain economy, rising crime, and natural disasters trouble us. Is there anything certain? What can we really hang on to in a time of crisis?

Many people are finding answers in *It Is Written* television's new set of *Search for Certainty* Bible guides authored by Mark Finley.

If ever there was a time to seek answers to the deepest questions of the human heart, it is today. If ever there was a time to understand the Bible for ourselves, it is today. The *Search for Certainty* lessons make Bible study fascinating and easy to understand. These lessons will answer such questions as: What does the Bible teach about the end times? What are the signs of the coming of Jesus? How can I get answers to my prayers? What happens when you die? What is heaven really like? These and many other questions will be answered as you personally explore the great teachings of Scripture.

These lessons are yours absolutely free. There is no cost. Your only commitment is to faithfully complete the lessons. If you would like to deepen your faith by participating in this Bible study adventure, **mail the enclosed card today.** You will understand answers to questions you have asked all of your life. We will be delighted to deliver your lessons immediately upon receiving your card. Be assured you are poised on the verge of thrilling new discoveries that will bring you greater peace of mind, deeper joy, and meaning to your life.

Sincerely, your friend,

Dear Friend:

Occasionally, I come across a book that brings me such inspiration that I want to share it. Recently, I read *To Hope Again* by my good friend Mark Finley, of *It is Written* television. This small volume outlines the great prophetic chapters of the Bible, focusing especially on the second coming of Christ. It is filled with hope. It describes the signs of Christ's soon return as well as how to prepare for the second coming of Christ.

Each chapter is a description of the events that will occur in connection with the second coming of Christ. This book will give you insight into what is coming upon the world. It is yours absolutely free. I will be delighted to present it to you as a gift. I am personally convinced that we are living in the days when Bible prophecy is being fulfilled.

This book will help you prepare for the events that will soon take place in our world. Our loving Lord desires you to be ready for His return. He desires that your family meet Him in peace and live with Him forever. This book, *To Hope Again*, will provide you with inspiration, hope, and courage.

Please mail the enclosed card today to receive your free copy of *To Hope Again*. We will deliver your book immediately.

Sincerely in Christ,

Dear Friend:

I would like to give you a personal invitation to attend the Unsealing Daniel's Mysteries seminar.

History has been following Daniel's prophecies of named kings, rulers, and empires before their appearance in history.

During this twelve-session seminar, we will cover such topics as:

- The future of the world
- How to survive tough times
- How to discover truth
- How to be ready for the coming of Christ
- When church and state unite
- The truth about the end time
- The longest time prophecy in the Bible, and many more topics

I have enclosed a brochure for the Unsealing Daniel's Mysteries seminar. Be sure to attend and receive twelve free lessons on the prophetic themes of Daniel that contain charts, diagrams, and supplementary material.

During the Unsealing Daniel's Mysteries seminar, you will see the prophecies of Daniel come to life. You can review the lessons at home as you study the Bible prophecies of Daniel. You will be among the many who are saying, "I never knew Bible prophecy could be so clear."

Tens of thousands testify that these prophecies have changed their lives. Be sure to attend the Unsealing Daniel's Mysteries seminar that begins:

Date:

Time:

Location:

It Is Written television is sponsoring the Unsealing Daniel's Mysteries seminar. There is no charge. I look forward to seeing you there.

Sincerely, your friend,

Dear Friend:

Here's some good news you will not want to miss. Mark Finley, the speaker for *It Is Written* television, will be conducting a series of meetings on Bible prophecy via video, titled Revelation of Hope. Revelation of Hope has been conducted around the world to packed audiences. Tens of thousands have appreciated hid dynamic presentations on the Bible's last book, Revelation.

During this hope-filled series, you will learn more than you ever have in your life about Revelation's end-time prophecies. You will discover answers to such questions as:

- Who is the beast?
- What does the mysterious number 666 mean?
- What and where is the battle of Armageddon?
- Who are the four horsemen of the Revelation?
- What is America's role in Bible prophecy?
- Does the Bible predict one thousand years of peace?

Discover for yourself God's outline for the future. You can face the future with new confidence. Revelation of Hope is a gripping multimedia presentation that will hold your attention from the first minute of the program until the end.

We have enclosed a colorful brochure describing the program in detail. We also have a free place reserved especially for you. To make your reservation, please call 000-0000.

We look forward to seeing you at the Revelation of Hope Bible prophecies series beginning _____ (date), at_____. Join the thousands who testify that, "This is the most powerful, hope-filled presentation I have ever attended!"

Sincerely, your friend,

ENLISTMENT FORM FOR COMMITTEES

_____**Prayer Ministry**

- I will pray daily for the evangelistic meetings.
- I will be a part of a prayer group that prays before every meeting.

_____**Ushers**

- Distribute materials in your section
- Collect the offering
- Pass out and collect decision cards
- Get acquainted with as many people as possible in your area

_____**Hosts and Hostesses**

- Welcome all guests as they enter the auditorium
- Hand out program schedules
- Give ticket book or scanner card to every person the first night
- Distribute copies of the lecture at the end of the meeting

_____**Registration Personnel**

- Registers all new people after the first night
- Takes care of all back lecture magazines
- Gives out all gifts

_____**Attendance Record Personnel**

- Collects all tickets each evening from the hosts and hostesses
- Enters all names and addresses into the computer
- Enters all decision card information in the computer
- Enters all ticket numbers into the computer
- Scans the person's card as they come into the meeting

_____**Bible School**

- Gives out lessons to the guests
- Receives completed lessons
- Corrects the completed _Search for Certainty_ lessons

_____Parking Attendants

- Assist in helping people to park
- Direct guests to the auditorium

_____Children's Meeting

- Four leaders—One for each night of the week (Sunday is combined with Saturday)
- Tell Bible stories
- Give nature nuggets/health talks/character-development stories
- Help with crafts
- Helpers

_____Babysitting

- Take care of babies from birth to four years old.

_____Resource Center

- Sells books, music, and materials relating to the meeting

ESSENTIAL SUPPLIES FOR A PUBLIC EVANGELISTIC CAMPAIGN

For Public Advertising

- Handbills
- Postcard handbills
- Posters
- Reserved seat tickets
- There are many more advertising devises, but these are at least the essentials

For Platform

- Backdrop (Can be very simple)
- Decorations
- Pulpit or stand
- Chairs

For Preaching

- Bible
- 1 set sermons on CD-Rom containing all 26 sermons with graphics
- 1 or 2 computers (1 for graphics audience sees—1 for graphics and sermon notes speaker sees)
- Remote control devise for changing graphics
- 1 projector
- Screen
- TV monitor (If using computer for sermon notes)

For Sound

- PA system
- Lapel microphone for speaker
- Microphones for musicians
- Tape/CD deck (If mastering sermons)

For Appeals

- Decision Cards
- Pencils
- Buckets

For Music

- Piano

For Registration

- Table cloths for tables
- Five-drawer roller case for supplies
- Tickets or scanner cards and envelopes
- Pens
- Previous meeting lecture magazines

For Gift Incentives

- Bibles
- Sermon lecture magazine
- Books
- Pictures

For Questions

- Question Box
- Paper/4x6 cards
- Pens

For Record Keeping

- Revelation of Hope tracking system
- Computers
- Networking system
- Printer
- Paper

For Office

- Copy machine
- Copy paper
- 1 five-drawer roller case for all supplies
- Name tags (For personnel—ushers, host, hostesses, etc.)
- Pens/pencils
- Paper clips
- Rubber bands
- Scissors

For Bible School

- *Search for Certainty* Bible lessons
- File boxes
- File folders
- Alphabetical dividers

For Resource Center/Sales

- Sermon magazines
- Sermon CDs/DVDs
- Music CDs
- Books

For Children's Meetings

- Bible study felts (Bible stories)
- Craft materials

For Babysitting

- Cribs
- Safe toys

For Parking

- Flashlights
- Umbrellas

For Promotion—Building Audience

- Small gift books and small Nathan Greene pictures

For Visitation

- Books

For Baptism

- Baptismal robes
- Baptismal bags

Search for Certainty Lessons

1. How to Understand the Bible
2. Our Day in the Light of Bible Prophecy
3. A World in Turmoil
4. The Manner of Christ's Coming
5. How to Find Personal Peace
6. The Secret of a New Life
7. Good God! Bad World! Why?
8. Revelation's Most Thrilling Message
9. The Bible's Longest and Most Amazing Prophecy
10. A Date With Destiny: The Judgment
11. What's Behind Rising Crime, Violence, and Immorality?
12. Christ's Special Sign
13. Tampering with Heaven's Constitution
14. Modern Cults Identified Five Ways

SEARCH FOR CERTAINTY
BIBLE SCHOOL REGISTRATION FORM

DATE ENROLLED: _____NIGHT # _____

DATE OF MEETINGS:

SERIES OF MEETINGS: Revelation of Hope

PLACE:

Name _____ Date _____

Address _____

City_____ State _____ Zip _____

Phone _____

E-Mail _____

This is the first time I have studied the Bible systematically. ____Yes ____No

FOR INSTRUCTOR USE ONLY

LESSONS COMPLETED: PLEASE CIRCLE LESSONS COMPLETED

1 2 3 4 5 6 7 8 9 10 11 12 13 14 15 16 17

18 19 20 21 22 23 24 25 26 27 28 29 30

Name of Bible Instructor: _____

BAPTISM—A STATEMENT OF FAITH CLASS #1

MY PERSONAL COMMITMENT

1. I believe there is one God: Father, Son, and Holy Spirit, a unity of Three co-eternal Persons.
   - 2 Corinthians 13:14
   - Deuteronomy 6:4
   - Matthew 28:19
   - Ephesians 4:4–6

2. I accept the death of Jesus Christ on Calvary as the atoning sacrifice for my sins and believe that through faith in His shed blood I am saved from sin and its penalty.
   - Ephesians 2:8
   - Romans 3:23
   - Romans 6:23
   - Romans 8:1–4

3. I renounce the world and its sinful ways, and have accepted Jesus Christ as my personal Savior, believing that God, for Christ's sake, has forgiven my sins and given me a new heart.
   - 1 John 1:9
   - Hebrews 8:12
   - Acts 3:19
   - 2 Corinthians 3:17, 18

4. I accept by faith the righteousness of Christ, my Intercessor in the heavenly sanctuary, and accept His promise of transforming grace and power to live a loving, Christ-centered life in my home and before the world.
   - Hebrews 7:25
   - Philippians 4:13
   - 2 Corinthians 5:17
   - Hebrews 4:15, 16

5. I believe that the Bible is God's inspired Word, the only rule of faith and practice for the Christian. I covenant to spend time regularly in prayer and Bible study.
   - 2 Timothy 3:16
   - 2 Peter 1:21
   - John 17:17
   - Psalm 119:105

6. I accept the Ten Commandments as a transcript of the character of God and a revelation of His will. It is my purpose by the power of the indwelling Christ to keep this law, including the fourth commandment, which requires the observance of the seventh day of the week as the Sabbath of the Lord and the memorial of Creation.
   - John 14:15
   - Genesis 2:1–3

- Exodus 20:8–11
- Mark 2:27, 28

7. I look forward to the soon coming of Jesus and the blessed hope when "this mortal shall put on immortality." As I prepare to meet the Lord, I will witness to His loving salvation, and by life and word help others to be ready for His glorious appearing.
   - John 14:1–3
   - 1 Thessalonians 4:16, 17
   - Revelation 1:7
   - Revelation 19:11–16

Name _____ Date _____

Address _____

City_____ State _____

Zip _____ Phone _____

Baptism—Class #2

My Personal Commitment

1. I accept the teaching of spiritual gifts and believe the gift of prophecy is one of the identifying marks of the remnant church.
   - Revelation 12:17
   - Revelation 19:10
   - 1 Corinthians 1:4–8
   - 1 Peter 1:10, 11

2. I believe in church organization. It is my purpose to support the church by my tithes and offerings and my personal effort and influence.
   - Haggai 1:3–11
   - Malachi 3:8–12
   - 1 Corinthians 9:8–14
   - Romans 15:26, 27

3. I believe my body is the temple of the Holy Spirit and will honor Him by caring for it, avoiding the use of that which is harmful; abstaining from all unclean foods, from the use, manufacture, or sale of alcoholic beverages, the use, manufacture, or sale of tobacco in any of its forms for human consumption, and from the misuse of or trafficking in narcotics or other drugs.
   - Romans 12:1, 2
   - 1 Corinthians 6:19, 20
   - Leviticus 11:1–12
   - 1 Corinthians 10:31

4. I know and understand the fundamental Bible principles as taught by the Seventh-day Adventist Church. I purpose by the grace of God to fulfill His will by ordering my life in harmony with these principles.
   - 1 John 2:6
   - 1 John 2:15–17

5. I accept the New Testament teaching of baptism by immersion and desire to be so baptized as a public expression of faith in Christ and His forgiveness of my sins.
   - Matthew 28:19, 20
   - John 3:5
   - Mark 16:16
   - Colossians 2:12

6. I accept and believe that the Seventh-day Adventist Church is the remnant church of Bible prophecy and that people of every nation, race, and language are invited and accepted into its fellowship. I desire to be a member of this local congregation of the world church.
   - Philippians 4:8

- 2 Corinthians 10:5
- Revelation 12:17
- Revelation 14:6, 7, 12
- Revelation 18:1, 2
- Matthew 16:16–18

Name _____ Date _____

Address _____

City _____ State _____

Zip _____ Phone _____

Seven Steps in Helping People Quit Smoking

1. **Recognize that smoking is a sin** against your body and your God. "I beseech you therefore, brethren, . . . that you present your bodies a living sacrifice, holy, acceptable to God, which is your reasonable service" **(ROMANS 12:1)**.

2. **Acknowledge your weakness and inability to quit on your own.** Like the woman with the "issue of blood" in Scripture, you may have sought help for years. Or like the man by the Pool of Bethseda for thirty-eight years, you may be desperate in your attempt to stop smoking **(SEE JOHN 5:5–8)**. Admit that you are weak. Acknowledge you cannot do it on your own. "Without Me you can do nothing" **(JOHN 15:5)**.

3. **By faith believe that although you are weak, He is strong.** Although you cannot do it, He is all powerful. When we choose to surrender our weak, wavering will to His all-powerful will, all the power in the universe is at our disposal **(PHILIPPIANS 4:13; 1 JOHN 5:14, 15)**.

4. **Surrender yourself and all of your tobacco to God** **(JOSHUA 24:15; 2 CORINTHIANS 6:2)**.

5. **Believe that victory is yours now and thank God right now** for giving you victory over smoking **(1 CORINTHIANS 15:57; MATTHEW 7:7; 1 JOHN 5:4)**.
   You may have a craving to smoke as the result of the physiological effect of nicotine deposited in the cell system. But you need not smoke.
   Smoking is a choice. There is a difference between the craving and the victory. The victory is yours by faith in Jesus.

6. **Destroy all of your tobacco.** Throw it away. Don't leave any around. "Therefore submit to God. Resist the devil" **(JAMES 4:7)**.

7. Believe that victory is yours now. To sustain the victory, thank God for it! **Praise Him because you are delivered and follow the physical habits listed below** to rid your body of nicotine.
   - When you get a craving, take slow deep breaths repeatedly until the craving passes.
   - Drink ten to twelve glasses of water a day for the next five days.
   - Relax in a warm (*not hot*) bath before going to bed.
   - Plan to get at least eight hours of sleep a night.
   - Avoid all coffee and alcohol.
   - Take two, thirty-minute walks each day.

Continually praise God that His power is greater than tobacco **(1 JOHN 4:4)**.

Response Cards

My Response—Child Born in the Middle East

- ❑   I believe Jesus is the Divine Son of God.

- ❑   I accept Jesus as my personal Savior.

- ❑   I have drifted away but tonight recommit my life to Jesus.

- ❑   I would like more reading material to grow in Jesus.

Name: _____

Address: _____

City: _____State: _____ Zip: _____

Phone: _____ Ticket Number: _____

My Response—Hope Beyond Tomorrow

- ❑   I believe Jesus will come literally, personally, visibly, and audibly.

- ❑   I desire to be ready for Jesus' return.

- ❑   I would like to be baptized soon.

- ❑   I would like more reading material on Jesus' coming.

Name: _____

Address: _____

City: _____State: _____ Zip: _____

Phone: _____ Ticket Number: _____

My Response—Remedy for Stress

❑   I desire to obey Jesus fully.

❑   I accept the Bible Sabbath as the true Lord's day.

❑   I love Jesus and desire to keep the seventh-day Sabbath holy.

❑   I desire more reading material on the Bible Sabbath.

Name: _____

Address: _____

City: _____ State: _____ Zip: _____

Phone: _____ Ticket Number: _____

My Response—Mysteries of the Mummies

❑   I accept God's plan of health for my life.

❑   I surrender my body as the temple of the Holy Spirit.

❑   I choose to give up alcohol, tobacco, harmful drugs, and unclean foods.

❑   I would like to be baptized soon.

Name: _____

Address: _____

City: _____ State: _____ Zip: _____

Phone: _____ Ticket Number: _____

My Response—How to Bury the Past

❑ I believe biblical baptism is by full immersion.

❑ I would like to be baptized soon.

❑ I would like to be rebaptized soon.

❑ I have already been baptized by immersion and would like to unite with God's commandment-keeping people.

Name: _____

Address: _____

City: _____ State: _____ Zip: _____

Phone: _____ Ticket Number: _____

My Response—Revelation's Four Horsemen

❑ I desire all of the truth God has for me.

❑ I choose to be obedient to all of God's commandments.

❑ I desire to be baptized soon.

❑ I would like to recommit my life to Christ.

Name: _____

Address: _____

City: _____ State: _____ Zip: _____

Phone: _____ Ticket Number: _____

Prayer Request

❑ Please pray for me. I need help in solving a problem.

❑ Please pray for my financial needs.

❑ Please pray for my health.

❑ Please pray for me to be able to break an undesirable habit.

Please pray for_____.
_____

Name: _____

Address: _____

City: _____State: _____ Zip: _____

Phone: _____ Ticket Number: _____

My Response—The Mark of the Beast

❑ I choose to lovingly obey Christ.

❑ I do not want to worship the beast.

❑ I accept the true Bible Sabbath.

❑ I would like to be baptized soon.

Name: _____

Address: _____

City: _____State: _____ Zip: _____

Phone: _____ Ticket Number: _____

REVELATION OF HOPE

Presents

This Certificate of Completion

Awarded to

Upon completion of the *Search for Certainty* Bible School

On the _____ day of _____ in the year of our Lord _____

Mark Finley

"Grace Be Unto You, And Peace, From God"

COLOSSIANS 1:2, KJV